British Library Cataloguing in Publication Data

Fallon, John P.
   Marks of London goldsmiths and silversmiths — 1697–1837
— 2nd ed.
   1. London goldware & silverware. Makers' marks,
1697–1837 — Lists
   I. Title
   739.2'0278

   ISBN 0–7153–5447–7

First published 1972
New and revised edition 1988

First published in the United States
by Charles E. Tuttle Co., Inc., 1988

ISBN 0-8048-7028-4
Library of Congress Catalog Card No. 88- 50740

Published by the Charles E. Tuttle Co., Inc.
of Rutland, Vermont & Tokyo, Japan
with editorial offices at
Suido 1-chome, 2-6, Bunkyo-ku, Tokyo, Japan

Printed in Great Britain
by Butler & Tanner, Frome
for David & Charles Publishers plc
Brunel House Newton Abbot Devon

CONTENTS

PREFACE

When in 1363, it was enacted that every maker of silver should have a mark of his own to be stamped beside the 'King's Mark', the object was to prevent fraudulent practices which were rife at the time. The maker's mark on old silver is now of the greatest interest to the connoisseur and to the collector. Unfortunately, due to a fire in the Assay Office at Goldsmiths' Hall in the late seventeenth century the early records of makers' marks were destroyed, but from 1697 to the present day they are almost complete with only two books missing. Therefore the majority of London makers' marks entered during this period can be identified from the registers at Goldsmiths' Hall. What has previously been lacking, however, is a publication for easy reference which is both accurate and not too voluminous. This small book will supply the need.

The entries in the registers at Goldsmiths' Hall are in the form of inked impressions from the actual punches used by the makers and in most cases the signature and address of the maker are included in addition to the date of entry. The illustrations which follow were traced from photographs of the original impressions and I can readily vouch for the care taken by the author to ensure their accuracy. To keep the book down to pocket size he has wisely omitted many lesser known makers and instead included a bonus in the form of a number of biographical notes. Both the casual collector and the expert should find this book invaluable.

J. S. Forbes
Former Deputy Warden
of the Goldsmiths' Company
1987

ACKNOWLEDGEMENTS

The author wishes to thank the following people for their assistance in compiling this book:

Mr J. S. Forbes,
Former Deputy Warden

Mr J. C. Furmedge,
Formerly of the Assay Office   Worshipful Company of
Goldsmiths, London

Miss S. Hare,
Librarian

Messrs Christie's, London

Messrs Sotheby's, London

INTRODUCTION

For many years, Sir Charles Jackson's book 'English Goldsmiths and their Marks' was the standard work for identifying makers and their marks. In compiling his book he apparently did not consult the original records at Goldsmiths' Hall since numerous discrepancies occurred, presumably due to this lack of information. In recent years, as a result of increased interest and further research, many of these discrepancies have come to light, particularly concerning London makers and their marks. In 1972 'Marks of London Goldsmiths and Silversmiths' was published and, since it had been compiled by direct consultation with the original records at Goldsmiths' Hall, some of these discrepancies were rectified, at least where the better-known London makers were concerned. At the same time it served as a useful reference book giving biographical details of the makers illustrated.

Since then Arthur Grimwade's book 'London Goldsmiths 1697-1837', published in 1976, has increased this knowledge far beyond any previous publication and become the standard work on London goldsmiths of this period. Even so, demand remains for the pocket sized 'Marks of London Goldsmiths and Silversmiths' to carry around antique shops, museums and auctions and it was felt that a revised edition would continue to be a useful reference book for all who have an interest in antique silver.

This edition has been arranged in four main sections: a revised section on makers together with their marks and biographical information; an addendum giving further information on particular makers; an updated list of London Assay marks; and an index of makers' marks. To trace a maker by means of a mark, simply locate it in the index by looking up the first letter of the mark; this will give the name of the maker which can then be located alphabetically in the makers' section. Where more than one maker has the same name, numerical classification has been used for reference purposes. It must be remembered that although this book contains over three hundred of the principal makers registered from 1697 to circa 1837, it only represents about one sixth of those to be found in the records during this period.

Unless otherwise stated, all makers' marks illustrated in the book are accurate drawings of those entered in the records at Goldsmiths' Hall, London. Those which have not been copied from the records were taken from actual articles of silver and the date given is generally that of the piece of silver on which the mark occurred.

All the drawings are from approximately one-and-a-half times to twice the size of the original punch marks. This means that where two or more different makers have used very similar marks to one another, for example the same initials in a rectangular surround, the only really conclusive check on the true maker is to compare the punch mark for size as well as shape with its original counterpart entered at Goldsmiths' Hall.

Makers and their Marks

Entries in the records were made by the actual metal punch used on the silverware. The punch tip was coated with a special ink and then pressed on to the appropriate page in the record book, thus leaving an ink impression of the punch mark. This was not always done very carefully with the result that some entries are smudged and blurred, while others are indistinct or have missed printing in part due to insufficient ink. It is because of this that drawings of the marks have been used as illustrations.

The earliest marks illustrated herein originate from 15 April 1697, the date when records were first kept in book form at Goldsmiths' Hall. Prior to this date, according to a work written in 1677 called 'The Touchstone for Gold and Silver Wares', lists of makers' marks were kept in the form of columns in the Assay Office at Goldsmiths' Hall. These marks were struck one below the other on to a column of hardened lead that was coupled with an adjoining column of parchment or vellum on which was written the corresponding maker's name. Records in this form are thought to have been in use for some two hundred years but unfortunately no example has survived to modern times. The columns were possibly destroyed when Goldsmiths' Hall was burnt out in the Great Fire of 1666 or probably in the Assay Office fire of November 1681. However, there still exists a copper plate with makers' marks stamped on it covering the period from 1675 to 1697. Unfortunately, as this plate does not give the makers' names or dates of entry of their marks, one can only recognise those marks which are known from other sources or which have been re-entered as Old Standard marks in the written records after 1 June 1720.

On 25 March 1697, the standard of silver for wrought plate was raised from 92.5% to 95.84% pure; i.e. from 925 parts to 958.4 parts of pure silver to every 1000. This was known as the New Standard or Britannia Standard, indicated on silverware by a mark depicting the figure of Britannia. Under this new standard, which remained compulsory until 31 May 1720, the old maker's mark was prohibited and a new one required to be used composed of the first two letters of the surname. In many instances this mark has the letters 'N.S.' after its entry in the records, thus indicating that it was a New Standard mark.

When the Old Standard of 92.5% pure was restored on 1 June 1720, the old form of maker's mark, namely the initials of the Christian and surname, was resumed. This mark often has the letters 'O.S.' after its entry in the records, thus indicating that it was an Old Standard mark. At the same time, the New Standard with its corresponding marks was retained as an optional alternative for silversmiths to use whenever they desired. This continued until 1739 when New Standard makers' marks were abandoned, although New Standard silver remains in use to the present day. Thus in many instances of silverware made between 1720 and 1739, it is possible to determine the standard of silver used according to the type of maker's mark stamped on the article.

In 1773, an enquiry was made by a Committee of the House of Commons as to 'the names and trades of the Wardens and Assayers of the Goldsmiths' Company, London, and when, at what time and by whom they were respectively elected.' The result of this enquiry was an account known as the

Parliamentary Return of 1773, which contained the names and addresses of all goldsmiths, silversmiths, plateworkers, etc whose marks had been entered at the Assay Office and who were still active members of the Company on 8 March 1773. It also stated the trade of each person, whether it was plateworker, goldsmith and goldworker, spoonmaker, haft and hilt maker or candlestick maker. In order to draw up this account, volumes of the Goldsmiths' records were submitted to the Parliamentary Committee but apparently two volumes containing makers' marks were never returned. These consisted of Small Workers marks from 24 May 1739 to 13 July 1758 and of Large Workers marks from 30 September 1759 to 7 March 1773. It may well be that these volumes still exist and are filed away with other records in the archives of Parliament, provided they survived the fire of 16 October 1834 when the old Houses of Parliament were largely destroyed. Because of the missing volumes, some silverware made during these two periods cannot always be attributed conclusively to a particular maker. However, one sometimes comes across a piece of silver made during one of these periods which is stamped with a maker's mark corresponding exactly with a mark entered at a later date. This is undoubtedly the same maker, his original mark being presumably in one of the missing volumes and for some reason, such as a change of address, he has entered his mark again at a later date.

Sometimes a maker's mark is found to be only similar to one entered in the records. In this case, provided it has a distinctive design already associated with that particular maker, one can usually assume it to be a variation of the mark already entered. Probably he did not bother to have it entered since it was so similar to the recorded mark and yet sufficiently distinctive not to be mistaken for any other maker. An example of this is to be found under the maker John Tuite. Occasionally a maker reverted to one of his earlier marks without re-recording it. Such a situation might occur after the termination of a partnership with another maker, which is what appears to have happened to Daniel Smith and Robert Sharp after Richard Carter disappeared from the partnership in 1780

An article of silver stamped with a maker's mark could have been made either by that particular craftsman or by one of his journeymen in the workshop. Consequently, the larger the workshop, the more journeymen employed and the greater the likelihood that the mastercraftsman only supervised the article's manufacture. Generally a maker, having already served an apprenticeship of at least seven years, had the ability to produce his own article of silverware, if so required. However, exceptions could and did occasionally occur. For example, a person who became a member of the Goldsmiths' Company by Patrimony had not necessarily served an apprenticeship, and the widow of a member who had recently died was usually permitted to take over her late husband's business without being a silversmith herself. In that instance, manufacturing would be carried out by the journeymen whilst she ran the design side perhaps or kept the books. Yet there were instances where women did serve apprenticeships and proved themselves competent silversmiths in their own rights. Where a widow has entered her own mark at Goldsmiths' Hall it is usually easily distinguished by its diamond-shaped surround, a design borrowed from ancient heraldry where widow's arms were enclosed in a similar frame called a lozenge.

Methods of Entry to the Goldsmiths' Company

Becoming a member or Freeman of the Goldsmiths' Company could be achieved in any one of three possible ways; by Service, by Redemption or by Patrimony.

1. Service: to serve and complete an apprenticeship to a Freeman of the Goldsmiths' Company. The period was generally seven years, sometimes more.
2. Redemption: to be nominated and seconded by members of the Goldsmiths' Company and then pay an entrance fee if elected by the Company's Court of Assistants.
3. Patrimony: to receive the freedom of the Company automatically upon application provided that the applicant's

father, at the time of the applicant's birth, was already a Freeman. If the father became free after the birth, then the applicant could not claim freedom by Patrimony

Occasionally a member of a Goldsmiths' Company in another part of the country wished to work in London and become a member of the London Company. Transference of membership was arranged through a Letter of Attorney giving proof to the new Company of existing freedom.

Structure of the Goldsmiths' Company

The general members of the Company were called Freemen. Above them was the Livery composed of approximately two hundred Liverymen who had been elected from the Freemen. One of their annual duties was to combine with the Liverymen of other Companies in the city for the purpose of electing the Lord Mayor of London. Over this group, governing the whole Goldsmiths' Company, was the Court of Assistants. In 1722, the Court consisted of sixty members but it was gradually reduced during the eighteenth century until, in 1827, the number was fixed at twenty-five members. Within the Court, four Assistants were elected annually to serve as senior members called Wardens. These Wardens were also placed in order of seniority, namely fourth, third, second and Prime Warden. In structure, it was rather like a modern board of directors with the Prime Warden in the place of the Chairman. This Court also appointed a Touch Warden or Deputy Warden who was in charge of the Assay Office and its workings. Before being elected to either the Livery or the Court of Assistants, a member asked to be nominated and then paid an entrance fee upon election. The same procedure is followed today, although the Court of Assistants has been substantially enlarged.

Originally any craftsman or tradesman working within London's city boundaries was required to be a member of a Company representative of one of the crafts or trades, eg Goldsmiths, Broderers, Turners, Watchmakers, Blacksmiths, Carpenters, etc. The fact that a craftsman was a member of a different Company to the one representing the craft in which he worked did not matter because, once he had gained the Freedom of any Company, and thereby the Freedom of the City, he was at liberty to work within the city boundaries at the craft or trade of his choice. Hence, several esteemed city goldsmiths included in this book were not members of the Goldsmiths' Company but had gained their Freedom from other Companies. After the Great Fire of London in 1666, the Goldsmiths' Company, together with others, found it increasingly difficult to enforce this regulation with the result that the occasional maker who was not a Freeman did manage to work within the city precincts. Outside the city boundaries it was optional whether or not they became members, with the result that numerous makers working outside the city precincts, chose not to become Freemen of the Company.

However, goldsmiths were permitted to work within the city boundaries without being Freemen, provided they worked in certain districts of the city called 'Liberty Areas'. These were privileged regions within the City of London which, prior to 1697, were exempt from the jurisdiction of the city and its civil laws and possessed rights of sanctuary. Each area elected its own sheriff and gave freedom from arrest to persons within its precincts. These concessions were subsequently abused and the Liberty Areas became the resorts of criminals and miscreants, hence the privileges were abolished by Act of Parliament in 1697 and the areas were again brought under the jurisdiction of the City, although they continued to be used by craftsmen trading within the areas who were not members of a City Company. The Liberty Areas included St Martins-Le-Grand (favoured by goldsmiths because of its proximity to Goldsmiths' Hall); Blackfriars; Whitefriars; St Katherine's by the Tower; the Temple; Duke's Place, Aldegate and Tower liberties, Minories precinct.

In the biographical notes within the main body of this book, the trades of individual people, if known, are stated in brackets. Where the stated trade commences with a capital letter, it indicates that the person so named was a Freeman of that particular Company. Where the word 'Citizen' is included in brackets, it indicates that the person so named was a Freeman of the City of London. Thus, Peter Archambo (No 1) (goldsmith, Citizen and Butcher) indicates that he traded as a goldsmith, was a Citizen of London and a Freeman of the Butchers' Company.

Assaying

Then as now, all articles of silver were required to be sent to the Assay Office for testing to ensure that the correct standard of silver had been used. For this, scrapings were removed from the article, weighed, wrapped in lead foil, and then heated in a small cup called a cupel. This cupel, being made of bone ashes, absorbed all the alloy metals leaving a residue of pure silver. The residue was weighed and the result compared with the weight of the original scrapings. If the difference was more than a certain amount, it meant that the silver was below standard and consequently the article was rejected. This method has now been superseded by a more accurate procedure for assaying silver.

In the Goldsmiths' Company, each assay year ran from 19 May (St Dunstan's Day) to 18 May of the following year. This meant that with each May a new date letter was introduced for the coming year which partially spanned two normal calendar years (eg May 1749 to May 1750). This procedure continued to apply until the end of 1974, except that in recent years the changeover occured at a convenient time in mid-May. From 1 January 1975 the changeover has been standardised for all Assay Offices. It now occurs on 1 January of each year.

Until 31 December 1751, the entries of makers' marks in the registers were dated according to a registration year which generally commenced on 25 March and finished on 24 March of the following year. At the end of 1751, the normal calendar year was introduced and is still in use today for the registration of marks. Thus, prior to 1751, any mark registered between 1 January and 24 March in any year was dated as having been entered in the previous calendar year, because the Office's new year started on the 25 March. For example, dates which actually occurred from 1 January to 24 March

1751 were recorded as being in 1750, but for the subsequent year, these three months were given as per the actual calendar year, namely 1752. Therefore, because of this changeover, no registration dates were recorded as being from 1 January to 24 March 1751, since it was then 1752.

Apprenticeship and Freedom Records

The dates of apprenticeships and freedoms have been obtained from the actual records of the time, the majority of which are to be found at Goldsmiths' Hall. Here again, up to 31 December 1751, apprenticeship and freedom dates were recorded in accordance with the Gregorian calendar wherein any date between 1 January and 24 March was given as being in the previous year to that in which it occurred. After 31 December 1751, the normal calendar year was introduced and has remained in use to the present day.

Most of the apprenticeship and freedom dates have been taken from the Goldsmiths' records except where makers were apprenticed to or gained freedom of other City Companies. In these cases, the information has been obtained from records held by the pertinent Company or from the Guildhall library where may Companies' records are now kept. Occasionally, the date when a maker undertook an apprenticeship can be traced without finding any record of his freedom date, usually about seven years later. This is generally due to the fact that he never completed his apprenticeship. Again, in rare instances, his freedom date is missing because he became free of another Company and this is often discovered solely by noticing his name in the records of that other Company. In the Guildhall library are preserved London Directories. These are records of censuses taken at irregular intervals during the eighteenth century, listing the names and addresses of all tradesmen in the city. It is sometimes possible to trace a goldsmith or silversmith in these directories in order to discover if he was still trading at a particular time and occasionally there is a clue suggesting the Company of which he was a Freeman. Although the apprenticeship and freedom records at Goldsmiths' Hall are comprehensive, those of some other Companies are much depleted, the records having been misplaced over the years, lost through general deterioration, or destroyed by local fires or bombing during the last war.

References

London Goldsmiths 1697-1837, Their Marks & Lives by Arthur G. Grimwade

The Halls of the Fishmongers' Company by Priscilla Metcalf

George Wickes 1698-1761 by Elaine Barr

A Directory of Newcastle Goldsmiths by Margaret A.V. Gill

The Huguenot Family of Courtauld by S.L. Courtauld

English Goldsmiths and their Marks by Sir Charles J. Jackson

Old English Plate by Wilfred Joseph Cripps

The London Goldsmiths by Ambrose Heal

Hester Bateman by David S. Shure

Paul Storr by N.M. Penzer

Barraud by E.M. Barraud

The Lengthening Shadow of Rundells by Shirley Bury

The Phipps Family & Edward Robinson by Sir Eric Sachs

Huguenot Goldsmiths in England & Ireland by Joan Evans

The Hennells Identified by Percy Hennell (Connoisseur Magazine, December 1955)

The Copper Plate of the Goldsmiths Company of Newcastle-upon-Tyne by J.W. Clark

Ancestors and descendants of Pezé Pilleau the London Goldsmith by C.T. Clay

The Goldsmiths' Company, London, for records of apprenticeships, freedoms, makers marks and Court minutes.

The following companies for records of apprenticeships and freedoms:

The Blacksmiths' Company
The Brewers' Company
The Broderers' Company
The Butchers' Company
The Clothworkers' Company
The Girdlers' Company
The Haberdashers' Company
The Longbow String Makers' Company
The Merchant Taylors' Company
The Pewterers' Company
The Skinners' Company
The Wax Chandlers' Company

William Abdy (No 1)

 24 June 1763
Noble Street

Moved to Oat Lane
26 February 1765

 5 October 1767
Oat Lane,
Noble Street

 10 May 1769
Oat Lane,
Noble Street

 15 October 1779
Small worker
5 Oat Lane

 1 September 1784
Plate worker
5 Oat Lane,
Noble Street

William Abdy (No 1) obtained his freedom of the Goldsmiths' Company by Redemption on 2 July 1752. He was made a Liveryman in June 1763 and died on 6 September 1790.

His two sons, William (No 2) and John, obtained their freedoms by Patrimony on 4 April 1781 and 4 October 1786 respectively. Another son, Thomas, was apprenticed to him on 6 August 1777.

It seems that William (No 2), after obtaining his freedom, worked with his father and eventually took over the firm. This possibly occurred in 1784, when new marks were entered in the records noting him as a plate worker instead of a small worker or, more likely, in September 1790 when new marks were entered following the death of William (No 1).

William Abdy (No 2)

15 September 1790
Plate worker
5 Oat Lane,
Noble Street

16 October 1790
5 Oat Lane,
Noble Street

Removed to 11 Wilson Street,
Finsbury, 3 February 1821

He was the son of William Abdy (No 1) and obtained his freedom by Patrimony on 4 April 1781. He was made a Liveryman in February 1791 and resigned from the Company on 3 December 1823, presumably having left the trade.

Robert Abercromby

11 May 1731
with George Hindmarsh
Christopher's Court,
St Martins-le-Grand

5 October 1731
Living in new Rents,
St Martins-le-Grand

23 June 1739
O.S.
In new Rents
St Martins-le-Grand

29 April 1740
N.S.
In new rents,
St Martins-le-Grand

He was not apprenticed through the Goldsmiths' Company nor was he a Freeman of the Company.

His address of St Martins-le-Grand, although within the city, was known as a 'liberty' area which meant it was exempt from the city's civil laws. Because of this he was not obliged to be a Freeman of a Company while trading in this locality.

Stephen Adams (No 1)

(No date. Probably February) 1759
with William Jury
Lilypot Lane

29 October 1759
with William Jury
Lilypot Lane

8 October 1760
Lilypot Lane

23 February 1762
Lilypot Lane

11 January 1764
St Ann's Lane

4 April 1765
St Ann's Lane

15 May 1766
St Ann's Lane

18 June 1767
St Ann's Lane

15 August 1769
St Ann's Lane

5 February 1774
Buckle maker
3 St Ann's Lane

26 March 1776
Buckle maker
3 St Ann's Lane

30 May 1781
3 St Ann's Lane

6 March 1782
3 St Ann's Lane

24 February 1787
3 St Ann's Lane

5 February 1802
3 St Ann's Lane

He was a Freeman of the Lorimers' Company.

His son, Stephen (No 2), obtained his freedom of the Goldsmiths' Company in 1784 and entered his own marks concurrently with Stephen (No 1) from the same address. Heal records the firm of Stephen Adams & Son from circa 1790 to 1796.

24 May 1792
Buckle maker
3 St Ann's Lane

21 May 1795
3 St Ann's Lane

17 June 1807
3 St Ann's Lane

14 November 1813
Plate worker
3 St Ann's Lane

2 May 1815
St Ann's Lane

Removed to 8 Wingrove Place,
Clerkenwell, 13 March 1824

Removed to 70 Chapel Street,
Islington, 21 January 1825

He was the son of Stephen Adams (No 1) (Citizen and Lorimer) and was apprenticed to Joseph Walton (oilman, Citizen and Goldsmith) of Little Britain on 1 October 1777. He obtained his freedom on 6 October 1784, was made a Liveryman in February 1791 and died on 15 July 1840.

Apparently he worked from the same premises as his father since his first three marks, signed 'Stephen Adams Junior', were entered concurrently with Stephen (No 1) from the same address.

N.B. An oilman was a purveyor of sweet oils such as olive oil.

Charles Aldridge

19 August 1775
with Henry Green
Plate workers
62 St Martins-le-Grand

20 September 1786
Plate worker
18 Aldergate Street

25 September 1780
18 Aldergate Street

He was the son of Charles Aldridge (staymaker) of Slimbridge, Gloucestershire and was apprenticed to his brother, Edward Aldridge (No 2) (Citizen and Goldsmith), on 5 July 1758. On the same day he was turned over to Edward Aldridge (No 1) (Citizen and Clothworker) who was probably his uncle. He obtained his freedom of the Goldsmiths' Company on 5 February 1766 by which time Edward (No 1) was dead.

His partnership with Henry Green was listed in the Parliamentary Return of 1773, giving their address as Aldersgate Street so presumably an earlier partnership mark to that of 1775 was entered at Goldsmiths' Hall in the now missing volume of Large Workers' marks 1759-73.

His brother, Edward (No 2), was turned over to Edward (No 1) in 1751 and obtained his freedom in 1758. He was made a Liveryman in 1763 and died between 1802 and 1811.

(See Addendum for further information on the Aldridge family)

Edward Aldridge (No 1)

5 February 1724
St Leonard Court,
Foster Lane

29 June 1739
Lillypot Lane
Clothworker

Removed to Foster Lane,
20 April 1743

20 July 1753
with John Stamper

He was the son of William Aldridge and obtained his freedom of the Clothworkers' Company by Patrimony on 4 February 1724. On 19 October 1723 he married Elizabeth Parker by whom he had three daughters and a son.

In June 1742 he and five other goldsmiths were charged with counterfeiting assay marks on wrought plate to avoid paying duty and assay charges. By August 1742 he had been prosecuted, tried and acquitted of the charge against him.

Two relatives who were turned over to him are thought to have been his nephews. They were Edward Aldridge (No 2) in 1751 and Charles Aldridge in 1758. Both obtained their freedom of the Goldsmiths' Company, Edward (No 2) in 1758 and Charles in 1766.

William Plummer was apprenticed to him in 1746 and obtained his freedom of the Clothworkers' Company in 1755.

Edward (No 1) died in December 1765 leaving all his estate to his widow, Elizabeth.

(See Addendum for further information on the Aldridge family)

Joseph Allen & Company

9 March 1730
with Mordecai Fox
Living in St Swithin's Lane,
near Lombard Street

21 August 1739
with Mordecai Fox
At the Sun,
in St Swithin's Lane

He was not a Freeman of the Goldsmiths' Company. Possibly he was a Freeman of another Company thereby permitting him to trade within the city precincts. His partner, Mordecai Fox, was apprenticed to silversmith, Francis Garthorne who was a member of the Girdlers' Company. Fox therefore became a member of the same Company when he obtained his freedom on 15 July 1712.

Joseph Allen

20 May 1761
Featherstone Street,
Bunhill Row

Later moved to Old Bailey

He was the son of John Allen (brasier) of St Luke's, Middlesex and was apprenticed to John Pierce on 6 March 1745. He obtained his freedom on 7 December 1757.

7 October 1811
Plate worker
55 Compton Street,
Clerkenwell

8 April 1824
55 Compton Street,
Clerkenwell

31 January 1831
with John Angell (No 1)
Plate workers
55 Compton Street,
Clerkenwell

6 July 1840
with Joseph Angell (No 2)
Plate workers
55 Compton Street,
Clerkenwell

Removed to 25 Panton Street,
Haymarket, 13 October 1842

He was the son of Joseph Angell (weaver) of Cow Cross,
London who apparently changed his trade to silversmith at
some time between 1799 and 1808. Joseph Angell (No 1)
was apprenticed to Henry Nutting (Goldsmith) on 5 October
1796 and obtained his freedom on 3 October 1804. He died
circa 1851-53.

He had two brothers; John (No 1) and Abraham. John (No 1)
was apprenticed to William Elliott (Goldsmith) on 6 February

Joseph Angell (No 1) continued

1799 and obtained his freedom on 7 January 1807. Abraham was apprenticed to Joseph Angell (No 1) on 6 July 1808 but there is no record of his having obtained his freedom.

Joseph Angell (No 1) also had three sons; Charles, Joseph (No 2) and Thomas John. Charles was apprenticed to his father on 2 February 1825 but there is no record of his having obtained his freedom. Joseph (No 2) obtained his freedom by Patrimony on 3 February 1836 and was made a Liveryman in 1842. He entered his own mark on 20 October 1849, recording his address as 10 Strand, London with a manufactory at 25 Panton Street, Haymarket. Presumably he had recently taken over his father's business at Panton Street. He died on 13 September 1891. Thomas John became a solicitor and obtained his freedom by Patrimony on 1 December 1841.

Nathaniel Appleton

 26 July 1771
with Ann Smith
Aldersgate Street

He was the son of George Appleton (cordwainer) of St Giles without Cripplegate and was apprenticed to James Waters on 2 August 1751. He obtained his freedom on 7 March 1759.

Peter Archambo (No 1)

9 March 1721
N.S.
At the Golden Cup,
in Green Street
Freeman of the Butchers' Company

2 November 1722
O.S.
Green Street

Later he removed to Hemings Row

27 June 1739
At the Golden Cup,
Coventry Street, Piccadilly

He was the son of Peter Archambo (staymaker) and was apprenticed to Jacob Margas, a member of the Butchers' Company, on 6 April 1710. He obtained his freedom of the Butchers' Company on 7 December 1720 and died in 1767. His will, dated 20 May 1759, was proved on 7 August 1767. About 1722, he married Elizabeth Troubee by whom he had four daughters, Martha, Ann, Elizabeth and Esther and a son, Peter (No 2).

Peter (No 2) was apprenticed to both him and Paul De Lamerie in December 1738 and obtained his freedom in February 1748.

(See Addendum for Peter Archambo's will)

Peter Archambo (No 2)

18 January 1750
with Peter Meure
At the Golden Cup,
Coventry Street

He was the son of Peter Archambo (No 1) (goldsmith, Citizen and Butcher). On 5 December 1738 he was apprenticed to Paul de Lamerie (Goldsmith) and on the same day turned over to his father. This enabled him to serve his apprenticeship under his father, a working goldsmith, but still become free of the Goldsmiths' Company instead of the Butchers' Company because he was originally apprenticed to a Freeman of the Goldsmiths' Company. He obtained his freedom on 3 February 1748 and died at some date prior to 5 February 1768 when a second probate was granted to his father's will.

His partner and cousin, Peter Meure, was apprenticed to Peter Archambo (No 1) on 6 December, 1721 and obtained his freedom of the Butchers' Company on 5 July 1739.

John Bache

(No date. Probably April 1697)
with William Denny
Dove Court
Lombard Street

1 November 1700
In Lombard Street

20 June 1720
O.S.
In Lombard Street

He was the son of Thomas Bache (yeoman) of Avely, Salop and was apprenticed to William Harrison (Goldsmith) on 28 February 1673. He obtained his freedom of the Goldsmiths' Company on 5 March 1680 and was made an Assistant in 1703. He became 4th Warden in 1718, 3rd Warden in 1722, 2nd Warden in 1723 and Prime Warden in 1726.

His first wife, Margaret, who died in 1682, gave him a son, John, in 1681. In 1683 he married Suzanna Moore by whom he had three sons and four daughters between 1684 and 1701.

William Bainbridge

April 1697
Catherine Wheel Alley,
Whitechapel

He was the son of Thomas Bainbridge (clerk) of Bookford,
Derbyshire and was apprenticed to Robert Peak on 19 October
1683. He obtained his freedom on 22 October 1690 and died
in 1707 when his wife took over the business and entered
her own mark.

Mary Bainbridge

21 April 1707
Oat Lane
Widow of William Bainbridge

She was the wife of William Bainbridge and, upon his
death, took over the business entering her own mark in
1707.

Thomas Bamford

 5 January 1720
N.S.
Gutter Lane

 27 June 1720
O.S.
Gutter Lane

 18 July 1739
Foster Lane

He was the son of Thomas Bamford (malster) of Uttoxeter, Staffordshire and was apprenticed to Charles Adam (Goldsmith) on 18 August 1703. He obtained his freedom of the Goldsmiths' Company on 5 September 1711.

He and his wife, Judith, had three sons and two daughters between 1718 and 1726. The eldest son, Thomas, was born in 1718 and died in 1732.

Samuel Wood was apprenticed to him in 1721.

Thomas Bamford specialized in manufacturing casters as did his master, Charles Adam, and his apprentice, Samuel Wood.

Edward Barnard (No 1)

14 October 1808
with Rebecca Emes
Plate workers
Amen Corner, Paternoster Row
(These two marks were entered by
'Virtue of a Power of Attorney' and
signed by William Emes and Edward
Barnard (No 1))

29 April 1818
with Rebecca Emes
I enter one mark for Rebecca Emes
(Signed by Edward Barnard (No 1))

20 February 1821
with Rebecca Emes
Amen Corner, Paternoster Row

28 October 1825
with Rebecca Emes
Amen Corner, Paternoster Row

25 February 1829
with Edward (No 2), John (No 1)
and William Barnard
Plate workers
Amen Corner

Removed to Angel Street,
St Martins-le-Grand, 18 June 1838

His father, Edward Barnard, a silver flatter of Aldersgate, London, was born on 2 March 1735, married Mary Gastineau of London on 4 April 1763 and died on 23 February 1808. Mary, who had nine children, was born on 17 May 1734 and died on 30 April 1800.

Edward (No 1) was born on 30 November 1767 and apprenticed to Charles Wright on 5 December 1781. On 4 February 1784 he was turned over to Thomas Chawner and on 4 February 1789 he obtained his freedom of the Goldsmiths' Company, remaining with the Chawner firm as one of its employees in the workshop. In the years that followed, he saw Thomas Chawner's son, Henry, take over the firm, then John Emes became Henry's partner. Eventually Emes became head of the firm with Edward (No 1) as leading journeyman. After John Emes died in 1808, his widow, Rebecca Emes, took Edward (No 1) into the firm as a partner. Edward (No 1) was made a Liveryman in June 1811 and died on 4 January 1855.

On 28 January 1791, Edward (No 1) married Mary Boosey, a cousin of William Boosey who founded the well-known firm of music publishers. They had ten children, five boys and five girls. Three of the sons, Edward (No 2), John (No 1) and William, were apprenticed to their father to learn the trade of silversmith. Edward (No 2) was apprenticed on 7 February 1810, obtained his freedom of the Goldsmiths' Company on 5 March 1817 and was made a Liveryman in January 1822. John (No 1) was apprenticed on 1 January 1812 and obtained his freedom on 6 January 1819. On 14 March 1826 he married Margaret Faraday, sister of Michael Faraday the scientist. William was apprenticed on 5 July 1815 and obtained his freedom on 5 February 1823. Another son, George, became a landscape painter and art master at Rugby School.

Of the daughters, Mary married William Ker Reid, silver-smith, on 11 February 1812; Elizabeth married David Reid, silversmith and brother of William Ker, on 26 August 1815; Sarah married Michael Faraday, the scientist, on 12 June 1821.

George Baskerville

9 February 1738
at the Sign of Golden Acorn,
Chandos Street

26 July 1745
Cock Court,
St Martins-le-Grand

1 February 1751
Removed into Round Court,
in the Strand

27 January 1755
with William Sampel
New Inn Passage,
Clare Market

3 September 1755
New Inn Passage,
Clare Market

6 May 1775
with Thomas Morley
Plate workers
8 Albion Buildings

3 March 1780
Small worker
8 Albion Buildings

George Baskerville continued

He was the son of George Baskerville (yeoman) of Winterbourne Bassett, Wiltshire and was apprenticed to Joseph Sanders on 4 May 1732 for a term of seven years. There is no record of his having obtained his freedom and it seems that he must have terminated his apprenticeship in February 1738, after less than six years, in order to establish himself with his own mark. He died prior to March 1782, this being when his will was proved. (See Addendum for George Baskerville's will)

Ann Bateman

 * 2 May 1791
with Peter Bateman
Plate workers
Bunhill Row

 * (Between 1 and 3) January 1800
with Peter & William Bateman (No 1)
Plate workers
Bunhill Row

Born in 1748, she was the daughter of James and Ann Olympe Dowling. In May 1769 she married Jonathan Bateman at St Luke's, Old Street. They had seven children including a Jonathan and William (No 1) both of whom were apprenticed to their father.

When her mother-in-law, Hester, retired, Ann's husband and his brother Peter took over the family business. They entered their first partnership marks on 7 December 1790. On 19 April 1791 Jonathan died of cancer leaving Ann his share of the firm. On 2 May 1791, Ann and Peter, her brother-in-law, entered their first partnership marks. Also during 1791 the family business moved to 108 Bunhill Row, the premises at 107 being let to an Adam Travers.

In January 1800 her son, William (No 1), joined the partnership. In 1805, Ann retired due to increasing ill health from dropsy and died before 1813.

* Mark entered in two sizes.

Hester Bateman

 16 April 1761
In Bunhill Row

 9 January 1771
Bunhill Row

 17 June 1774
Spoon maker
107 Bunhill Row

 3 December 1774
Plate worker
107 Bunhill Row

 5 June 1776
107 Bunhill Row

 21 February 1778
107 Bunhill Row

 25 November 1781
107 Bunhill Row

 28 June 1787
Plate worker
Bunhill Row

 3 August 1787
Bunhill Row

40

Hester Bateman continued

The daughter of Thomas Needham, she was born in 1708 at Clerkenwell. In 1730 she is thought to have gone through a form of marriage to John Bateman, jeweller and chain maker. Their first child, John, was born in March 1730. Her official church marriage to John Bateman was at St Botolph, Aldersgate on 20 May 1732. They had a further five children, Letticia born 1733, Ann 1736, Peter 1740, William 1745 and Jonathan 1747. John the eldest, worked for the family firm until his death in 1778. Letticia married Richard Clarke, jeweller and goldsmith, in 1755 and had six children who actually suvived infancy, one of whom, Sarah, married Crispin Fuller, goldsmith. Peter and Jonathan were both apprenticed to Richard Clarke and eventually took over the family firm when Hester retired in 1790. When Hester's husband died of consumption on 16 November 1760, Hester carried on the family firm and entered her first mark on 16 April 1761. She appears to have been illiterate, as her only signature in the records is the crude intials, 'H.B'. In 1790 Hester handed over the firm to her sons, Peter and Jonathan, and retired to live at Holborn with her widowed daughter, Letticia. On 16 September 1794, Hester died aged 85 years.

(Note: In Hester Bateman's will and the proving of the will, her daughter's name is spelt in four different ways; Letisia, Letticia, Lettitia and Letitia).

(See Addendum for details of Hester Bateman's will)

Jonathan Bateman

  * 7 December 1790
with Peter Bateman
Plate workers
Bunhill Row

 * 9 December 1790
with Peter Bateman
Bunhill Row

The youngest son of Hester and John Bateman, he was born on 18 November 1747. Although he completed his apprenticeship to Richard Clarke, his brother-in-law, in April 1769, it was not until 7 April 1784 that he obtained his freedom of the Goldsmiths' Company by Redemption. In May 1769 he married Ann Dowling. They had seven children including a Jonathan and William (No 1) both of whom were apprenticed to their father to become goldsmiths. After Hester's retirement, Jonathan senior and his brother Peter took over the family business and entered their partnership marks on 7 December 1790. On 19 April 1791, Jonathan died of cancer and Ann, his widow, inherited his share of the business.

Jonathan junior was apprenticed to his father on 7 July 1784 and, following his father's death, was turned over to his mother, Ann, on 1 June 1791, eventually obtaining his freedom on 5 October 1791.

William (No 1) was apprenticed to his father on 7 January 1789 and turned over to Ann on 6 July 1791, obtaining his freedom on 6 February 1799.

* Mark entered in two sizes.

Peter Bateman

* 7 December 1790
with Jonathan Bateman
Plate workers
Bunhill Row

* 9 December 1790
with Jonathan Bateman
Bunhill Row

* 2 May 1791
with Ann Bateman
Plate workers
Bunhill Row

* (Between 1 and 3) January 1800
with Ann and William Bateman (No 1)
Plate workers
Bunhill Row

* 8 November 1805
with William Bateman (No 1)
Plate workers
Bunhill Row

The son of Hester and John Bateman, he was born on 25 January 1740. On 15 September 1755 he was apprenticed to Richard Clarke, his brother-in-law, but although he served the apprenticeship, he never took up his freedom of the Goldsmiths' Company. He first married Elizabeth Beaver (widow) in 1763 and lived at 86 Bunhill Row. Following her death, he returned to his mother's home where he remained until he

43

Peter Bateman continued

remarried in 1776. Upon this marriage he bought and moved into 106 Bunhill Row where he lived for the rest of his life. He never had any children by either marriage.

Following Hester's retirement from the firm, Peter and his brother, Jonathan, entered their first partnership marks on 7 December 1790. After Jonathan's death in April 1791, Ann, his widow, entered into partnership with Peter, their first marks being recorded on 2 May 1791.

In January 1800, Ann's son, William (No 1), joined the partership and, in 1805, Ann retired leaving Peter and William (No 1) to continue running the firm. In 1815, Peter retired and eventually died on 19 November 1825 aged 85 years.

* Mark entered in two sizes.

William Bateman (No 1)

 * (Between 1 and 3) January 1800
with Peter and Ann Bateman
Plate workers
Bunhill Row

 * 8 November 1805
with Peter Bateman
Plate workers
Bunhill Row

 15 February 1815
Plate worker
108 Bunhill Row

The son of Ann and Jonathan Bateman, he was born in 1774. On 7 January 1789 he was apprenticed to his father to be a goldsmith but following his father's death in April 1791, he was turned over to his mother on 6 July 1791 to continue his apprenticeship. On 6 February 1799, he obtained his freedom and in January 1800 he entered his first marks in partnership with his mother and uncle. Later that year he married Ann Wilson. They had eight children, five daughters and three sons including William (No 2).

In 1802 William (No 1) and his family moved into 107 Bunhill Row. In 1805, his mother retired from the family business due to her increasing ill health from dropsy. Following his uncle's retirement, William entered his own marks on 15 February 1815.

In 1816 he became a Liveryman and in 1828 an Assistant. He was now living at Stoke Newington, the premises at Bunhill Row being entirely workshops.

He became 4th Warden in 1833, 3rd Warden in 1834, 2nd Warden in 1835 and Prime Warden in 1836. He again became 4th Warden in 1847, 3rd Warden in 1848, 2nd Warden in 1849 but failed to become Prime Warden again as he died in January 1850 when 76 years old.

*Mark entered in two sizes.

Wiliam Bateman (No 2)

9 February 1827
Plate worker
Bunhill Row

(These marks for 1827
and 1830 were entered
at Goldsmiths' Hall
by William (No 2)
although at the time
his father was still
in control of the
firm.)

22 May 1830
Bunhill Row

31 December 1839
with Daniel Ball
Plate workers
Bunhill Row

The son of Ann (née Wilson) and William Bateman (No 1), he was born soon after their marriage in 1800. On 1 February 1815, he was apprenticed to his father to be a silversmith and obtained his freedom on 4 December 1822. He did not get on very well with his father, particularly after marrying Elizabeth Parratt, a serving girl.

In 1829 he was made a Liveryman. In 1839 he assumed control of the family firm and took Daniel Ball as his partner. He died in 1875.

John Bayley

21 March 1751
Wood Street

He was the son of Richard Bayley (Citizen and Goldsmith) of London and was apprenticed to James Smith (No 1) on 6 June 1732. On 13 February 1737 he was turned over to his father for the residue of his term, with the consent of James Smith's executors. He obtained his freedom by Patrimony on 2 May 1740 and was made a Liveryman in March 1750.

Richard Bayley

29 March 1708
N.S.
Foster Lane

16 July 1720
O.S.
Foster Lane

19 June 1739
Foster Lane

He was the son of Antony Bayley (yeoman) of Hampton, near Highworth, Wiltshire and was apprenticed to Charles Overing on 28 April 1699. He was turned over to John Gibbons on 26 April 1704 and obtained his freedom on 11 December 1706. He was made a Liveryman in 1712, an Assistant in 1732, 4th Warden in 1748 and Prime Warden in 1751.

His son, John, was turned over to him on 13 February

Richard Bayley continued

1737 for the residue of his apprenticeship but obtained his freedom by Patrimony on 2 May 1740.

Among his apprentices were Richard Gurney, Thomas Cooke and Henry Brind.

His mark is frequently found on tea and coffee pots and tankards.

Richard Beale

 1 October 1733
At the Unicorn,
in Henrietta Street,
Covent Garden

 23 June 1739
Henrietta Street
Covent Garden

The son of ----Beale (draper) of Hull, Yorkshire, he was apprenticed to Jonathan Newton on 13 June 1722 and turned over to John Le Sage on 23 July 1725. There is no record of his obtaining his freedom but presumably he did not take it up since it was not required when working outside the city precincts.

William Bell

 10 February 1759
Monkwell Street

Removed to Featherstone Street,
31 October 1759

 22 March 1763
Featherstone Street

Removed to Silver Street,
3 April 1764

 8 March 1769
Bridgewater Square

 4 August 1772
Rolls Buildings

 28 October 1774
10 Rolls Buildings,
Fetter Lane

 6 August 1777
Rolls Buildings

He was the son of John Bell (linen draper) of Reading, Berkshire and was apprenticed to William Burton on 3 February 1748. He obtained his freedom on 9 April 1755, was made a Liveryman in March 1758 and resigned from the Livery in August 1778.

He appears to be the 'William Bell' who was appointed Junior Weigher in the Assay Office on 9 December 1763.

Charles Bellassyse

21 July 1740
Eagle Street,
near Red Lion Square

He was the son of William Bellassyse (Citizen and Merchant Taylor deceased) of London and was apprenticed to James Wilkes on 5 February 1734. On 27 July 1738 he was turned over to Marmaduke Daintry and obtained his freedom on 2 July 1741.

Heal records him as being at The Mitre, Eagle Street, Red Lion Square in 1740. Note that a mitre is incorporated in his mark.

William Bellassyse

16 March 1717
N.S.
In Monkwell Street,
Freeman of Merchant Taylors

3 July 1723
O.S.
In Holborn
Freeman of Merchant Taylors

He was the son of Richard Bellassyse (clerk deceased) of Haughton, Durham and was apprenticed to Seth Lofthouse, a Freeman of the Merchant Taylors' Company who traded as a goldsmith, on 5 October 1709. On 7 November 1716 he obtained his freedom of the Merchant Taylors' Company.

He died prior to 1734 when his son, Charles, was apprenticed to James Wilkes.

Joseph Bird

April 1697
Foster Lane
Free Brewer

(No date or address entered. Possibly entered 10 July 1702 when another maker's entry was written in what appears to be the same ink.)

19 June 1724
O.S.
Foster Lane
Free Brewer

He was apprenticed to an unknown member of the Brewers' Company and obtained his freedom of that Company on 19 June 1690. Heal records his having died in 1735.

Matthew Cooper (No 1) was turned over to him in 1693.

Edmund Boddington

 8 October 1725
Gutter Lane
Free Goldsmith

 5 July 1727
O.S.
Foster Lane

He was the son of Edmund Boddington (Citizen and Apothecary deceased) of London and was apprenticed to John Boddington (Goldsmith) on 7 May 1706. It is likely that John Boddington was his uncle. Edmund was turned over to Giles Edmunds (Turner) on 24 September 1706 and obtained his freedom on 5 May 1714. Heal records him as being insolvent in 1729 yet he was made a Liveryman in March 1736.

Thomas Heming was apprenticed to him on 7 February 1738 but was turned over to Peter Archambo (No 1) (goldsmith and Butcher) on the same day. This enabled Heming to serve his apprenticeship under Archambo, a working goldsmith, yet still obtain his freedom of the Goldsmiths' Company because of being apprenticed to Boddington in the first instance.

John Boddington

April 1697
Foster Lane

He was the son of John Boddington (clerk deceased) of Marston, Leicestershire and was apprenticed to Jacob Harris on 2 November 1677. He obtained his freedom on 18 July 1688 and was made a Liveryman in April 1705. In 1692 he married Elizabeth Franklyn by whom he had two daughters, Elizabeth in 1693 and Anne in 1696 and a son, John, who was apprenticed to him on 1 May 1718. John junior was turned over to Samuel Gatcliff (jeweller) in December 1718 and then turned over to a Mr Wright in 1722.

Having become bankrupt in 1714, John senior petitioned for the vacant position of Beadle of the Goldsmiths' Company. On 15 February 1715 he was appointed to the post which he held until his death in January 1728.

Edmund Boddington, who was probably his nephew, was apprenticed to him in 1706.

Pierre Bouteiller

13 February 1727
St Martin's, South Court

He was not apprenticed through the Goldsmiths' Company nor was he a Freeman of the Company.

John Bridge

13 November 1823
Plate worker
76 Dean Street,
Soho

25 November 1823
76 Dean Street,
Soho

He was born on 21 January 1755, the eldest son of Mary and Thomas Bridge of Piddletrenthide, Dorset. Mary and Thomas died in 1779 and 1792 respectively. John was apprenticed to William Rogers (jeweller) of Bath in 1769. He came to London in 1777 where he was employed by the firm of Pickett & Rundell as shopman then, in 1788, he became Rundell's partner. Rundell had been apprenticed to Rogers in Bath in 1760.

It is said that in 1789, George III was visiting Weymouth when he was introduced to a John Bridge, farmer, of Wynford Eagle near Bridport. They discussed agricultural matters and during their conversation John Bridge recommended his cousin, John Bridge, a partner of Rundell & Bridge, goldsmiths, on Ludgate Hill. George III subsequently gave his support to the firm, transferring his patronage from Thomas Heming to Rundell & Bridge and, in 1797, the firm was appointed Goldsmiths and Jewellers to the King.

John Bridge continued

A similar warrant was received from George, the Prince of Wales. The firm retained the royal warrant until 1830 when it was acquired by the firm of Garrard.

From 1807 until 1819, Paul Storr ran the manufacturing side of the firm using his own mark on all gold and silverware. When Storr left, Philip Rundell, the senior partner, entered his own mark at Goldsmiths' Hall. Then, when Rundell retired in 1823, John Bridge entered his own mark. He retired in 1830 and died in 1834 without ever becoming a Freeman of the Goldsmiths' Company. Following his death, the firm's name was changed to Rundell, Bridge & Co and continued trading until its closure at the end of 1843.

At Piddletrenthide school there is a bust of John Bridge dated 1821 which states 'during a period of more than fifty years' residence in London, never forgot this his native village'. When, in 1826, Westminster Abbey disposed of its old gates, John Bridge acquired them to use as playground gates at the village school.

Bridge's nephew, John Gawler Bridge, joined the firm in 1804, obtained his freedom by Redemption on 5 June 1816 and became a partner in 1817. He was made a Liveryman in 1818, became Prime Warden in 1839 and died in June 1849.

Henry Brind

 6 May 1742
Foster Lane

He was the son of William Brind (victualler deceased) of Highworth, Wiltshire and was apprenticed to Richard Bayley on 5 March 1734. He obtained his freedom on 6 May 1742 and was made a Liveryman in September 1746. His brother was Walter Brind (Goldsmith).

Walter Brind

 7 February 1749
Foster Lane

 31 August 1751
Foster Lane

 11 October 1757
Foster Lane

26 February 1781
Plate worker
34 Foster Lane

Walter Brind continued

He was the son of William Brind (innholder deceased) of Highworth, Wiltshire and was apprenticed to John Raynes on 7 October 1736. On 2 July 1742 he was turned over to his brother, Henry Brind (Goldsmith), and obtained his freedom on 8 November 1743. He was made a Liveryman in March 1758 and died between 1795 and 1801.

His wife, Anne, died on 11 January 1791. They had three daughters and four sons, William, Henry, Thomas and Walter, who were apprenticed to their father in 1763, 1769, 1774 and 1778 respectively. Thomas was turned over to Thomas Clements In 1777 and Walter to George Jackson in 1780.

William Burwash

16 August 1802
Case maker
3 Red Lion Street,
Clerkenwell

23 June 1803
3 Red Lion Street
Clerkenwell

7 October 1805
with Richard Sibley
Plate workers
14 Bartholomew Close

6 July 1812
Plate worker
14 Bartholomew Close

10 August 1812
14 Bartholomew Close

23 April 1813
14 Bartholomew Close

He was not apprenticed through the Goldsmiths' Company nor was he a Freeman of the Company.

His son, George, was apprenticed to Richard Sibley on 1 January 1806 and another son, William, to William Chawner (No 2) on 6 November 1816.

William Burwash's sister, Mary, married William Chawner (No 2) on 16 June 1816.

Abraham Buteux

13 May 1721
N.S.
Green Street
near Leicesterfield
Freeman of the Skinners

13 May 1721
O.S.
Green Street,
near Leicesterfield
Freeman of the Skinners

The son of Elizabeth and Isaac Buteux (weaver deceased) of Stepney, London, he was baptized on 13 June 1698 with Simon Pantin as his godfather. He was apprenticed to William West, a member of the Skinners' Company, on 4 December 1711 and obtained his freedom of that Company on 4 August 1719.

He married Elizabeth Pantin at St Paul's Cathedral on 11 February 1720. Probably she was Simon Pantin's daughter.

When he died in 1731 his widow, Elizabeth, took over the family business and entered her own mark.

Elizabeth Buteux

 15 November 1731
Norris Street,
St James

Elizabeth was probably the daughter of Simon Pantin
(Goldsmith). On 11 February 1720, she married Abraham
Buteux at St Paul's Cathedral. Following his death in 1731,
she took over the business and entered her own mark on 15
February 1731.

On 6 February 1732, she married Benjamin Godfrey
(goldsmith) but, following his death in 1741, she entered
a further mark of her own on 29 June 1741. (See under
Elizabeth Godfrey.)

John Cafe

 21 August 1740
Foster Lane

Removed to Carey Lane,
13 April 1741

 13 December 1742
This new mark was entered
the old one being broke
(No address, presumably Carey Lane)

Removed to Gutter Lane,
31 May 1743

He was the son of Anne and Giles Cafe (yeoman) of Blackford, Somerset and was apprenticed to James Gould (Goldsmith) on 15 December 1730. He did not obtain his freedom until 5 March 1741 although he had already entered his first mark in August 1740. He was made a Liveryman in September 1746 and died in 1757 leaving a wife, Elizabeth, and five children, Mary, John, Anne, Elizabeth and Susanna.

Among the nine apprentices whom he accepted between 1741 and 1754 were his younger brother, William Cafe, William Gamble and Thomas Hannam.

Like his master, James Gould, John Cafe specialized in manufacturing candlesticks and tapersticks of which he was one of the most prolific makers of his time.

(See Addendum for details of John Cafe's will)

16 August 1757
Gutter Lane

Circa 1758 (This mark is not recorded at Goldsmiths' Hall. Presumed to be William Cafe and possibly entered in the missing volume of Large Workers marks 1759-73.)

He was the son of Anne and Giles Cafe (yeoman) of Blackford, Somerset and was apprenticed to his elder brother, John, on 11 March 1742. On 19 March 1747 he was turned over to Simon Jouet (Goldsmith) whose family came from Exeter. Presumably William completed his apprenticeship about 1749 although he did not take up his freedom of the Company until 5 October 1757. He was made a Liveryman in March 1758 and became bankrupt in 1772. He died in 1802 leaving a second wife, Jane, and a married daughter, Mrs. Elizabeth Upstone.

Thomas Hannam was apprenticed to John Cafe in 1754 and turned over to William Cafe in 1757, following John's death.

(See Addendum for further information on William Cafe.)

Christopher Canner (No 1)

April 1697
Gutter Lane

He was the son of Edward Canner (hosier deceased) of Tewkesbury, Gloucestershire and was apprenticed to Francis Archbold on 18 June 1680. He obtained his freedom on 20 June 1688, was made a Liveryman in April 1705 and died in January 1708.

He and his wife, Mary, had two daughters and a son, Christopher (No 2) who obtained his freedom in 1716. Christopher (No 1) seems to have specialized in manufacturing casters.

Richard Watts was apprenticed to Christopher (No 1) in 1698 and obtained his freedom in 1707.

Christopher Canner (No 2)

30 May 1716
N.S.
Maiden Lane

8 July 1720
O.S.
Foster Lane

Born in 1692, he was the son of Christopher Canner (No 1) and obtained his freedom by Patrimony on 18 May 1716. He married Mary Page of Holborn on 16 February 1723 and had two sons, both named Christopher, who died in 1723 and 1725 respectively.

John Carter

 21 September 1776
Plate worker
Bartholomew Close

 30 October 1776
Bartholomew Close
 Left the trade (retired)
20 January 1777

He was not apprenticed through the Goldsmiths' Company nor was he a Freeman of the Company.

Presumably it was his son, Richard Carter, who entered his mark from the same address upon John Carter's retirement in 1777.

John Carter specialized in candlesticks and salvers. He bought large numbers of candlesticks manufactured in Sheffield which he then overstruck with his own mark before re-selling in London.

Richard Carter

20 January 1777
with Robert Makepeace (No 1)
Plate workers
Bartholomew Close

9 December 1778
with Daniel Smith
and Robert Sharp
Plate workers
14 Westmoreland Buildings

He was not apprenticed through the Goldsmiths' Company nor was he a Freeman of the Company. Presumably he was the son of John Carter and entered his mark with Robert Makepeace on the day of John Carter's retirement in January 1777.

It is possible that Richard Carter retired or died early in 1780, this being the date when Smith and Sharp re-entered the partnership mark of 9 December 1778 but with Carter's initials removed.

Benjamin Cartwright (No 1)

BC
22 June 1732
At the Three Horseshoes,
Pedlars Lane,
Cow Cross

20 June 1739
At the Crown and Pearl,
Bartholomew Close

19 May 1748
At the Crown and Pearl,
Bartholomew Close

18 February 1757
At the Crown and Pearl,
Bartholomew Close

He was not apprenticed through the Goldsmiths' Company
nor was he a Freeman of the Company.

His son was Benjamin Cartwright (No 2), a member of the
Blacksmiths' Company.

Benjamin Cartwright (No 2)

 22 April 1754
Smithfield

 7 September 1756
At the 'Kings Arms & Snuffers',
in the Strand

 2 January 1770
Pall Mall

He was never a Freeman of the Goldsmiths' Company. He was
the son of Benjamin Cartwright (No 1) and was apprenticed
to James Cartwright, a member of the Blacksmiths' Company,
on 6 February 1746. Presumably James was a relation,
possibly an uncle or elder brother.

Benjamin obtained his freedom of the Blacksmiths' Company on 1 March 1754.

Daniel Chartier

23 March 1740
Hemings Row,
St Martin's Lane

He was the son of Jean Chartier (Citizen and Goldsmith) of London and was apprenticed to his father on 25 October 1720. There is no record of his obtaining his freedom but this would not have been a requirement since he was working outside the city precincts.

Jean Chartier

April 1698
N.S.
Hemings Row
St Martin's Lane in the Fields

10 July 1723
O.S.
Hemings Row
Free Goldsmith

He and his wife, Suzanne Garnier, were Huguenot refugees from Blois, France. He obtained his freedom by Redemption (by order of the Court of Aldermen) on 13 April 1698. His wife, Suzanne, was related to the goldsmith, Daniel Garnier. Possibly she was his sister.

Suzanne had three sons, Jean, Daniel and Issac. Jean, born in December 1697, does not appear to have become a Freeman or have been apprenticed through the Goldsmiths' Company. Daniel was apprenticed to Jean senior in 1720 and, although he appears to have eventually taken over the family business, he never took up his freedom of the Goldsmiths' Company. Issac, the third son, obtained his freedom of the Goldsmiths' Company by Patrimony on 2 July 1746. Jean senior also had a daughter, Henriette. She married his apprentice, Alexis Pezé Pilleau, in 1724. Pilleau had been apprenticed to him in 1710 and had taken up his freedom of the Goldsmiths' Company in 1724.

11 November 1786
Plate worker
Amen Corner

31 August 1787
Amen Corner

27 August 1796
with John Emes
Plate workers
Amen Corner

He was born on 14 November 1764, the son of Sarah and Thomas Chawner (Goldsmith), and obtained his freedom by Patrimony on 7 December 1785.

According to Burke, *Landed Gentry*, he was married on 3 March 1788 to Mary Hore, only daughter and heiress of Edward Hore of Esher, Surrey. However, according to *The Gentleman's Magazine*, he was married on 2 March 1789 to Miss Hore, only daughter of Mr Hore.

He was made a Liveryman in April 1791, an Assistant in May 1801 and died on 10 March 1851 when 86 years old. He lived out his retirement at Newton Manor House, Newton Valence, Hampshire. This house was still the family residence in 1935.

He and his wife, who died in 1848, had two sons and three daughters. The sons were, Captain Edward Hore Chawner (4th Dragoon Guards), born 1802, died 1868 and the Rev. Charles Fox Chawner (rector of Bletchingly, Surrey), born 1807, died 1888.

Mary Chawner

  14 April 1834
Spoon maker
16 Hosier Lane

 25 March 1835
16 Hosier Lane

 3 August 1840
with George William Adams
Spoon makers
16 Hosier Lane

She was the wife of William Chawner (No 2) and took over the family business when her husband died on 20 March 1834.

Their son, William, who had been apprenticed to his father in 1831, was turned over to Mary at this time and obtained his freedom in 1838.

Thomas Chawner

 Circa 1763-64 (These marks are not recorded at the Goldsmiths' Hall. They are assumed to be Thomas and William Chawner and were probably entered in the missing volume of Large Workers marks 1759-73.)

Circa 1765-66

Circa 1768-69

15 October 1773
60 Paternoster Row

1 November 1775
60 Paternoster Row

 31 May 1783
Plate worker
9 Ave Maria Lane

Thomas Chawner continued

Born 1734, the son of John Chawner (gentleman) of Church Broughton, Derbyshire and Anne, daughter of Edmund Chaloner of Marston, Derbyshire, Thomas was sent to London where he was apprenticed to Ebenezer Coker on 4 December 1754. He obtained his freedom on 13 January 1762, was made a Liveryman in December 1771 and died between 1802 and 1811. He married Sarah, daughter of Robert Emery of Doveridge, Derbyshire by whom he had a son, Henry, born on 14 November 1764.

Thomas Chawner's partnership with his brother, William (No 1), at 60 Paternoster Row commenced circa 1763-64 and lasted until 1773.

Among his apprentices were William Fearn, Thomas Northcote, Edward Barnard (No 1), Henry Nutting and William Sumner (No 1).

William Chawner (No 1)

	Circa 1763-64	(These marks are not recorded at the Goldsmiths' Hall.
	Circa 1765-66	They are assumed to be Thomas and William Chawner and were probably entered in the missing
	Circa 1768-69	volume of Large Worker's marks 1759-73.)

William Chawner (No 1) continued

17 November 1774
with George Heming
Plate workers
Bond Street

15 February 1781
with George Heming
Old Bond Street

He never became a Freeman of the Goldsmiths' Company. He was apprenticed to Francis Pigott, a Freeman of the Pewterers' Company and obtained his freedom of that Company on 20 October 1757. He was made a Liveryman of the Pewterers' Company on 29 June 1761 but paid the necessary fine to be excused as Steward of the Company in 1768 and again as Renter Warden in 1777.

His partnership with his brother, Thomas, at 60 Paternoster Row commenced circa 1763-64 and lasted until 1773. Heal records him both alone and with Thomas at 60 Paternoster Row from 1759 to 1768.

In 1774 William went into partnership with George Heming. This lasted until circa 1790-91 when William probably retired or died.

William Chawner (No 2)

 10 April 1808
with William Eley (No 1)
and William Fearn
Spoon makers
2 Lovell's Court,
Paternoster Row

 9 February 1815
Spoon maker
16 Hosier Lane,
West Smithfield

 13 August 1819
16 Hosier Lane

 27 January 1820
16 Hosier Lane

 14 February 1820
16 Hosier Lane

 11 August 1820
16 Hosier Lane

 11 June 1823
16 Hosier Lane

 14 October 1833
16 Hosier Lane

William Chawner (No 2) continued

He was the son of Jonathan Chawner (tanner) of Horncastle, Lincolnshire and was apprenticed to William Fearn (Goldsmith) on 4 January 1797. He obtained his freedom on 4 April 1804, was made a Liveryman in January 1824 and died on 20 March 1834.

His wife, Mary, took over the family business upon his death. She had been Mary Burwash, presumably the sister of William Burwash, and had married William Chawner on 16 June 1816.

They had a son, William (No 3), born on 31 March 1817 and a daughter, Mary Ann, born on 26 April 1818. William (No 3) was apprenticed to his father on 6 April 1831 but when William (No 2) died in 1834, he was turned over to his mother and eventually obtained his freedom on 2 May 1838.

Pierre Le Cheaube

21 November 1707
In Pall Mall

27 June 1726
Living in Glass House,
Glass House Street
Free Goldsmith

He took out papers of denization on 20 March 1700. He was the son of Thomas Le Cheaube of Metz, France and was apprenticed to David Willaume (No 1) on 11 July 1700. He obtained his freedom on 21 November 1707.

Ann Chesterman

20 April 1775
Small worker
Fleet Market

As the widow of Charles Chesterman (No 1), she carried on the family business following her husband's death in 1775.

Their son, Charles (No 2), appears to have taken over the business and entered his own mark on 14 February 1780 following Ann's death earlier that year.

Samuel Wheatley was apprenticed to Ann in 1777 and turned over to Charles (No 2) in April 1780, by consent of Sarah Chesterman the executor of Ann's will.

Charles Chesterman (No 1)

7 July 1741
Horton Street
Clare Market

2 October 1752
Removed into Carey Lane

Removed into Rose and Crown Court,
Foster Lane, 1 August 1754

20 November 1771
Fleet Market

He was the son of Thomas Chesterman (Citizen and Joiner) of London and was apprenticed to George Greenhill Jones on 21 May 1734. He eventually took up his freedom of the Goldsmiths' Company on 2 November 1748. When he died in 1775, his widow, Ann, continued running the business.

Their son, Charles Chesterman (No 2), was apprenticed to him in 1776.

Charles Chesterman (No 2)

14 February 1780
Small worker
62 Fleet Market

6 March 1801
62 Fleet Market

He was born on 5 May 1752, the son of Ann and Charles Chesterman (No 1) (Citizen and Goldsmith) of London. He was apprenticed to his father on 2 July 1766 and obtained his freedom of the Goldsmiths' Company on 4 May 1774.

When his father died in 1775, his mother continued running the family business but upon her death early in 1780, Charles (No 2) took over the business himself.

25 September 1713
N.S.
Wood Street
Later of Lombard Street

 23 June 1720
O.S.
Love Lane

 15 December 1721
O.S.
In Lombard Street

He was the son of Francis Clare (Citizen and Baker) of London and was apprenticed to Nathaniel Lock on 17 February 1702. He obtained his freedom on 4 November 1712 and was made a Liveryman in October 1721. Heal records his death as being in 1728.

His son was Joseph Clare (No 2).

Joseph Clare (No 2)

2 March 1763
Deans Court,
St Martin's-le-Grand

1 October 1767
Deans Court,
St Martin's-le-Grand

16 September 1768
Deans Court
St Martin's-le-Grand

He was the son of Joseph Clare (No 1) (Citizen and Goldsmith deceased) of London and was apprenticed to Jeremiah Marlow junior on 6 June 1732. There is no record of his obtaining his freedom but this would not have been a requirement since he was working in a 'liberty' area. This was a locality which was exempt from the city's civil laws although it was within the city precincts.

Richard Clarke

 31 May 1787
Case maker
58 Featherstone Street,
Bunhill Row

Removed to 126 Bunhill Row,
26 February 1789

Removed to 67 Wheler Street,
Spitalfield, 12 April 1790

 27 January 1792
Case maker
67 Wheler Street,
Spitalfield

 18 April 1796
Watch case maker
15 Ratcliff Row,
City Road

Removed to 4 Ship Court,
Old Bailey, 3 February 1800

 27 November 1805
(No address. Probably 4 Ship Court)

He was not apprenticed through the Goldsmiths' Company
nor was he a Freeman of the Company.

Nicholas Clausen

10 June 1709
In Orange Street,
near Leicester Fields
Free Haberdasher

29 July 1720
O.S.
(Address as before)

He was not a Freeman of the Goldsmiths' Company. He obtained his freedom of the Haberdashers' Company by Redemption on 1 July 1709.

Ebenezer Coker

 27 March 1738
Clerkenwell Green

 25 June 1739
Clerkenwell Green

 24 May 1745
Clerkenwell Green

 20 December 1751
Clerkenwell Green

He was the son of William Coker (cheesemonger) of Berkhampstead, Hertfordshire and was apprenticed to Joseph Smith on 21 October 1728. He eventually took up his freedom on 7 February 1740 when he had already entered his first mark. On 1 December 1739, when a widower, he married Elizabeth Ramsey.

Heal records him as being in partnership with a Thomas Hammond (?Thomas Hannam). Apparently this was dissolved in 1760. In the Parliamentary Return of 1773 he was listed as a goldsmith of Clerkenwell Close. Presumably his partnership mark with Thomas Hammond (?Hannam) and subsequent solo mark were entered in the missing volume of Large Workers marks 1759-1773.

He became bankrupt in 1781 and died on 2 August 1783.

Mainly he manufactured candlesticks and salvers.

Lawrence Coles

 April 1697
Foster Lane

He was the son of Hugh Coles (maltster) of Northampton and was apprenticed to John Smith (Goldsmith) on 17 August 1660. He obtained his freedom on 23 October 1667 and was made an Assistant in 1698. He became 4th Warden in 1712, 3rd Warden in 1715 and 2nd Warden in 1716. Possibly he died in 1717 as he did not become Prime Warden that year. Heal records him as a goldsmith 1669-97 and as a plateworker 1697-1714 although he specialized in manufacturing spoons.

Lawrence and his wife, Francis, had a daughter, Francis, born on 5 March 1686 and buried on 13 April 1687 at St Michael le Quern. Their son, John, was buried there on 8 April 1689 as was Lawrence's wife on 8 April 1692.

Thomas Cooke

7 June 1727
Foster Lane
became Free Goldsmith

19 October 1727
with Richard Gurney
At the Golden Cup,
Foster Lane

23 December 1734
with Richard Gurney
At the Golden Cup,
Foster Lane

28 June 1739
with Richard Gurney
Foster Lane

17 February 1749
with Richard Gurney
Foster Lane

30 July 1750
with Richard Gurney
Foster Lane

Thomas Cooke continued

He was the son of John Cooke (weaver) of Warwick and was apprenticed to Richard Bayley (Goldsmith) on 11 June 1719. He obtained his freedom on 22 September 1726, was made a Liveryman in 1739 and an Assistant in 1752. He appears to have died about 1761.

Matthew Cooper (No 1)

2 May 1702
N.S.
Foster Lane

13 July 1720
O.S.
Foster Lane

He was the son of William Cooper (yeoman deceased) of Newport Pagnell, Buckinghamshire and was apprenticed to Robert Cooper, his brother, on 20 January 1693. On 19 May 1693 he was turned over to Joseph Bird. He obtained his freedom on 21 April 1702 and was made a Liveryman in October 1708.

Heal records him as insolvent in 1738 but other sources state he was bankrupt in December 1731.

He seems to have been primarily a candlestick maker as was his master, Joseph Bird.

Matthew Cooper (No 2)

30 June 1725
O.S.
Spectacle maker
In the Minories

9 September 1725
N.S.
In the Minories

21 July 1726
In Pump Yard,
Bishopsgate Street,
near Norton Folgate

He was not apprenticed through the Goldsmiths' Company
nor was he a Freeman of the Company.

Robert Cooper

April 1697
In the Strand

He was the son of William Cooper (yeoman) of Lathbury, Newport Pagnall, Buckinghamshire and was apprenticed to Thomas George on 8 January 1664. He obtained his freedom on 15 February 1670, was made a Liveryman in June 1682 and an Assistant in 1693. He became 4th Warden in 1707, 3rd Warden in 1711, 2nd Warden in 1712 and Prime Warden in 1717.

His brother, Matthew Cooper (No 1), ws apprenticed to him in 1693.

William Fawdery was apprenticed to him in 1686 and John White in 1711.

Isaac Cornasseau or Cornafleau

At the Acorn
in Drury Lane

(No date of entry given. Presumably entered between 20 July 1722 and 8 December 1724, these being the preceding and following entry dates of other makers' marks in the records.)

He was not apprenticed through the Goldsmiths' Company nor was he a Freeman of the Company.

Edward Cornock

 14 July 1707
Carey Lane

 25 November 1723
O.S.
Carey Lane

He was the son of Thomas Cornock (taylor deceased) of St Leonard, Foster Lane, London and was apprenticed to Henry Grant (Goldsmith) on 9 February 1698. He obtained his freedom on 27 March 1708.

He specialized in manufacturing tobacco boxes.

Augustin Courtauld (No 1)

 23 December 1708
Church Court,
St Martin's Lane

 7 October 1729
Chandos Street

 6 July 1739
Chandos Street,
St Martin's in the Fields
Goldsmith

He was born in 1686, the son of Julie and Augustin Courtauld, a merchant of Saint Pierre d'Oleron, France. He was one of four children of whom only he and a sister survived childhood. His father, who was born in 1661 and died in 1706, had married Julie Giraud on 19 August 1677 when they were both sixteen years old. Julie died in 1686, possibly in giving birth to Augustin (No 1). His father then came to England circa 1688 leaving Augustin (No 1) in France with his grandfather, Pierre Courtauld.

In March 1689, his father married for a second time. She was Esther Poitier and was thirty-two years old at the time. They had only one child, Peter, born on 10 January 1690. This half brother to Augustin (No 1) also became a goldsmith.

In 1696 Augustin (No 1) left France to join his father in London, since his grandfather had been taken seriously ill and feared he might die. Arriving in England, Augustin (No 1) was made a denizen on 20 July 1696. He was apprenticed to Simon Pantin (Citizen and Goldsmith) on 9 August 1701. In the record of his apprenticeship, his father is described as a Wine Cooper of St Anne's, Westminster, Middlesex. He obtained his freedom on 20 October 1708 and entered his first mark on 23 December 1708. During 1708, he was contracted to marry Anne Ribouleau but the marriage never took place. Presumably, she was a relation of Isaac Ribouleau, goldsmith, who was apprenticed to Augustin (No 1) from 1716 to 1724.

In 1709, Augustin (No 1) married Anne Bardin and they had eight children of whom five survived their parents. One was Samuel (No 1) who became a goldsmith and had George Cowles apprenticed to him. Another child was Anne who married John Jacob, goldsmith, in 1738. They had several children, one of whom, Judith, married George Cowles.

In March 1751, Augustin's wife, Anne, died and the following month Augustin (No 1) died, bequeathing all his patterns and tools to his son, Samuel (No 1).

Edward Feline was apprenticed to Augustin (No 1) in 1709.

Louisa Perina Courtauld

 1765 (Not recorded at Goldsmiths' Hall. Presumed to be Louisa Courtauld and entered in the missing volume of Large Workers marks 1759-73.)

 1768 (Not recorded at Goldsmiths' Hall. Presumed to be with George Cowles and entered in the missing volume of Large Workers marks 1759-73. This partnership recorded in the Parliamentary Return of 1773 as being at 21 Cornhill.)

 16 October 1777
with Samuel Courtauld (No 2)
Plate workers
Cornhill

Born at Poitou, France in 1729, she was one of a family of nine children. Her parents were Pierre Ogier and his wife, Catherine Rabaud, of Sigournay in Poitou.

Soon after 1730, Louisa came to England where, in August 1749, she married Samuel Courtauld (No 1). They had eight children of whom four survived their parents. One was Samuel (No 2) who was born on 20 October 1752.

In February 1765, Samuel Courtauld (No 1) died, leaving Louisa to carry on the family business. She is presumed to have entered her own mark at this time in one of the missing volumes of makers' marks.

On 8 May 1765, her husband's apprentice, George Cowles, obtained his freedom, she having taken over his apprenticeship when her husband died. In 1768, George Cowles married her niece-in-law, Judith Jacob, the daughter of goldsmith, John Jacob. In 1769, Louisa took George Cowles into partnership and presumably they entered their joint mark at Goldsmiths' Hall in the now missing volume of Large Workers marks.

On 16 October 1777, Louisa and her son, Samuel (No 2), entered their joint mark, George Cowles having left the firm. However, Samuel (No 2) did not take up his freedom, which was by Patrimony, until 4 March 1778. In 1780, Samuel (No 2) emigrated to America so Louisa, then 51 years old, sold the business to John Henderson. Louisa died at Clapton on 12 January 1807 when 77 years old and was buried at Spitalfields Church.

Meanwhile, Samuel (No 2) married a widow, Sarah Norris Wharton, in Philadelphia and eventually died near Wilmington in the State of Delaware in 1821. His wife died in 1836.

Peter Courtauld

15 June 1721
N.S.
Litchfield Street,
St Ann's, Westminster

21 July 1721
O.S.
Litchfield Street,
St Ann's, Soho

The only son of Esther and Augustin Courtauld (vintner), he was born on 10 January 1690. His mother was Augustin's second wife, the first having died in France before Augustin came to England circa 1688. One of the four children by this first marriage was Peter's half brother, Augustin (No 1).

On 28 March 1705, Peter was apprenticed to Simon Pantin, as had been Augustin (No 1) before him. On 5 February 1709, when 19 years old, Peter married Judith Pantin the daughter of Esaie Pantin, a goldsmith of St James. Doubtless a relation of Simon Pantin.

On 3 December 1712, Peter obtained his freedom but did not register his first mark until 15 June 1721. In 1729 he died when only 39 years old.

Samuel Courtauld (No 1)

6 October 1746
Chandos Street,
near St Martin's Lane

23 November 1751
Removed to Cornhill

The son of Anne and Augustin Courtauld (No 1), he was born on 10 September 1720. On 12 November 1734, he was apprenticed to his father and on 6 October 1746, he entered his first mark at Goldsmiths' Hall although he did not obtain his freedom until 3 February 1747.

In August 1749, he married Louisa Perina Ogier who had been born at Poitou, France in 1729. They had eight children, including Samuel (No 2) who was born on 20 October 1752.

In June 1763, Samuel (No 1) was made a Liveryman and in February 1765 he died leaving his wife, Louisa, to carry on the family business.

His sister, Anne, married the goldsmith, John Jacob, in 1738 and had several children, including Judith, born in 1741. Judith married the goldsmith, George Cowles, in 1768.

George Cowles was apprenticed to Samuel (No 1) on 6 September 1751.

Robert Albion Cox

 10 July 1752
Fetter Lane

17 December 1755
(removed to) LIttle Britain

 12 July 1758
Little Britain

 27 June 1759
Little Britain

He was the son of Edward Cox (gentleman) of Brewham, Somerset and was apprenticed to Humphrey Payne on 16 January 1745. On 13 March 1751, he was turned over to Humphrey Payne's son, John, and obtained his freedom on 2 July 1752. Humphrey Payne had retired in April 1751 leaving his business to his son, John.

Although Robert Albion Cox commenced his working life as a goldsmith, he gradually digressed over the years to build up a considerable family business in banking and the refining of precious metals. His refinery became the largest in London. It was known as Cox & Marle in 1781, Marle & Co in 1817 and Marle, Son & Co (bankers & gold refiners) of 2 Cox's Court, Little Britain from 1818 to 1821.

When Robert Albion Cox died in 1790, he left a personal estate of some £70,500.

Note: In his apprenticeship and freedom records, his Christian names are given as Robert Albin but in the Parliamentary Return of 1773 they are recorded as Robert Albion. Also, in his will he signed himself as Robert Albion Cox.

(See Addendum for details of his will and family)

Joseph Cradock or Craddock

15 August 1806
with Thomas and Joseph Guest
Plate workers
67 Red Lion Street,
Holborn

24 February 1808
with Thomas and Joseph Guest
67 Red Lion Street,
Holborn

Removed to 67 Leather Lane,
Holborn, 15 June 1808

8 June 1812
with William K. Reid
Plate workers
67 Leather Lane

19 August 1819
with William K. Reid
3 Carey Street,
Lincoln's Inn Fields

24 September 1824
with William K. Reid
3 Carey Street,
Lincoln's Inn Fields

Joseph Cradock or Craddock continued

 13 October 1825
Plate worker
3 Carey Street,
Lincoln's Inn Fields

 10 November 1827
3 Carey Street,
Lincoln's Inn Fields

He was not apprenticed through the Goldsmiths' Company nor was he a Freeman of the Company.

His son, Charles Tyrwhitt Cradock was apprenticed to Alexander Thomas (silver planisher) of Kirby Street, Hatton Garden on 2 July 1823 to learn the trade of silver planisher. There is no record of his obtaining his freedom of the Company.

Sebastian Crespel (No 1) and James Crespel (No 1)

 Circa 1762

(This mark is not recorded at Goldsmiths' Hall. It is thought to be Sebastian and James Crespel and was probably entered in the missing volume of Large Workers marks 1759-73.)

Neither Sebastian nor James Crespel (Nos 1) ever became Freemen of the Goldsmiths' Company.

Probably they were brothers who, from about 1762 to 1773, traded from premises in Whitcomb Street, Leicester Fields.

(See Addendum for further information on the Crespel family)

Sebastian Crespel (No 2)

3 August 1820
Large worker
11 James Street,
Haymarket

Removed to 11 White Hart Court,
Castle Street, Leicester Square,
12 October 1836

He was the son of James Crespel (No 1) (silversmith) of Whitcomb Street, Leicester Fields and later of Panton Street, Haymarket. On 3 June 1801, he was apprenticed to his brother, Honorius Crespel (silver flatter and Goldsmith). Following his brother's death in the spring of 1806, he was turned over to his brother-in-law, Robert Garrard (No 1) (silversmith and Grocer), on 7 May 1806 and obtained his freedom of the Goldsmiths' Company on 3 May 1809. It seems likely that he continued working for Robert Garrard's firm until he set up on his own in 1820.

Sebastian (No 2) had three brothers who entered the silversmithing trade and became Freemen of the Goldsmiths' Company. They were Honorius, apprenticed to John Wakelin in 1779 and free in 1786, Andrew (No 1) apprenticed to John Wakelin in 1785 and free in 1792 and James (No 2) apprenticed to Thomas Gardner in 1803 and free in 1810.

Sebastian (No 2) had a son, Andrew (No 2), who obtained his freedom of the Goldsmiths' Company by Patrimony on 6 May 1846.

Thomas Parker, who subsequently entered into partnership with Andrew (No 2), was apprenticed to Sebastian (No 2) in 1839 and obtained his freedom in 1847.

Paul Crespin

(No date. Between July 1720
and December 1721)
N.S.
Compton Street

(No date. Between July 1720
and December 1721)
O.S.
Compton Street,
Freeman of the
Longbow String

4 July 1739
At the Golden Ball,
Compton Street,
St Ann, Soho

7 November 1740
N.S.
At the Golden Ball,
Compton Street,
St Ann, Soho

22 January 1757
At the Golden Ball,
Compton Street,
St Ann, Soho

Paul Crespin continued

Born in 1694, he was the son of Daniel Crespin of St Giles, Westminster. On 24 June 1713, he was apprenticed for seven years to Jean Pons, a member of the Longbow String Makers' Company and on 26 April 1721, he obtained his freedom of that Company by Redemption. This was by virtue of an order given by the Court of Aldermen of the City of London dated 25 April 1721. (See apprenticeship and freedom records of the Longbow String Makers' Company now held by the Fletchers' Company, which still survive for this period.)

He and his wife, Mary Branboeuf, had five children; Magdelaine Benine born 1729 and later wife of Francis Barraud (watchmaker), Lewis Vincent Paul born 1732, Elias David born 1734, Paul born 1739 and Sarah born 1743. Both Lewis and Paul appear to have died young. Elias David became a clergyman and was Dean of Guernsey from 1765 until his death in 1795.

Paul senior appears to have retired in 1759. He died at Southampton on 25 January 1770 when 76 years old. In his will, dated 17 December 1759 and proved on 26 March 1770, he bequeathed everything to his wife, his sole executor. She died on 15 December 1775.

William Cripps

 31 August 1743
At the Crown and Ball,
Compton Street

 16 July 1746
Removed to the Golden Ball,
St James Street

 16 November 1751

He was the son of Edward Cripps (yeoman deceased) of
Newport, Buckinghamshire and was apprenticed to David
Willaume (No 2) on 8 January 1731. He obtained his freedom
on 2 May 1738 and was made a Liveryman in January 1750.

Presumably he died or retired by 25 April 1767 when
his son, Mark Cripps, entered his own mark from the same
address.

Richard Crossley

1 May 1775
with William Sumner (No 1)
Plate workers
1 Clerkenwell Close

27 January 1776
with William Sumner (No 1)
1 Clerkenwell Close

10 May 1777
with William Sumner (No 1)
1 Clerkenwell Close

27 January 1780
with William Sumner (No 1)
1 Clerkenwell Close

5 April 1782
Plate worker
21 Foster Lane

(Removed to)
14 Giltspur Street,
12 November 1783

9 December 1785
14 Giltspur Street

RC	6 January 1795 14 Giltspur Street
RC	5 February 1802 14 Giltspur Street
RC	14 May 1804 14 Giltspur Street
RC GS RC GS	9 April 1807 with George Smith (No 4) Spoon makers Giltspur Street
RC RC	2 January 1812 Plate worker 14 Giltspur Street

He obtained his freedom of the Goldsmiths' Company by Redemption on 1 May 1782. Presumably he considered it advisable to become a Freeman when he moved within the city precincts to his new address in Foster Lane. He was made a Liveryman in February 1791 and died in April 1815.

John Crouch (No 1)

 Circa 1767

 Circa 1773

(These two marks are not recorded at Goldsmiths' Hall. They are assumed to be J. Crouch (No 1) and T. Hannam and possibly entered in the missing volume of Large Workers marks 1759-73.)

He was the son of Christopher Crouch (yeoman deceased) of St Sepulchre parish, Middlesex and was apprenticed to Richard Rugg on 8 November 1758. He obtained his freedom on 4 December 1765. His partnership with Thomas Hannam was recorded in the Parliamentary Return of 1773 as being at 28 Giltspur Street. Heal records them together at 23 Giltspur Street from 1766 to 1793 and at 37 Monkwell Street in 1790. Crouch (No 1) appears to have retired or died by 1799 when Hannam entered a new mark with the son, John Crouch (No 2). John Crouch (No 2) had been apprenticed to his father in 1790 and had obtained his freedom in 1797.

Crouch (No 1) and Hannam specialized in manufacturing salvers, trays and some candlesticks. Both of them would have gained knowledge of candlestick manufacture from their masters. Rugg had been apprenticed to James Gould and Hannam to John and William Cafe, all of whom were specialist candlestick manufacturers.

William Frisbee was apprenticed to John Crouch (No 1) in 1774.

John Crouch (No 2)

 13 April 1799
with Thomas Hannam
Plate workers
37 Monkwell Street

 11 February 1808
Plate worker
37 Monkwell Street

He was the son of John Crouch (No 1) (Citizen and Gold
smith) of Gilspur Street and was apprenticed to his fathe
on 6 January 1790. He obtained his freedom on 1 Februar
1797, was made a Liveryman in March 1829 and died i
January 1837.

Francis Crump (No 1)

 9 November 1741
Newcastle Street,
near Fleet Market

 14 May 1745

Removed to Fenchurch Street,
opposite Grace Church

 30 March 1750
Third mark

Removed to Nine Elms,
Battersea Parish,
20 July 1750

22 November 1753
with Gabriel Sleath
Gutter Lane

26 March 1756
Gutter Lane

17 October 1761
Gutter Lane,
near Cheapside

He was the son of John Crump (cap maker) of Bewdley, Worcestershire and was apprenticed to Gabriel Sleath on 30 August 1726. He obtained his freedom on 6 November 1741. On 19 February 1760, he married Sarah Bulbeck of Woolwich. They had four children, Mary, John, Francis and Sleath between 1761 and 1767.

Francis Crump (No 2), who was the son of Daniel Crump (cordwainer) of Bewdley, was apprenticed to Gabriel Sleath on 5 October 1752. He obtained his freedom on 6 May 1761. Although there is no record of his mark at Goldsmiths' Hall, it could have been entered in the missing volume of Large Workers marks 1759-73. Possibly he was the nephew of Francis Crump (No 1) as they both originated from Bewdley.

In the Parliamentary Return of 1773, a Francis Crump was entered as a plateworker of Gutter Lane.

1 December 1703
Panton Street

 1 December 1703
Panton Street

He took out letters of denization on 8 May 1697 and obtained his freedom by Redemption on 1 December 1703. He was made a Liveryman in October 1708 and died on 14 December 1733.

His son, Samuel, was apprenticed to him on 14 November 1710 and turned over to Daniel Shawe (Lorimer) at some date between 8 January and 27 February 1711. Samuel obtained his freedom of the Goldsmiths' Company in 1724.

John Denziloe

27 October 1774
Plate worker
3 Westmoreland Buildings,
Aldersgate Street

He was the son of William Denziloe (haberdasher deceased)
of Bridport, Dorset and was apprenticed to Charles Wright on
9 January 1765. He obtained his freedom on 6 May 1772, was
made a Liveryman in March 1781 and died in December 1820.

Isaac Dighton

April 1697
Gutter Lane
Free Haberdasher

He was never a Freeman of the Goldsmiths' Company. He
was the son of Henry Dighton (gentleman) of Bristol and was
apprenticed to William Brown, a member of the Haberdashers' Company, on 26 May 1665. He obtained his freedom
of that Company on 7 June 1672. His death was registered
on 28 February 1707 at St Vedast, Foster Lane. His widow,
Catherine, was buried there on 3 July 1712.
Anthony Nelme, who was apprenticed to Richard Rowley in
November 1672, was turned over to Isaac Dighton at some
later date during his apprenticeship.

William Eaton (Nos 1 and 2)

19 March 1781
Buckle maker
6 Albion Buildings,
Aldersgate Street

22 April 1784
Buckle maker
3 Addle Street,
Wood Street

8 May 1786
Buckle maker
3 Addle Street,
Wood Street

** 20 August 1801
Buckle maker
3 Addle Street,
Wood Street

18 May 1813
Plate worker
30 Addle Street

5 March 1824
30 Addle Street

*18 October 1825
30 Addle Street

Removed to 16 Jewin Crescent,
Jewin Street, 20 December 1825

5 September 1828
Plate worker
16 Jewin Crescent,
Jewin Street

Removed to 2 Lovell's Court,
Paternoster Row, 10 December 1828

*31 December 1828
Plate worker
2 Lovell's Court,
Paternoster Row

30 September 1830
2 Lovell's Court,
Paternoster Row

2 January 1834
Spoon maker
2 Lovell's Court,
Paternoster Row
& 16 Jewin Crescent

*27 January 1836
2 Lovell's Court,
Paternoster Row

2 June 1837
Manufactory and residence
removed to 16 Jewin Crescent

* 22 February 1840

A manufactory at 32 Banner Street,
St Luke's, 1 October 1844

It would appear that these are the marks of two William Eatons, probably father and son, who were buckle maker of 3 Addle Street and plater worker of 30 Addle Street respectively. This assumption has been made since the signatures against the marks of the buckle maker were not written by the same William Eaton as those against the marks of the plate worker. Hence, all those marks entered from and including 18 May 1813 are probably by William Eaton (No 2).

There is no record of either William Eaton being apprenticed through the Goldsmiths' Company or of their becoming Freemen of the Company. However, they could have been Freemen of another City Company which further research might disclose.

* Mark entered in two sizes
** Mark entered in three sizes

John Eckford (No 1) or Eckfourd

31 December 1698
In Red Lion Court, Drury Lane
Free Draper

(No date. Probably entered 1720)
O.S.
Red Lion Court, Drury Lane

He was the son of William Eckford (blacksmith deceased) of Berwick-on-Tweed and was apprenticed to John Whitfield (tobacconist and member of the Drapers' Company) on 12 April 1682. On 11 September 1682, he was apprenticed to Anthony Nelme (Goldsmith) but this entry in the Goldsmiths' Company apprentice register was subsequently scored out for some unknown reason. Eventually, he obtained his freedom by Service on 29 June 1698. In the Goldsmiths' Company records of marks he is noted as a Free Draper, whereas in the Drapers' Company quarterage book he is listed as a tobacconist and silversmith. When his son, John Eckford (No 2), was turned over to him in 1712, John (No 1) was recorded as Citizen and Goldsmith in the Goldsmiths' Company apprentice register.

John (No 1) was buried at St Paul's, Covent Garden on 14 July 1730.

His mark is often found on tobacco boxes.

John Eckford (No 2)

23 June 1725
N.S.
Three Tun Court,
Red Cross Street
Goldsmith

23 June 1725
O.S.
Three Tun Court,
Red Cross Street
Goldsmith

20 June 1739
In the Inner Court,
Red Cross Street

He was the son of John Eckford (No 1) and was apprenticed to John Fawdery on 24 January 1712. He was turned over to John Eckford (No 1) on 14 February 1712 and again to Philip Rollos on 29 June 1714. He obtained his freedom of the Goldsmiths' Company on 4 July 1723.

Edward Edwards (No 1)

10 June 1811
with John Edwards
Plate workers
1 Bridgewater Square

19 September 1816
1 Bridgewater Square

Removed to 48 Banner Street,
St Luke's, 5 March 1823

Removed to 5 Radnor Street,
St Luke's, 18 March 1825

He was the son of John Edwards (silversmith) of London and was apprenticed to John Mewburn (Goldsmith) on 7 Novemeber 1797. He obtained his freedom on 6 March 1811 and entered his first mark with his father on 10 June 1811.

Edward Edwards (No 2)

11 April 1828
Small worker
42 Fetter Lane, Clerkenwell

Removed to 60 Red Lion Street,
18 June 1829

12 May 1840
(No address recorded)

13 January 1841
(No address recorded)

He was not apprenticed through the Goldsmiths' Company nor was he a Freeman of the Company.
  Possibly he was the son of Edward Edwards (No 1).

Charles Eley

14 July 1824
with Henry and William Eley (No 2)
Plate workers
1 Lovell's Court,
Paternoster Row

19 January 1825
Spoon maker
2 Lovell's Court,
Paternoster Row

He was the son of William Eley (No 1) and was apprenticed to his father on 1 May 1811 to learn the trade of a silversmith. He obtained his freedom on 4 November 1818 and presumably remained working with the family firm.

Following his father's death in March 1824, he and his brothers Henry and William (No 2), entered a partnership mark in July 1824. Apparently he set up on his own in January 1825 but, by 10 December 1828, his premises at 2 Lovell's Court were occupied by William Eaton (No 2).

Charles Eley died on 15 November 1875 and was buried at St Lawrence, Isle of Wight.

William Eley (No 1)

 11 November 1777
with George Pierrepont
Spoon makers
46 Little Bartholomew Close

 3 November 1778
Small worker
4 New Street, Cloth Fair

 1 December 1778
2 George Street,
St Martins-le-Grand

 29 April 1785
Buckle maker
14 Clerkenwell Green

 12 March 1790
14 Clerkenwell Green

 5 May 1795
14 Clerkenwell Green

 4 January 1797
with William Fearn
Plate workers
14 Clerkenwell Green

Removed to 1 Lovell's Court,
Paternoster Row, 29 January 1802

10 April 1808
with William Fearn
and William Chawner (No 2)
Spoon makers
2 Lovell's Court,
Paternoster Row

6 October 1814
with William Fearn
Spoon makers
Lovell's Court,
Paternoster Row

25 November 1817
with William Fearn

He was the son of George Eley (yeoman) of Foston, Derbyshire and was apprenticed to William Fearn on 7 November 1770 to learn the trade of a goldsmith. He obtained his freedom on 4 November 1778, was made a Liveryman in October 1806 and died in March 1824.

His three sons, William (No 2), Charles and Henry were apprenticed to him in 1808, 1811 and 1814 respectively. William (No 2) obtained his freedom in 1815, Charles in 1818 and Henry in 1822.

William Eley (No 2)

14 May 1824
with William Fearn
Plate workers
1 Lovell's Court,
Paternoster Row
(This entry signed by
William Eley (No 2) only)

14 July 1824
with Charles and Henry Eley
Plate workers
1 Lovell's Court,
Paternoster Row

19 January 1825
Plate worker
3 Lovell's Court,
Paternoster Row

22 June 1825
3 Lovell's Court

20 June 1826
3 Lovell's Court

5 December 1826
3 Lovell's Court

He was the son of William Eley (No 1) and was apprenticed to his father on 3 February 1808 to learn the trade of a silversmith. He obtained his freedom on 1 March 1815, was made a Liveryman in April 1816 and died in June 1841.

Following the death of his father in March 1824, it appears he entered into a short-term partnership with his father's partner, William Fearn. At the time Fearn would have been about 76 years old and probably was a sleeping partner. Two months later (July 1824) he entered into a new partnership with his two brothers, Charles and Henry.

Charles was apprenticed to his father on 1 May 1811, obtained his freedom on 4 November 1818 and entered his own mark on 19 January 1825 from 2 Lovell's Court.

Henry was apprenticed to his father on 2 February 1814 and obtained his freedom on 6 February 1822. Later, he took Holy Orders and, subsequently, became vicar of Broomfield, Essex in 1841.

27 August 1796
with Henry Chawner
Plate workers
Amen Corner

10 January 1798
Plate worker
Amen Corner

21 July 1802
Amen Corner

He was the son of William Emes (surveyor) of Bowbridge Field, near Derby and was apprenticed to William Woollett (Goldsmith and engraver) of Green Street on 7 October 1778. He obtained his freedom of the Goldsmiths' Company on 5 July 1786. In 1796, he became a partner in Henry Chawner's firm and within two years was running the business, Henry Chawner having taken semi-retirement. Chawner had married an heiress in 1788 and, presumably, no longer needed to work as a goldsmith.

John Emes died intestate in June 1808 and on 25 June his wife, Rebecca, and brother, William Emes, were granted letters of Administration of his estate.

Rebecca Emes

30 June 1808
with William Emes
Plate workers
Amen Corner,
Paternoster Row
(These two marks were entered by
'Virtue of a Power of Attorney'
and signed by William Emes)

14 October 1808
with Edward Barnard (No 1)
Plate workers
Amen Corner,
Paternoster Row
(These two marks were entered by
'Virtue of a Power of Attorney'
and signed by William Emes and
Edward Barnard (No 1))

29 April 1818
with Edward Barnard (No 1)
I enter one mark for Rebecca Emes
(Signed by Edward Barnard (No 1))

20 February 1821
with Edward Barnard(No 1)
Amen Corner,
Paternoster Row

28 October 1825
with Edward Barnard (No 1)
Amen Corner,
Paternoster Row

Rebecca was the wife of John Emes and, following his death in June 1808, she took over the firm. Because John Emes died intestate, Rebecca, and his brother, William Emes, were granted Letters of Administration of the estate on 25 June 1808. Also, they were appointed the curators and guardians of his two children, Sarah and Ellen, until they were twenty-one years old. (Public Record Office. PROB/6/184.)

Rebecca's partnership with William Emes was only a temporary measure for, three and a half months later, she formed a new partnership with her late husband's leading journeyman, Edward Barnard (No 1). This lasted until her death late in 1828. Edward Barnard (No 1) then brought his three sons into the partnership and entered a joint mark in February 1829.

Edward Farrell

 27 April 1813
Plate worker
18 King's Head Court,
Holborn Hill

 20 May 1813
18 King's Head Court,
Holborn Hill

Removed to 24 Bridge Street,
Covent Garden, 26 September 1818

 17 March 1819
 Plate worker
24 Bridge Street,
Covent Garden

He was not apprenticed through the Goldsmiths' Company
nor was he a Freeman of the Company.

Ann Farren

 19 December 1743
St Swithin's Lane

Presumably she was the wife of Thomas Farren and, following his death, entered her own mark in 1743.

Thomas Farren

 16 October 1707
St Swithin's Lane

 11 November 1720
St Swithin's Lane

 15 June 1739
St Swithin's Lane

He was the son of John Farren (maltster) of Tewkesbury, Gloucestershire and was apprenticed to William Denny (Goldsmith) on 8 April 1695. He obtained his freedom on 3 October 1707, was made a Liveryman in 1721 and an Assistant in 1731. Presumably, he died in 1743 when his wife, Ann Farren, took over the business and entered her own mark.

John Pero was apprenticed to him in 1709 and obtained his freedom in 1717.

Thomas Whipham was apprenticed to him in 1728 and obtained his freedom in 1737.

William Williams was apprenticed to him in 1731 and obtained his freedom in 1738.

Hester Fawdery

 28 September 1727
O.S.
Goldsmith Street,
near Cheapside

She was the wife of William Fawdery and took over the business when her husband died in 1727.

John Fawdery (No 1)

April 1697
Foster Lane

He was the son of John Fawdery (yeoman) of Clevley (?Cleveley), Oxfordshire and was apprenticed to Anthony Nelme on 18 January 1688. He obtained his freedom on 11 September 1695 and was made a Liveryman in April 1705. He was buried on 16 January 1724.

His brother was William Fawdery.

John Fawdery (No 2)

27 February 1729
Hemings Row,
St Martin's Lane

He was the son of John Fawdery (No 1) (Goldsmith) of London and was apprenticed to Edward Cornock on 29 July 1719 but there is no record of his obtaining his freedom. This would not have been a requirement since he was working outside the city precincts. He married Hester Pain of Spitalfields on 1 April 1731.

William Fawdery

 April 1697
Goldsmith Street

 28 July 1720
N.S.
Goldsmith Street

 28 July 1720
O.S.
Goldsmith Street

He was the son of John Fawdery (gentleman) of Enstone, Oxfordshire and was apprenticed to Robert Cooper on 15 December 1686. He obtained his freedom on 8 August 1694, was made a Liveryman in October 1708 and died in 1727. His wife, Hester, took over the business and entered her own mark in September 1727.

His brother was John Fawdery (No 1).

William Fearn

April 1769
5 Brownlow Street,
Holborn

13 May 1774
Spoon maker
75 Wood Street

3 November 1786
with George Smith (No 3)
Plate workers
60 Paternoster Row

Removed to 1 Lovell's Court,
Paternoster Row, 29 June 1790

4 January 1797
with William Eley (No 1)
Plate workers
14 Clerkenwell Green

Removed to 1 Lovell's Court,
Paternoster Row, 29 January 1802

10 April 1808
with William Eley (No 1)
and William Chawner (No 2)
Spoon makers
2 Lovell's Court,
Paternoster Row

6 October 1814
with William Eley (No 1)
Spoon makers
Lovell's Court,
Paternoster Row

25 November 1817
with William Eley (No 1)

14 May 1824
with William Eley (No 2)
Plate workers
1 Lovell's Court,
Paternoster Row
(This entry signed by
William Eley (No 2) only)

He was the son of William Fearn (farmer) of Sedbury, Derbyshire and was apprenticed to Thomas Chawner on 6 October 1762. He obtained his freedom on 7 February 1770. In the Parliamentary Return of 1773 he is recorded as being at 5 Brownlow Street and 75 Wood Street. *The Gentleman's Magazine* records him as being bankrupt in July 1777.

Following the death of William Eley (No 1) in March 1824, it appears that he entered into a short-term partnership with Eley's son, William Eley (No 2). At the time, Fearn would have been about 76 years old and probably was a sleeping partner.

William Eley (No 1) was apprenticed to him in 1770 and William Chawner (No 2) in 1797.

Edward Feline

 25 September 1720
N.S.
Rose Street,
Covent Garden

 25 September 1720
O.S.
Rose Street,
Covent Garden

 15 June 1739
King Street,
Covent Garden

He was the son of Peter Feline (tailor) of St Martin's in the Fields and was apprenticed to Augustin Courtauld (No 1) on 31 March 1709. He obtained his freedom on 6 April 1721, was made a Liveryman in April 1731 and presumably died in 1753 when his wife, Magdalen, took over the business.

His son, Edward, was apprenticed to him in 1745 and eventually obtained his freedom in 1763.

Fuller White was apprenticed to him in 1733 and obtained his freedom in 1744.

Magdalen Feline

 15 May 1753
King Street,
Covent Garden

 18 January 1757
King Street,
Covent Garden

She was the wife of Edward Feline and presumably she took over the business when her husband died in 1753. She appears to have continued working until 1762.

William Fleming

 April 1697
Maiden Lane,
Cripplegate Without

He was the son of John Fleming (Citizen and Haberdasher) of London and was apprenticed to Nathaniel Lock on 22 February 1688. He obtained his freedom on 20 March 1695 and was made a Liveryman in October 1708.

Andrew Fogelberg

17 July 1780
with Stephen Gilbert
Plate workers
29 Church Street,
St Ann's

He was not apprenticed through the Goldsmiths' Company nor was he a Freeman of the Company. Possibly he served his apprenticeship in Sweden since he was of Swedish origin. It has been suggested that he may have been an Anders Fogelberg, born circa 1732 and apprenticed to Berent Halck in Stockholm circa 1746.

By 1770, he had arrived in England from Gothenburg. In the Parliamentary Return of 1773, he was recorded as a plate worker of Church Street, Soho, therefore he would have had a mark registered at Goldsmiths' Hall prior to that date. Presumably it had been entered in the now missing volume of Large Workers marks 1759-73.

Andrew Fogelberg probably retired in 1793 when Paul Storr apparently took over his premises in Church Street.

Thomas Folkingham

 3 February 1707
N.S.
St Swithin's Lane

 6 February 1721
O.S.
St Swithin's Lane

He was the son of Thomas Folkingham (clerk deceased) of Derbyshire and was apprenticed to John Bache on 9 March 1693. He obtained his freedom on 23 June 1703 and was made a Liveryman in October 1708. On 7 May 1700, he married Elizabeth Denny. Probably she was the daughter of William Denny who was John Bache's partner circa 1697.

Thomas Folkingham appears to have become a banker goldsmith and is reputed to have left upwards of £30,000 when he died on 23 October 1729.

Simon Jouet was turned over to him in 1722.

William Fordham

31 January 1707
Lombard Street
Free of the Wax Chandlers

He was never a Freeman of the Goldsmiths' Company. He was the son of Richard Fordham (gentleman) of Tharfield, Staffordshire and was apprenticed to Melior Benskin, widow of Richard Benskin, a member of the Wax Chandlers' Company, on 1 December 1686. He obtained his freedom of that Company on 18 September 1093, was made a Liveryman on 13 August 1694 and a Steward on 29 September 1705. On 24 June 1710, he became an Assistant of the Wax Chandlers' Company but, soon afterwards, he was, 'Removed for non-attendance' at Court meetings.

William Fountain

29 July 1791
with Daniel Pontifex
Plate workers
13 Hosier Lane,
West Smithfield

1 September 1794
Plate worker
47 Red Lion Street,
Clerkenwell

30 June 1798
47 Red Lion Street,
Clerkenwell

Removed to King Street,
Clerkenwell, 1 April 1811

5 February 1821
Plate worker
Hartford Place,
Huggerstone Bridge

He was the son of John Fountain (shipwright deceased) of Poplar, Middlesex and was apprenticed to Fendall Rushforth (Goldsmith) of Goldsmiths' Hall on 1 October 1777. He was turned over by consent on the same day to Daniel Smith (Merchant Taylor) of Adlermanbury, London. When he obtained his freedom on 2 February 1785, it was of the Goldsmiths' Company because he was apprenticed initially to a Freeman of that Company.

Charles Fox (No 1)

*20 October 1801
with James Turner
Plate workers
3 Old Street
Goswell Street

5 September 1804
Plate worker
139 Old Street
Goswell Street

He was not apprenticed through the Goldsmiths' Company
nor was he a Freeman of the Company. He appears to have
retired in 1822 when his son, Charles (No 2), took over the
firm. Charles (No 1) died in 1838.

* Mark entered in two sizes.

Charles Fox (No 2)

19 February 1822
Plate worker
139 Old Street

27 January 1823
139 Old Street

*21 August 1823
139 Old Street

23 September 1823
139 Old Street

 10 December 1823
139 Old Street

 9 May 1838
139 Old Street

He was not apprenticed through the Goldsmiths' Company nor was he a Freeman of the Company. Born in 1777, he was the son of Charles Fox (No 1). Apparently he assumed a leading position in his father's firm since his signature, with the appendage 'Junior', appears in the records beside all those marks entered in 1822 and 1823. The same signature appears beside the 1838 entry but this time with the appendage 'Senior'. This would suggest that he had become head of the firm due to his father's death prior to this entry.

Charles (No 2) died on 14 March 1850 at 3 Albion Place, Barnsbury as the result of an attack of bronchitis that lasted for six weeks (Somerset House. Death Cert. No 7529G). He married Catherine Goodson who died on 6 May 1862, her will being proved on 27 August 1862. They are known to have had a daughter and four sons; Mary, Yonge William who was dead by October 1860, Charles Thomas born 1801, Frederick born 1810 and George born 1816.

The two sons, Charles Thomas and George, took over the family firm and entered their own mark in July 1841. Frederick eventually set up on his own, entering his first mark in August 1852.

(See Addendum for Catherine Fox's will)

* Mark entered in two sizes.

Mordecai Fox

 9 March 1730
with Joseph Allen
St Swithin's Lane

 21 August 1739
with Joseph Allen
St Swithin's Lane

 21 January 1747
St Swithin's Lane

 18 June 1755
St Swithin's Lane

He never became a Freeman of the Goldsmiths' Company.
On 2 October 1704, he was apprenticed to the silversmith,
Francis Garthorne, a Freeman of the Girdlers' Company.
Mordecai became a Freeman of that Company on 15 July
1712, as stated in the Girdlers' Company records.

James Fraillon

17 January 1711
Maiden Lane,
Covent Garden

Later moved to
Lancaster Court, in the Strand

6 March 1723
Lancaster Court,
in the Strand

He was the son of Claude Fraillon (brewer) of St Martin's Lane, Middlesex and was apprenticed to Philip Roker (No 1) on 25 April 1699. He obtained his freedom on 1 May 1706.

He appears to have died between September 1727 and June 1728 when his widow, Blanche, took over the business and entered her own mark.

William Frisbee

12 April 1791
with John Edwards
Plate workers
48 Jewin Street

11 January 1792
Plate worker
5 Cock Lane,
Snowhill

2 May 1792
with Paul Storr
Plate workers
5 Cock Lane
Snowhill

23 June 1798
5 Cock Lane
Snowhill

2 June 1801
Plate worker
Inner Court,
Bridewell Hospital

10 September 1811
with John Frisbee
Plate workers
Bridewell Hospital

William Frisbee continued

11 May 1814
with John Frisbee
Bridewell Hospital

He was the son of John Frisbee (Citizen and Tallow Chandler) of the Old Bailey and was apprenticed to John Crouch (No 1) on 5 October 1774, to learn the trade of a goldsmith. He obtained his freedom on 6 February 1782, was made a Liveryman in October 1806 and died on 9 December 1820.

His son, John, was apprenticed to him in 1799 and obtained his freedom in 1806. John entered a partnership mark with his father in 1811 and again in 1814.

Two other sons were apprenticed to William. They were William in 1806 and Daniel Luffman in 1809.

Crispin Fuller

 * 29 December 1792
Plate worker
42 Monkwell Street

 *11 July 1796
42 Monkwell Street

Removed to 3 Windsor Court,
Monkwell Street, 14 August 1797.

 *5 August 1823
(No address. Presumably
at Windsor Court.)

He was not apprenticed through the Goldsmiths' Company
nor was he a Freeman of the Company. He married Sarah,
daughter of Letticia and Richard Clarke and granddaughter
of Hester Bateman.

* Mark entered in two sizes.

Philip Garden

12 June 1738
Gutter Lane
Free Goldsmith

23 June 1739
Gutter Lane

12 March 1744
Removed to St Paul's Churchyard

29 October 1748
Mark entered as
'old one being broke'

18 April 1751

28 April 1756

He was the son of John Garden (Citizen and Draper deceased) of London and was apprenticed to Gawen Nash (Goldsmith) on 4 February 1730 on payment of £5 from the charity of Christ's Hospital, London. He obtained his freedom on 3 October 1738 and was made a Liveryman in September 1746.

Following Paul De Lamerie's death in August 1751, he purchased some of his patterns and tools when they were subsequently auctioned.

Philip Garden continued

In 1762, he became bankrupt and, on 9 December 1763, resigned from the Goldsmiths' Company. Presumably as a result of his bankruptcy in 1762 and his ensuing financial difficulties, he resolved to apply to the Goldsmiths' Company for the return of his Livery Fine paid when he first became a Liveryman.

In the Minutes of the Court of Assistants meeting held on 9 December 1763, it is noted that Garden had petitioned for the return of his Livery Fine of £20, paid when he became a Liveryman in 1746. It continues, 'thro divers Losses and unavoidable Misfortunes he is now reduced to very low Circumstances and in great want of some Charitable Assistance'. His petition was granted and his £20 returned upon his releasing his privileges as a Liveryman.

Daniel Garnier

April 1697
In the Pall Mall

He was the son of Michael Garnier, a Huguenot refugee. In 1697, he took out letters of denization, then obtained his freedom by Redemption on 29 May 1696 by order of the Court of Aldermen. In October 1698, he was made a Liveryman.

He was related to Jean Chartier's wife, Suzanne Garnier. Possibly she was his sister.

Robert Garrard (No 1)

20 October 1792
with John Wakelin
Plate workers
Panton Street

11 August 1802
Plate worker
Panton Street,
Haymarket

Born in December 1758, Robert (No 1) was the son of Miriam (née Richards) and Robert Haslefoot Garrard (linendraper) of Cheapside, London. He was apprenticed to Stephen Unwin (hardwareman) of Cheapside who was a Freeman of the Grocers' Company. The unusual fee for this apprenticeship was 'Love and Affection'. When Robert (No 1) obtained his freedom of the Grocers' Company by Service on 2 November 1780, he had already joined the firm of Wakelin & Co, goldsmiths, of Panton Street, Haymarket. Although only employed on the retail side of the business, he was taken into partnership by John Wakelin in 1792 and eventually took over the firm, Wakelin & Garrard, entering his own mark at Goldsmiths' Hall in August 1802.

By 1793, he had married Sarah Crespel who is thought to have been the daughter of either James or Sebastian Crespel (Nos 1). Robert (No 1) and Sarah had ten children of whom eight were still living at the time of Robert's death on 26 March 1818. They were Robert (No 2), James, Sebastian, Stephen, Henry, Sarah, Miriam and Caroline.

Robert (No 2), together with James and Sebastian, continued running the firm after their father's death in 1818 but Henry emigrated to Australia where he became a farmer and married Mary Mortimer in 1831.

Robert Garrard (No 1) continued

It is interesting to note that George Garrard ARA, a brother of Robert (No 1), married Matilda, the daughter of the well known artist, Sawrey Gilpin RA.

(See Addendum for details of Robert Garrard's (No 1) will)

Robert Garrard (No 2)

16 April 1818
Panton Street
(Note that an Old English E was used
in this mark in mistake for a G)

17 January 1822
Panton Street,
St Martin's

Removed to 29 Panton Street,
27 February 1836

29 June 1847
29 Panton Street

Born on 13 August 1793, he was the eldest son of Sarah and Robert Garrard (No 1). He was apprenticed to his father on 1 June 1809 and obtained his freedom of the Grocers' Company by Service on 4 July 1816. When his father died, he took over the firm, entering his own mark at Goldsmiths' Hall on 16 April 1818.

In 1830, the firm was appointed Goldsmiths and Jewellers to the King, a royal warrant which it has continued to hold to the present day.

On 11 June 1825, Robert (No 2) married Ester Whippy and they had three sons and three daughters. Ester died in 1848.

Robert (No 2) was made a Liveryman of the Grocers' Company in May 1818, 3rd Warden in 1844 and again in 1845, 2nd Warden in 1852 and Prime Warden or Master in 1853. He died on 26 September 1881.

Soon after Robert (No 2) took over the firm in 1818, he was joined by two of his brothers, James and Sebastian. James was born on 13 June 1795 and married Emily Van der Zee. He obtained his freedom of the Goldsmiths' Company by Redemption on 1 June 1825, was made a Liveryman in March 1829, and an Assistant in January 1842. He became 4th Warden in 1844, 3rd Warden in 1845, 2nd Warden in 1846 and Prime Warden in 1847 and again in 1850. He died in November 1870.

Sebastian was born in 1798 but apparently he did not become a Freeman of any Company. He married Harriet Fletcher, but they remained childless. When his brother, Henry, in Australia, sent his four eldest children, including James Mortimer, to be educated in England, they were looked after by Sebastian and Harriet. Sebastian died on 11 November 1870 and Harriet in 1873.

Eventually, James Mortimer Garrard took over the firm of Garrard and became Prime Warden of the Goldsmiths' Company in 1896.

Francis Garthorne

April 1697
St Swithin's Lane
Free Girdler

He never became a Freeman of the Goldsmiths' Company. Apparently he obtained his freedom of the Girdlers' Company at some date prior to 1604, this being as far back as the Company's existing Freedom records reach. In 1718, he became Master of the Girdlers' Company, as stated in the Company's records.

His son, Robert, having been apprenticed to him, obtained his freedom of the Girdlers' Company on 15 July 1712.

Mordecai Fox was apprenticed to Francis Garthorne and also obtained his freedom of the Girdlers' Company on 15 July 1712. Later, Fox entered into partnership with the silversmith, Joseph Allen.

George Garthorne was turned over to Francis Garthorne at some unknown date and obtained his freedom in 1680.

George Garthorne

April 1697
Keyre (Carey) Lane

He was the son of John Garthorne (farmer) of Cleasby, Yorkshire and was apprenticed to Thomas Payne on 18 August 1669. He was later turned over to Francis Garthorne and obtained his freedom on 11 August 1680.

Benjamin Gignac

28 February 1745
Deans Court,
St Martins-le-Grand

He was born in Amsterdam in 1713 where he was apprenticed in 1724. He came to London in 1735 but did not become a Freeman of the Goldsmiths' Company.

His address of St Martins-le-Grand, although within the city, was known as a 'liberty' area which meant it was exempt from the city's civil laws. Because of this, he was not required to be a Freeman while working in this locality.

In the Parliamentary Return of 1773 he was recorded as a plate worker of Deans Court, St Martins-le-Grand.

Stephen Gilbert

17 July 1780
with Andrew Fogelberg
Plate workers
29 Church Street,
St Ann's

He was the son of John Gilbert (yeoman deceased) of Hixton, Staffordshire and was apprenticed to Edward Wakelin on 8 May 1752. He obtained his freedom on 1 February 1764. Prior to his apprenticeship, he worked in Wakelin's workshop where his annual wages were £5 in 1750 and £6 in 1751. The payments ceased upon the commencement of his apprenticeship (Victoria and Albert Museum, Garrard MSS).

Following his freedom, he continued to work for Parker and Wakelin, possibly as an out-worker, until he went into partnership with Andrew Fogelberg in 1780.

Pierre Gillois

20 November 1754
Wardour Street

15 June 1782
Plate worker
25 Queen Street,
Seven Dials

He was not apprenticed through the Goldsmiths' Company nor was he a Freeman of the Company.

In the Parliamentary Return of 1773 he was recorded as a plate worker of Wardour Street, Soho.

He manufactured tea caddies and sugar boxes.

Thomas Gilpin

24 September 1730
At the Acorn in the Strand
Goldsmith

2 July 1739
Lincolns Inn,
Bargate

He was the son of Robert Gilpin (innholder deceased) of Hockliff, Bedfordshire and was apprenticed to John Wells on 7 January 1720. There is no record of his having obtained his freedom but this would not be required when working outside the city precincts.

Samuel Godbehere

 20 November 1784
Plate worker
 86 Cheapside

 27 November 1784
86 Cheapside

 13 September 1786
with Edward Wigan
Plate workers
86 Cheapside

14 August 1787
with Edward Wigan
86 Cheapside

 26 July 1792
with Edward Wigan
86 Cheapside

 15 March 1800
with Edward Wigan and James Bult
Plate workers
(No address)

 16 September 1818
with James Bult
Plate workers
86 Cheapside

Samuel Godbehere continued

He was not apprenticed through the Goldsmiths' Company nor was he a Freeman of the Company. On 13 November 1790, he married Miss Wood of Great George Street, Westminster. It is possible that he retired or died in 1819 since James Bult entered a mark of his own on 13 July 1819.

Benjamin Godfrey

3 October 1732
Hand, Ring and Crown,
In Norris Street,
St James, Haymarket

18 June 1739
Norris Street,
in St James, Haymarket

He was not apprenticed through the Goldsmiths' Company nor was he a Freeman of the Company.

On 6 February 1732, he married Elizabeth Buteux, widow of Abraham Buteux.

When Benjamin Godfrey died in 1741, Elizabeth, now widowed for a second time, continued running the business, entering her own mark on 29 June 1741.

Elizabeth Godfrey

29 June 1741
Norris Street,
in St James, Haymarket

She was the widow of Abraham Buteux, goldsmith, who
died in 1731. On 6 February 1732, she married Benjamin
Godfrey who may have been a journeyman in her workshop.
When he died in 1741, she continued running the business,
entering her own mark on 29 June 1741. She appears to have
continued working until circa 1758. (For her previous mark,
see under Elizabeth Buteux.)

James Gould

19 November 1722
N.S.
At the three Golden Lions
in Gutter Lane
Free of the Goldsmiths' Company

19 November 1722
O.S.
At the three Golden Lions
in Gutter Lane
Free of the Goldsmiths' Company

(No date. Between
October 1732 and July 1734.)
At the three Golden Lions
in Gutter Lane

James Gould continued

30 May 1739
Candlestick maker
Gutter Lane

Removed out of Gutter Lane
to the Golden Bottle
in Ave Maria Lane, 25 March 1741

6 June 1743
Mark entered,
the old mark being destroyed

31 August 1747
Mrs James Gould
Mark was entered

He was born circa 1698, the son of James Gould (grazier) who lived in the village of Kingsbury Episcopi, Somerset. From here, James junior was sent to London to be apprenticed through the Goldsmiths' Company to David Green (Goldsmith) on 26 October 1714. Green's business premises were in Foster Lane from where he operated as a plate worker and candlestick maker. It was under his guidance that James Gould learnt the craft of candlestick making.

James obtained his freedom on 8 November 1722, was made a Liveryman in March 1739 and elected an Assistant of the Court of the Goldsmiths' Company in May 1745.

His production of candlesticks and tapersticks was prolific during the 1730s but ceased in the late 1740s. He died on 25 February 1750 when 51 years old and was buried in the churchyard at Kingsbury Episcopi. (See Addendum for further biographical information on James Gould and James Gould's will.)

William Gould

20 October 1722
At the Wheatsheaf
in Gutter Lane

24 July 1734
At the Candlestick
in Foster Lane

15 June 1739
In Foster Lane
Goldsmith

1 June 1748
Mark entered

24 September 1753
William Gould in Old Street

14 May 1756
Removes in Foster Lane

He was the son of James Gould (gentleman) of Kingsbury Episcopi, Somerset and was apprenticed to his brother, James, on 9 January 1724. Presumably he completed his apprenticeship within the usual seven years but, for some reason, did not take up his freedom of the Goldsmiths' Company until 5 April 1733, although he had already entered his first mark in October 1732.

He was made a Liveryman in September 1746 but, in 1752, he was accused and convicted of fraud and eventually resigned from the Company on 14 December 1763 (see Addendum, William Gould, for details).

William Grundy

23 December 1743
Fetter Lane

24 June 1748
Pemberton Row
Goff Square

30 June 1748
Pemberton Row
Goff Square

26 May 1754
Removed to Fetter Lane

20 September 1777
Plate worker
Fetter Lane

23 February 1779
with Edward Fernell
119 Fetter Lane

He was the son of Charles Grundy (dyer deceased) of St Giles without Cripplegate and was apprenticed to Edward Vincent on 2 April 1731. He obtained his freedom on 6 February 1739 and was made a Liveryman in January 1750. Probably he retired or died by 19 January 1780 when Edward Fernell entered a mark of his own.

John Peter Guerrier

5 January 1717
At the Mitre
in the Strand

He was the son of John Guerrier (tailor) of St Anne's, Westminster and was apprenticed to Pierre Harache (No 2) on 26 September 1700. He obtained his freedom on 24 December 1716.

Richard Gurney

 19 October 1727
with Thomas Cooke
At the Golden Cup,
Foster Lane

 23 December 1734
with Thomas Cooke
At the Golden Cup,
Foster Lane

 28 June 1739
with Thomas Cooke
Foster Lane

 17 February 1749
with Thomas Cooke
Foster Lane

 30 July 1750
with Thomas Cooke
Foster Lane

He was the son of George Gurney (butcher) of Turrington, Bedfordshire and was apprenticed to Richard Bayley on 2 May 1717. He obtained his freedom on 3 September 1724, was made a Liveryman in 1736 and an Assistant in 1752. He became 4th Warden in 1763, 3rd Warden in 1764 and 2nd Warden in 1765.

William Priest was apprenticed to him in 1740.

Louis Hamon

18 March 1736
Great Newport Street
near Long Acre

4 August 1738
Church Street,
St Ann's, Soho

20 June 1739
Church Street,
St Ann's, Soho

He was not apprenticed through the Goldsmiths' Company
nor was he a Freeman of the Company.

Paul Hanet

7 March 1716
Great St Andrews Street,
in St Giles
Free Longbow String Maker

H A

17 September 1717
Great St Andrews Street,
in St Giles
Free Longbow String Maker

24 May 1721
(No address. Presumably
Great St Andrews Street)

He was not a Freeman of the Goldsmiths' Company. He obtained his freedom of the Longbow String Makers' Company by Redemption on 7 March 1716.

He appears to have been 2nd Warden or Lower Warden in 1726-7 and Prime Warden or Upper Warden in 1727-8. He was an Assistant of the Court in 1731, 1732 and 1733 and may have been so for further years but unfortunately the Accounts records for 1734 onwards appear to have been lost or destroyed.

He specialized in manufacturing spoons.

Thomas Hannam

Circa 1767 — (These two marks are not recorded at Goldsmiths' Hall. They are assumed to be J. Crouch (No 1) & T. Hannam and possibly entered in the missing volume of Large Workers marks 1759-73.)

Circa 1773

13 April 1799
with John Crouch (No 2)
Plate workers
37 Monkwell Street

He was the son of William Hannam (tallow chandler deceased) of Blackford, Somerset and was apprenticed to John Cafe on 6 November 1754. He was turned over to William Cafe by consent of John Cafe's executor, John Winning, on 13 October 1757 and obtained his freedom on 2 December 1761.

Heal records Ebenezer Coker and Thomas Hammond (Hannam?) as dissolving their partnership in 1760 followed by Thomas Hannam and Richard Mills in partnership in 1765. Heal then records Thomas Hannam in partnership with John Crouch from 1766 to 1793.

Following his partnership with Crouch (No 1), Hannam apparently entered into partnership with the son, John Crouch (No 2) in April 1799. Probably Hannam had either retired or died by 11 February 1808 when Crouch (No 2) entered a separate mark at Goldsmiths' Hall.

Both of the Crouch and Hannam partnerships specialized in manufacturing salvers and trays.

Francis Harache

16 February 1738
Silversmith
At the Seven Dials,
in Great St Andrews Street,
at the Blackmoor's Head,
St Giles

He was not apprenticed through the Goldsmiths' Company
nor was he a Freeman of the Company.

Jean Harache

22 June 1726
Foreigner
Riders Court,
St Ann's parish

He was not apprenticed through the Goldsmiths' Company
nor was he a Freeman of the Company. He may be the Jean
Harache who took out 'letters of denization' in December 1687.

Pierre Harache (No 1)

April 1697
Suffolk Street,
near Charing Cross

He was a Huguenot immigrant from France. He obtained his freedom of the Goldsmiths' Company by Redemption on 21 July 1682 by order of the Court of Aldermen and was made a Liveryman in November 1687. Heal records his death as being in 1700 but Simon Pantin (No 1) was apprenticed to him on an unknown date and obtained his freedom on 4 June 1701.

His son was Pierre Harache (No 2).

His daughter, Anne, married Estienne Hobbema, brother-in-law of Louis Mettayer on 1 April 1700.

Pierre Harache (No 2)

25 October 1698
Compton Street,
near St Ann's church,
Soho

He was the son of Pierre Harache (No 1) and obtained his freedom of the Goldsmiths' Company by Redemption on 24 October 1698 by order of the Court of Aldermen. He married Jeanne le Magnan at some date prior to 1690.

John Peter Guerrier was apprenticed to him in 1700.

Jonathan Hayne

***14 November 1808
Large worker
13 Clerkenwell Close

22 February 1810
with Thomas Wallis (No 2)
Plate workers
10 Red Lion Street,
Clerkenwell

**3 December 1817
with Thomas Wallis (No 2)
16 Red Lion Street

17 February 1820
with Thomas Wallis (No 2)
16 Red Lion Street

**3 July 1821
Plate worker
Red Lion Street,
Clerkenwell

*19 June 1823
Red Lion Street

29 October 1829
Red Lion Street

**12 April 1832
Red Lion Street

**13 May 1834
Red Lion Street

He was the son of Jonathan Hayne (surgeon deceased) of Red Lion Street, Clerkenwell and was apprenticed to Thomas Wallis (No 2) (Goldsmith), also of Red Lion Street, on 1 June 1796.

Presumably the death of Jonathan's father left the family in financial difficulties since the £5 apprenticeship fee due to Wallis (No 2) was paid by the charity of the Governors of Christ's Hospital, London. On 4 January 1804, the Governors paid a similar fee for Jonathan's brother, Samuel Holditch John, to be apprenticed likewise to Wallis (No 2).

Jonathan obtained his freedom of the Goldsmiths' Company on 4 January 1804 (the same day as his brother's apprenticeship began), was made a Liveryman in 1811 and an Assistant in 1836. He became 4th Warden in 1840, 3rd Warden in 1841, 2nd Warden in 1842 and Prime Warden in 1843. He died on 19 March 1848.

He had two sons who became Freemen of the Company by Patrimony, Samuel Holditch Thomas (silversmith of Red Lion Street) on 1 April 1835 and Watson Ward (gentleman of Croydon, Surrey) on 6 December 1843. Samuel, who was made a Liveryman in 1839 and an Assistant in 1850, resigned from the Company in 1854 and died on 4 August 1887. Watson, who was made a Liveryman in February 1847, died on 15 June 1893.

*Mark entered in two sizes.
** Mark entered in three sizes.
*** Mark entered in four sizes.

Thomas Hayter

7 January 1792
with George Smith (No 5)
Plate workers
4 Huggin Lane

21 May 1805
Plate worker
4 Huggin Lane,
Wood Street

15 March 1816
with George Hayter
Plate worker
Huggin Alley,
Wood Street

7 December 1821
with George Hayter
Huggin Alley
Wood Street

He was the son of John Hayter (carver) of Cavendish Street and was apprenticed to George Smith (No 5) of Huggin Lane to learn the trade of silversmith on 4 December 1782. He obtained his freedom on 3 February 1790, was made a Liveryman in October 1801 and died on 2 September 1840.

His son and partner, George Smith Hayter, obtained his freedom of the Goldsmiths' Company by Patrimony on 7 December 1814, was made a Liveryman in April 1816 and an Assistant in 1846. He twice held the position of Prime Warden, in 1854 and again in 1863. He died on 15 September 1887.

George Heming

 17 November 1774
with William Chawner (No 1)
Plate worker
Bond Street

 15 February 1781
with William Chawner (No 1)
 Old Bond Street

He was the son of Thomas Heming (Citizen and Goldsmith) of London and was apprenticed to his father on 2 March 1763. There is no record of his having obtained his freedom but this would not be obligatory since his premises were outside the city precincts.

In the Parliamentary Return of 1773, he was recorded as a goldsmith of Piccadilly. This indicates that he had an earlier mark which, presumably, was entered in the now missing volume of Large Workers marks 1759-73.

When his partnership with William Chawner (No 1) terminated circa 1790-91, he continued running the business at 151 New Bond Street. In 1794, a Richard Heming, possibly his son, was at this address.

Thomas Heming

 12 June 1745
Piccadilly

 Circa (This mark not recorded at
1760 Goldsmiths' Hall. Assumed
to be Thomas Heming and
possibly entered in the
missing volume of Large
Workers marks 1759-73.)

He was the son of Richard Heming (mercer) of Ludlow, Salop and was apprenticed to Edmund Boddington (Goldsmith) on 7 February 1738. On the same day he was turned over to Peter Archambo (No 1) (Goldsmith and Butcher). This enabled him to serve his apprenticeship under Archambo, a working goldsmith, yet still obtain his freedom of the Goldsmiths' Company because he was apprenticed to Boddington in the first instance. He obtained his freedom on 7 May 1746, was made a Liveryman in June 1763 and died between 1795 and 1801. In the Parliamentary Return of 1773, he was recorded as a goldsmith of New Bond Street. He had moved from Piccadilly to these premises circa 1765.

His sons were George Heming, apprenticed to him in 1763, and Thomas Heming, apprenticed to him in 1767. There is no record of either son obtaining his freedom but this was not obligatory since they were outside the city precincts.

David Hennell (No 1)

 23 June 1736
Kings Head Court,
Gutter Lane

 Circa 1739

(These two marks are not recorded at Goldsmiths' Hall. They have been proven from other sources and are presumed to have been entered in the missing volume of Large Workers marks 1759-73.)

 Circa 1756

 9 June 1763
with Robert Hennell (No 1)
Foster Lane

 9 July 1768
with Robert Hennell (No 1)
Foster Lane

David Hennell (No 1) continued

He was the son of Robert Hennell, a framework knitter of Newport Pagnell, Buckinghamshire who founded a drapery business and later, in 1707, became vicar of Newport Pagnell church.

David (No 1), born on 8 December 1712, was sent to London and apprenticed to Edward Wood on 6 September 1728. He obtained his freedom on 4 December 1735 and, in June 1736, set up in business under the sign of the 'Fleur-de-Lis and Star' in Gutter Lane.

William Hennell, his step-brother, was apprenticed to him on 7 April 1737 and obtained his freedom on 12 June 1745. Probably he remained working for the firm.

David (No 1) married Hannah Broomhead on 1 March 1736. They had fifteen children; nine died before they were one year old and, of four sons called David, only one survived his father. One son, John, obtained his freedom by Patrimony on 3 June 1772 but did not take up the goldsmith's trade. Another son, Robert (No 1), was born in 1741 and apprenticed to David (No 1) in 1756. He obtained his freedom on 8 June 1763 and, the following day, entered a joint mark in partnership with his father.

David (No 1) was made a Liveryman in June 1763 and a Deputy or Touch Warden in 1773. About this time he retired, leaving Robert (No 1) to carry on the family business. He died in 1785.

David Hennell (No 2)

15 July 1795
with Robert Hennell (No 1)
Plate workers
11 Foster Lane

5 January 1802
with Robert Hennell (No 1)
and Samuel Hennell
Plate workers
11 Foster Lane

He was the son of Robert Hennell (No 1) and was born in 1767. He was apprenticed to his father on 6 February 1782 and obtained his freedom on 5 August 1789.

His two brothers, Robert and Samuel, were also apprenticed to their father. Samuel obtained his freedom in 1800 but there is no record of Robert having completed his apprenticeship.

In February 1791, David (No 2) was made a Liveryman and, in 1795, he and his father entered a partnership mark. In 1802, they entered another partnership mark, this time including Samuel. Later that year, David (No 2) appears to have retired from the firm, following which Samuel and his father entered their own partnership mark.

David (No 2) resigned his position of Liveryman in the Goldsmiths' Company on 4 December 1821 and died in 1829.

Robert Hennell (No 1)

 9 June 1763
with David Hennell (No 1)
Foster Lane

 9 July 1768
with David Hennell (No 1)
Foster Lane

 30 May 1772
Foster Lane

 9 October 1773
Salt maker
16 Foster Lane

 15 July 1795
with David Hennell (No 2)
Plate workers
11 Foster Lane

 5 January 1802
with David Hennell (No 2)
and Samuel Hennell
Plate workers
11 Foster Lane

Robert Hennell (No 1) continued

28 October 1802
with Samuel Hennell
Plate workers
11 Foster Lane

He was the son of David Hennell (No 1) and was born in 1741. He was one of fifteen children of whom nine died before they were one year old and only five reached maturity.

Robert (No 1) was apprenticed to his father on 5 May 1756 and obtained his freedom on 8 June 1763. The following day he entered his first partnership mark with his father. He was made a Liveryman in July 1763 and, when his father retired in 1772, he took over the business and entered his own mark.

His nephew, Robert Hennell (No 2), son of brother John, was apprenticed to him on 8 April 1778 and later founded his own firm.

Robert (No 1) had three sons, David (No 2), Robert and Samuel who were apprenticed to him. Samuel eventually took over the family business when Robert (No 1) died in April 1811.

Robert Hennell (No 2)

17 June 1808
with Henry Nutting
Plate workers
38 Noble Street,
Foster Lane

3 November 1809
Plate worker
35 Noble Street,
Foster Lane

Removed to 3 Lancaster Court,
Strand, 28 June 1817

RH
RH
11 August 1820
3 Lancaster Court,
Strand

23 January 1826
3 Lancaster Court,
Strand

Removed to 14 Northumberland Street,
Strand, 14 January 1828

Born in 1763, he was the son of John Hennell (draper, Citizen and Goldsmith) and nephew of Robert Hennell I (No 1).

John Hennell had obtained his freedom by Patrimony in 1772 but, instead of entering the goldsmith's trade, made a living out of his grandfather's drapery business at Newport Pagnell.

Robert Hennell (No 2) continued

Robert (No 2), therefore, was apprenticed to his uncle, Robert (No 1), on 8 April 1778 and two days later to John Houle, an engraver. Both apprenticeships were to run concurrently.

He obtained his freedom on 1 June 1785 and then moved to Windmill Court, Smithfield where he probably worked only at engraving. He did not enter his own mark until 1808 when he went into partnership with Henry Nutting as the senior partner. In 1809, Robert (No 2) moved from 38 to 35 Noble Street where he set up on his own.

On 25 May 1833, he announced his retirement in the *London Gazette* stating that his son, Robert (No 3), would take over his mark and thereby the family business. Robert (No 3) had been born in 1794 and obtained his freedom by Patrimony in 1834.

Samuel Hennell

5 January 1802
with Robert Hennell (No 1)
and David Hennell (No 2)
Plate workers
11 Foster Lane

28 October 1802
with Robert Hennell (No 1)
Plate workers
11 Foster Lane

22 June 1811
Plate worker
11 Foster Lane

6 April 1814
with John Terry
Plate workers
Foster Lane

27 July 1816
8 Aldermanbury

(This is a re-entry of the
same mark entered 22
June 1811)

Removed to 8 Charles Street,
Goswell Street, 19 September 1816

177

Removed to 11 Foster Lane,
7 August 1817

Removed to 5 Snowhill,
18 May 1818

He was the son of Robert Hennell (No 1) and was born in 1778. Although apprenticed to his father, he obtained his freedom by Patrimony on 2 December 1800.

His two elder brothers, David (No 2) and Robert, were also apprenticed to their father but only David obtained his freedom.

In 1802, Samuel joined his father and brother, David (No 2), in entering a partnership mark. Later that year, Samuel and his father entered another mark without David (No 2), presumably because he had retired from the firm. When Robert (No 1) died in April 1811, Samuel took over the business.

In 1814, he formed a partnership with John Terry who had married one of his nieces. After two years, Samuel returned to working on his own. On 23 August 1826, he entered his mark at the Sheffield Assay Office. This mark was similar to those in his entry of 27 July 1816 at Goldsmiths' Hall. He died in 1837.

Samuel's eldest son, Samuel, does not appear to have served an apprenticeship but his second son, Robert George, became a jeweller in Holborn.

George Hindmarsh

 11 May 1731
with Robert Abercromby
Christopher Court,
St Martin-le-Grand

 6 July 1731
Christopher Court,
St Martin-le-Grand

 (No date. Entered
between 24 December 1735
and 18 March 1736)
Glasshouse Yard,
Blackfriars

 27 June 1739
Glasshouse Yard,
Blackfriars

Removed to Essex Street,
in the Strand, 7 December 1748

Removed to the Strand,
9 July 1753

 15 September 1753

He was not apprenticed through the Goldsmiths' Company
nor was he a Freeman of the Company.
He specialized in manufacturing salvers and waiters.

Edward Holaday

 1 November 1709
Grafton Street

He was the son of Edward Holaday (husbandman) of Malling, Kent and was apprenticed to John Bache on 22 December 1699. He obtained his freedom on 14 September 1709, was made a Liveryman in December 1717 and died in June 1719. After his death, his widow, Sarah, continued running the business.

Matthew Perchard of Guernsey was apprenticed to him in 1717 and obtained his freedom in 1724. Perchard became Prime Warden of the Goldsmiths' Company in 1777.

Sarah Holaday

 22 July 1719
Grafton Street

 15 June 1725
O.S.
Grafton Street

She was the wife of Edward Holaday and took over the business following his death in June 1719.

Edmund Holliday

 3 August 1703
Horse-shoe Alley,
Bunhill Fields

He was the son of Edmund Holliday (cooper) of Norton
Folgate, Middlesex and was apprenticed to Benjamin Nelson
(Goldsmith) on 25 February 1691. He was turned over to
Thomas Elton on 26 October 1694 and eventually obtained
his freedom on 8 July 1703.

Samuel Hutton

7 October 1724
O.S.
At the Crown
Noble Street

7 January 1725
N.S.
At the Crown,
Noble Street

15 May 1734
At the Hat and Feather,
Goswell Street

21 January 1740
Goswell Street

He was the son of Samuel Hutton (Citizen and Glover) of London and was apprenticed to Edward Jennings on 4 April 1717. He obtained his freedom on 7 May 1724. Presumably he had died by 20 June 1740 when his wife, Sarah Hutton, entered her own mark. Both she and Samuel were spoon makers.

His son, Charles, obtained his freedom by Patrimony on 7 May 1760.

Sarah Hutton

20 June 1740
Goswell Street
Free Goldsmith

Removed to Noble Street,
near Goswell Street,
15 March 1748

She was the wife of Samuel Hutton and entered her own mark in June 1740, presumably following his death. She obtained her freedom of the Goldsmiths' Company by Patrimony on 7 April 1737 when still Sarah Penkethman, before her marriage to Samuel Hutton.

Hyam Hyams

12 April 1821
Plate worker
5 Castle Street,
Houndsditch

23 May 1821
5 Castle Street

29 June 1821
5 Castle Street

5 October 1821
5 Castle Street

6 October 1821
5 Castle Street

He was not apprenticed through the Goldsmiths' Company
nor was he a Freeman of the Company.

John Hyatt

26 January 1742
Little Britain

24 September 1757
with Charles Semore
Little Dean's Court,
St Martins-le-Grand
(Due to this mark in the Goldsmiths'
records being very blurred, it is
impossible to decipher the shape of
the central symbol. Here it is
illustrated as a dot only.)

Removed to Noble Street,
24 October 1758

He was the son of John Hyatt (clothier deceased) of Preston, Somerset and was apprenticed to James Gould on 10 May 1733. He obtained his freedom on 5 March 1741.

In the Parliamentary Return of 1773, his premises were recorded as being at Little Britain.

John Jackson

April 1697
Fleet Street

He was the son of William Jackson (clerk) of Bridgford, Nottingham and was apprenticed to Richard Bransfield on 10 October 1674 and later turned over to John Spackman (No 1). He obtained his freedom on 23 December 1681.

John Jacob

 3 May 1734
Hemings Row,
near St Martin's Lane

 20 June 1739
Hemings Row

 7 July 1760
Removed to Spur Street,
Leicester Fields

He was not apprenticed through the Goldsmiths' Company nor was he a Freeman of the Company. However, this would not be a requirement since he was working outside the city precincts.

In 1738, he married Anne, the daughter of Augustin Courtauld (No 1). They had several children one of whom, Judith born 1741, married the goldsmith, George Cowles, in 1768. Cowles had served his apprenticeship under Samuel Courtauld (No 1).

Peter Jouet

23 November 1723
Over against the Victualling Office,
Little Tower Hill

He was not apprenticed through the Goldsmiths' Company
nor was he a Freeman of the Company. Prior to coming to
London, he traded as a silversmith in Exeter.

Probably he retired or died in 1725 when his son, Simon,
took over the premises and entered a new mark.

Simon Jouet

(No date. Entered between
May and July 1725.)
N.S.
Maiden Lane

21 July 1725
O.S.
Over against the Victualling Office,
Little Tower Hill

Circa   (This mark not recorded at
1726   Goldsmiths' Hall. Presumed
to be Simon Jouet but not
entered due to similarity
with the previous mark.)

Simon Jouet continued

18 June 1739
At the White Hart,
Foster Lane

Removed to Carey Lane,
9 September 1746

29 February 1748

Now at Aldersgate,
5 April 1749

Removed to Kingsland,
27 March 1755

He was the son of Peter Jouet (goldsmith) of St Giles without Cripplegate and was apprenticed to John Orchard (Goldsmith) on 3 April 1718. He was turned over to Thomas Folkingham (Goldsmith) on 20 June 1722 and obtained his freedom on 27 May 1725. Presumably he had taken over his father's premises at Little Tower Hill by the time he entered his second mark on 21 July 1725.

William Cafe was turned over to him in 1746, having been apprenticed to John Cafe in 1741.

Charles Kandler (No 1)

29 August 1727
N.S.
with James Murray
St Martin's Lane

29 August 1727
O.S.
with James Murray
St Martin's Lane

29 August 1727
N.S.
St Martin's Lane

29 August 1727
O.S.
St Martin's Lane

Of German origin, he was not apprenticed through the Goldsmiths' Company nor was he a Freeman of the Company.

Evidently he was a relation of Charles Frederick Kandler, possibly his father, since Frederick used Charles' last new standard mark for his own in 1735. This probably occurred following Charles' death. A similar example of this occurrence was Francis Nelme using his father's marks in 1723.

However, it is thought possible that Charles (No 1) and Charles Frederick may have been the same person, although this would indicate a working life spanning some fifty years, unusual at that time.

Charles Kandler (No 2)

12 November 1778
Plate worker
100 Jermyn Street

He was not apprenticed through the Goldsmiths' Company
nor was he a Freeman of the Company.

Probably he was the son of Charles Frederick Kandler as
they were of the same address, namely Jermyn Street, in the
1770s. The Charles (No 2) entry of 1778 was probably due to
the death or retirement of Charles Frederick Kandler.

Charles Frederick Kandler

10 September 1735
N.S.
German Street,
near St James Church

10 September 1735
O.S.
German Street,
near St James Church

25 June 1739
Harman Street

24 June 1758
Harman Street

He was not a Freeman of the Goldsmiths' Company. Presumably he was a relation of Charles Kandler (No 1), possibly his son, since he re-entered Charles' new standard mark as his own in 1735. Charles (No 1) would have been dead at this time. Alternatively, it is a possibility that Charles Frederick and Charles (No 1) were the same person, although this would give him a working life of about fifty years.

In the Parliamentary Return of 1773, Frederick Kandler was recorded as a plate worker of Jermyn Street.

His son was probably Charles Kandler (No 2) who entered his mark in 1778 from the same address, Jermyn Street, following the retirement or death of Frederick Kandler.

Ann Kersill

 16 June 1747
Foster Lane

The wife of Richard Kersill, she took over the family business when her husband died in May 1747 aged about 25 years.

She gave birth to their second daughter, Mary, on 5 October 1747.

Richard Kersill

 20 April 1744
Foster Lane

He was the son of William Kersill (maltster) of Highworth, Wiltshire and was apprenticed to George Greenhill Jones on 1 July 1736. He obtained his freedom on 7 February 1744. When he died in May 1747 at the age of about 25 years, his wife, Ann, took over the family business.

They had a daughter, Ann, born on 9 July 1745 and another, Mary, born on 5 October 1747 following her father's death.

Richard's brother, Thomas, was apprenticed to Walter Brind in 1749 and obtained his freedom in 1757. He married Sarah Belbin in 1758.

William Kersill

 21 August 1749
Gutter Lane

 2 July 1757
Gutter Lane

He was not apprenticed through the Goldsmith's Company nor was he a Freeman of the Company.

Presumably he was related to Richard Kersill, possibly his brother.

Heal records him as being at 21 Aldersgate Street, 1772-77. In the Parliamentary Return of 1773 he was recorded as a small worker of the same address.

Jeremiah King

11 September 1723
O.S.
In Carey Lane
Imbroaderer

11 September 1723
N.S.
In Carey Lane
Imbroaderer

5 June 1736
In Foster Lane
Imbroaderer

18 June 1739
Foster Lane

26 January 1743
Due to the old mark
being broken

14 February 1744
Due to the old mark
being broken

He was apprenticed to William Scarlett of the Broderers' Company and obtained his freedom of that Company on 7 November 1722. He died in April 1750.

John Ladyman

1699 (between January and July)
Sherborne Lane

He was the son of John Ladyman (Citizen and Salter) of London and was apprenticed to George Watkins (Goldsmith) on 2 July 1675. He obtained his freedom on 28 September 1687 and was made a Liveryman in October 1698.

He and his wife, Sarah, had four sons and two daughters born 1692 to 1699 inclusive.

Thomas Sutton was apprenticed to him in 1702.

George Lambe

10 June 1713
Hemings Row,
St Martin's Lane

He was the son of William Lambe (weaver) of Llanterdine (?Leintwardine), Hertfordshire and was apprenticed to Joseph Barbutt on 23 May 1706. He obtained his freedom on 10 June 1713 and presumably died in 1720 when his wife, Jane, entered her widow's mark.

Their son, Edward John, was apprenticed to Jane Lambe on 2 April 1731 and obtained his freedom by Patrimony on 3 February 1742.

Both George and Jane Lambe specialized in manufacturing spoons and flatware.

Jane Lambe

(No date. Presume 1720)
N.S.
Chandos Street

(No date. Presume 1720)
N.S.
Chandos Street

She was the wife of George Lambe (Goldsmith) and took over the business when her husband died in 1720.

Their son, Edward John, was apprenticed to her in 1731 and obtained his freedom by Patrimony in 1742.

Heal records her as a plate worker in Chandos Street until 1732.

Jonathan Lambe

1699 (between January and July)
On London Bridge

He was the son of John Lambe (clerk) of Rayne Parva, Essex and was apprenticed to Richard Connyers (Goldsmith) on 26 March 1690. He obtained his freedom of the Goldsmiths' Company on 1 July 1697.

Paul De Lamerie

5 February 1713
N.S.
Windmill Street,
near the Haymarket

Circa (This mark not recorded at
1717 Goldsmiths' Hall. Presumed
to be Paul De Lamerie.)

17 March 1733
O.S.
At the Golden Ball,
Windmill Street,
St James

27 June 1739
Gerrard Street

He was the son of Paul Souchay de la Merie and Constance
le Roux, both French Huguenots of aristocratic birth. They
had fled to the Netherlands to escape from the religious
persecution that followed the repeal of the Edict of Nantes
by Louis XIV on 24 October 1685.

Young Paul was born in the Netherlands at Bois-le-Duc or
Hertogenbosch, this being its Dutch name, on 9 April 1688
and was baptised Paul Jacques at the local church on 14
April 1688. He arrived in England with his parents in March
1689 then, in 1691, they brought him to London where they

Paul De Lamerie continued

lived in a small house in Berwick Street, Soho.

As his father was not trained for any trade or profession, it is likely that their only income at times was a small pension from the Royal Bounty, a fund for assisting distressed Huguenot refugees. In 1703, this pension amounted to £6 for the year. Later, when young Paul was established in his own business, his mother came to live with him until her death in 1741, but for some reason his father and he were so estranged that he allowed him to become an inmate of the poor house where he died and had a pauper's funeral in 1735.

On 24 June 1703, young Paul took out letters of denization and on 6 August of that year he was apprenticed to the Huguenot silversmith, Pierre Platel. On 4 February 1713, he obtained his freedom of the Goldsmiths' Company and the following day entered his first mark at Goldsmiths' Hall. In 1717, he was made a Liveryman and, in 1731, an Assistant of the Court.

On 11 February 1717, he married twenty-three year old Louise Julliot, the daughter of Huguenot parents. They had six children of whom three died in childhood. These were Margaret born 1718, died 1724; Paul born 1725, died 1727; Daniel born 1727, died 1728. The three remaining children were Susan Mary born 1720; Susannah born 1729; Louisa Elizabeth born 1730. Susannah married Joseph Debaufre of the watch-making family in 1750 and Susan Mary married John Malliet in 1754, but Louisa Elizabeth remained a spinster until her death in 1761. Paul's wife, Louise, died on 8 June 1765.

Apparently Paul belonged to a militia organisation of some kind for, in 1736, he became a Captain and, from 1743, was Major until his death in 1751.

He became 4th Warden of the Goldsmiths' Company in 1743, 3rd Warden in 1746 and 2nd Warden in 1747. During 1750, his health began to fail and he died at his home in Gerrard Street on 1 August 1751.

Paul De Lamerie continued

As he had no son or heir to take over his business, he directed in his will that it should be closed and all plate in hand be completed and sold. Philip Garden purchased some of his patterns and tools when they were subsequently auctioned.

Peter Archambo (No 2) was apprenticed to him in 1738 and obtained his freedom in 1748.

John Lampfert

 12 November 1748
Little Windmill Street

 24 January 1749
The little mark was entered

Removed to Hemings Row,
24 November 1749

He was not apprenticed through the Goldsmiths' Company nor was he a Freeman of the Company.

He specialized in manufacturing spoons.

John Langlands (No 1)

3 March 1780
with John Robertson (No 1)
Plate workers
Newcastle-upon-Tyne
(These marks entered
at Goldsmiths' Hall
'by virtue of a
letter of Attorney')

He was apprenticed to Isaac Cookson, a Newcastle silver smith, on 2 October 1731. After completing his apprentice-ship, he remained with Cookson as one of his journeymen. When Cookson died in August 1754, he entered into part-nership with fellow journeyman, John Goodrick. Both he and Goodrick obtained their freedom of the Goldsmiths' Company of Newcastle on 24 September 1754. In April 1757, Goodrick died leaving Langland's (No 1) to continue running the business on his own.

In 1778, he took John Robertson (No 1) into partnership which lasted until Langland's (No 1) death on 10 April 1793. His widow then continued the partnership with Robertson (No 1), until dissolved on 10 June 1795.

Meanwhile, her son, John Langlands (No 2), obtained his freedom of the Newcastle Goldsmiths' Company by Patri-mony on 24 December 1793 but died on 5 May 1804 when only 31 years old leaving his widow, Dorothy, to continue running the firm until circa 1814.

N.B. Presumably these three marks above were entered in the London Goldsmiths' records for use on articles made or the London market. The firm's premises remained at Newcastle-upon-Tyne throughout this period.

These three marks are to be found likewise in the records of the Goldsmiths' Company of Newcastle-upon-Tyne where they are imprinted upon a copper plate.

Louis Laroche

19 November 1725
Lomber Court,
at corner of Seven Dials

31 July 1739
Lomber Court,
by Seven Dials

He was not apprenticed through the Goldsmiths' Company nor was he a Freeman of the Company.

In June 1742, he and five other goldsmiths were charged with counterfeiting assay marks on wrought plate to avoid paying duty and assay charges. By August 1742, he had been prosecuted, tried and convicted of the charge and was then residing in the Kings Bench Prison. The other five goldsmiths so charged were: Richard Gosling, Edward Aldridge, James Smith, David Mowden and Matthias Standfast.

Samuel Lea

13 July 1711
Castle Street,
near Hemings Row

12 December 1721
O.S.
(No address. Presumably as above)

He was the son of Joseph Lea (yeoman) of St Martin's in the Fields and was apprenticed to John Diggle (Goldsmith) on 8 June 1698. He was turned over to Philip Rollos (No 1) on 17 January 1699 and obtained his freedom of the Goldsmiths' Company on 13 July 1709.

John Leach

1699 (between January and July)
Distaff Lane
Haberdasher

He was the son of John 'Leitch' (tanner) of Chipping Norton, Oxon and was apprenticed to William Browne, a Freeman of the Haberdashers' Company, on 10 June 1675. He obtained his freedom of that Company on 14 July 1672.

Ralph Leake

1699 (between January and July)
Covent Garden

He was the son of Thomas Leake (yeoman) of Osbaston,
Salop and was apprenticed to Thomas Littleton on 15 July
1664. He obtained his freedom on 20 September 1671, was
made an Assistant in 1703 and 4th Warden in 1714.

Heal records him at Bridge Street, Covent Garden, 1686;
Angel, Catherine Street, Strand, 1692; and Covent Garden,
1697-1702.

Samuel Lee

14 August 1701
Newgate Street

1 July 1720
O.S.
(No address. Presumably as above)

He was the son of George Lee (grocer deceased) of Londo
and was apprenticed to William Swadling (Goldsmith) on
September 1692. He was turned over to John Penfold (Gold
smith) on 16 June 1696 and subsequently to Francis Archbol
(Goldsmith) on 25 June 1697. He eventually obtained hi
freedom on 7 August 1701.

Joseph Lejeune

 9 June 1760
Porter Street,
Seven Dials

ILI 5 February 1773
Litchfield Street,
Soho

He was not apprenticed through the Goldsmiths' Company
nor was he a Freeman of the Company.

John Lias (Nos 1 and 2)

8 November 1791
Buckle maker
15 Great Sutton Street

29 September 1792
with Dennis Charie
Buckle maker
16 Albemarle Street,
St John's Lane

3 July 1794
Buckle maker
Removed to 13 Bethnal Green Road
Removed to 8 Finsbury Street,
Moorefields. (No date given)

13 July 1799
Plate worker
8 Finsbury Street

15 March 1802
Plate worker
8 Finsbury Street,
Moorefields

25 November 1803
Plate worker
8 Finsbury Street

*17 August 1805
Plate worker
8 Finsbury Street

30 May 1810
Plate worker
8 Finsbury Street

*31 October 1812
Spoon maker
8 Finsbury Street

*16 June 1815
Spoon maker
8 Finsbury Street

14 March 1818
with Henry John Lias
Spoon maker
8 Finsbury Street

2 April 1818
with Henry John Lias
Spoon maker
8 Finsbury Street

*9 October 1819
with Henry Lias
Spoon maker
8 Finsbury Street

John Lias (Nos 1 and 2) continued

**7 August 1823
with Henry and Charles Lias
Plate workers
8 Finsbury Street

*3 March 1828
with Henry and Charles Lias
Plate workers
8 Finsbury Street

**24 September 1830
with Henry John and Charles Lias
Plate workers
8 Finsbury Street,
St Lukes

26 August 1835
with Henry John and Charles Lias
Plate workers
8 Finsbury Street,
St Lukes

*19 May 1837
with Henry Lias
Plate workers
Manufactory and residence
8 and 9 Finsbury Street,
St Lukes

28 November 1839
with Henry Lias
(Address as before)

*13 February 1843
with Henry Lias
(Address as before)
And a new manufactory
7 Salisbury Court,
Fleet Street

30 July 1845
with Henry Lias
(Address as before)

Trading under the firm of
John Lias & Son, 8 May 1848

It is likely that these are the marks of two John Lias's, presumably father and son, who were buckle maker and plate worker respectively. This possibility has been considered since the signatures against the marks of the buckle maker appear to be by a different John Lias from those against the plate worker. If this is correct, all those marks entered from 13 July 1799 onwards will be by John Lias (No 2).

Neither John Lias (No 1) nor John Lias (No 2) was apprenticed through the Goldsmiths' Company or became a Freeman of the Company.

Both Henry John and Charles, who were the sons of John Lias (No 2), joined their father in partnership, although only Henry John became a Freeman of the Goldsmiths' Company.

John Lias (Nos 1 and 2) continued

He was apprenticed to Isaac Boorman (silversmith, Citizen and Goldsmith) on 1 February 1809 and obtained his freedom on 7 August 1816. He eventually became Prime Warden of the Company in 1861 and died in 1877.

John Lias (No 2) appears to have retired or died by 7 February 1850 when Henry John (No 1) entered a new mark in partnership with his own son, Henry John (No 2).

*Mark entered in two sizes.
** Mark entered in three sizes.

Isaac Liger

2 October 1704
N.S.
Hemings Row,
near St Martin's Lane
'Free Imbroiderer'

5 September 1720
O.S.
Hemings Row,
near St Martin's Lane

He obtained his freedom of the Broderers' Company by Redemption on 19 September 1704 by order of a Court of Aldermen dated 14 September 1704.

On 16 October 1705, he married Marie Chemet at Swallow Street Church.

He appears to have died in 1730 when his son, John, entered his own mark from the same address. It is known that he was dead by 2 July 1735 when John obtained his own freedom of the Broderers' Company. Heal records Isaac Liger as a plate worker at Hemings Row until his death in 1730.

John Liger

9 December 1730
O.S.
At the sign of the Pearl,
in Hemings Row,
St Martin's Lane

He was the son of Isaac Liger (goldsmith and Broderer) and obtained his freedom of the Broderers' Company by Patrimony on 2 July 1735.

Nathaniel Lock

April 1697
without Cripplegate

24 January 1699
without Cripplegate

He was the son of John Lock (yeoman) of Warnford, Hampshire and was apprenticed to Roger Strickland on 21 May 1680. He obtained his freedom on 20 July 1697, was made a Liveryman in 1698 and an Assistant in 1709.

Heal records him as a plate worker at Blackwell Hall Court, Cripplegate 1692-98 and 1702-15.

William Fleming was apprenticed to him in 1687.

Mary Lofthouse

30 March 1731
Maiden Lane,
Wood Street

As the widow of Matthew Lofthouse (No 1), she carried on
the family business following her husband's death in 1731.

Their son, Matthew (No 2), obtained his freedom on 6
June 1732.

Matthew Lofthouse (No 1)

28 June 1705
N.S.
without Temple Bar
Free Wax Chandler

26 January 1721
O.S.
without Temple Bar

He was the son of Alvara Lofthouse (yeoman) of Menston,
Yorshire and was apprenticed to George Hewson, a Freeman of the Wax Chandlers' Company, on 20 February 1689.
He obtained his reedom of that Company on 29 September
1697 and was made a Liveryman in October 1716. In 1731,
he died leaving his widow, Mary, to carry on the business.

His son, Matthew (No 2), was first apprenticed to John
Boddington (Goldsmith) on 16 October 1724 and then turned
over to Matthew (No 1) (goldsmith and Wax Chandler) on 17
October 1724. This ensured that he became a Freeman of the

Goldsmiths' Company and not the Wax Chandlers' Company when he obtained his freedom on 6 June 1732.

Matthew (No 1)'s brother, Seth Lofthouse, was a Freeman of the Merchant Taylors' Company but traded as a goldsmith.

Seth Lofthouse

1699 (between January and July)
Bishopsgate Street

The above entry in the records states Seth Lofthouse was a Wax Chandler but this appears to have been added at a later date and to be an incorrect statement, since he was a Freeman of the Merchant Taylors' Company.

He was the son of Alvara Lofthouse of Menston, Yorkshire and was apprenticed to William Wakefield (goldsmith and Merchant Taylor) of St Nicholas Lane on 16 February 1675. Although Wakefield was a Freeman of the Merchant Taylors' Company he traded as a goldsmith. Seth obtained his freedom of the Merchant Taylors' Company on 25 September 1683 and was made a Liveryman on 5 December 1701. Heal records him as plate worker at White Horse, Fleet Street, near Fleet Bridge, 1712-22 and with Thomas Burgess as goldsmiths at White Horse, Fleet Street, 1719. He was dead by 7 February 1727 when one of his apprentices obtained his freedom.

His son, Joseph, was apprenticed to Matthew Derousseau, a Freeman of the Goldsmiths' Company, in 1705 but there is no record of his obtaining his freedom of the Company.

Seth's brother, Matthew Lofthouse (No 1), was a Freeman of the Wax Chandlers' Company but traded as a goldsmith.

William Bellassyse was apprenticed to Seth Lofthouse in 1709.

William Lukin

31 July 1699
In Gutter Lane

12 February 1702
In Gutter Lane

10 June 1725
O.S.
In the Strand

He was the son of Samuel Lukin (gentleman) of Bodicote, Oxfordshire and was apprenticed to St John Hoyte (Goldsmith) on 21 June 1692. On 1 June 1698, he was turned over to John Sheppard and obtained his freedom of the Goldsmiths' Company on 5 July 1699.

Heal records him as silversmith at the Golden Cup, Gutter Lane, 1699; at Blackamoor's Head, corner of York Buildings, Strand, 1712-34 and at Golden Cup, Strand, 1718.

He was made a Liveryman in October 1708, became bankrupt in August 1749 (*The Gentleman's Magazine*) and resigned from the Company on 15 October 1755.

He and his wife, Anne, had a daughter, Elizabeth, born 27 November 1700 and a son, Robert, buried 8 June 1703.

Jacob Marsh was apprenticed to him in 1726.

Jonathan Madden

 2 December 1702
Ball Alley,
Lombard Street

He was not apprenticed through the Goldsmiths' Company nor was he a Freeman of the Company.

Heal records him as plate worker at Lombard Street, 1702-06 and (?) Lombard Street, 1723-24.

Matthew Madden may have been his father.

Matthew Madden

 April 1697
Ball Alley,
Lombard Street

 April 1700
Ball Alley,
Lombard Street

He was not apprenticed through the Goldsmiths' Company nor was he a Freeman of the Company.

Heal records him as plate worker at Lombard Street, 1692-3 and 1697 and Lombard Street (?), 1695-1701.

Jonathan Madden may have been his son.

Robert Makepeace (No 1)

20 January 1777
with Richard Carter
Plate workers
Bartholomew Close

He obtained his freedom of the Goldsmiths' Company by Redemption on 4 April 1759, was made a Liveryman in 1763 and an Assistant in 1787. He became 4th Warden in 1792, 3rd Warden in 1793, 2nd Warden in 1794, and Prime Warden in 1795. He died circa 1796-1801.

It seems he entered marks at Goldsmiths' Hall prior to those of 1777, presumably in the now missing volume of Large Workers marks 1759-73. Heal records Robert (No 1), goldsmith at Serle Street, Lincoln's Inn from 1767 and in partnership with Richard Carter at 6 Serle Street, 1772-77.

Robert (No 1) had two sons, Robert (No 2) and Thomas. They were apprenticed to him in 1776 and 1778 respectively and both obtained their freedoms in 1788.

Heal records the firm as Robert Makepeace and Sons, goldsmiths of 6 Serle Street in 1784, so presumably both sons had been taken into the firm by that date.

Robert Makepeace (No 2)

*8 January 1794
with Thomas Makepeace
Plate workers
Serle Street,
Lincoln's Inn Fields

*20 January 1795
Plate worker
Serle Street,
Lincoln's Inn

He was the son of Robert Makepeace (No 1) (Citizen and Goldsmith) of Serle Street, Lincoln's Inn Fields and was apprenticed to his father on 7 February 1776. He obtained his freedom on 2 April 1788, was made a Liveryman in 1791 and an Assistant in 1801. He became 4th Warden in 1812, 3rd Warden in 1813 and Prime Warden in 1814. He died on 16 December 1827.

His brother, Thomas, was apprenticed to Robert Makepeace (No 1) on 7 October 1778 and obtained his freedom on 7 May 1788.

* Mark entered in two sizes.

Jacob Margas

19 August 1706
St Martin's Lane
Free of the Butchers' Company

September 1720
O.S.
St Martin's Lane

Born on 19 March 1684, he was the son of Samuel Margas (goldsmith) of St Giles in the Fields, Middlesex and was apprenticed to Thomas Jenkins, a Freeman of the Butchers' Company, on 2 January 1699. He obtained his freedom of that Company on 7 August 1706.

Heal records him as plate worker at St Martin's Lane, 1706-20 and bankrupt, 1725.

His brother, Samuel Margas, was apprenticed to him in 1708 and obtained his freedom in 1714.

Peter Archambo (No 1) was apprenticed to him in 1710 and obtained his freedom in 1720.

Samuel Margas

14 February 1715
N.S.
King Street,
Covent Garden

8 March 1721
O.S.
King Street,
Covent Garden

He was the son of Samuel Margas (goldsmith) of St Giles in the Fields, Middlesex and was apprenticed to his brother, Jacob Margas (goldsmith and Butcher), on 8 January 1708. Jacob was a Freeman of the Butchers' Company, although he traded as a goldsmith. Consequently, when Samuel obtained his freedom on 12 January 1714, it was of the Butchers' Company.

He married Judith de la Neuve Maison at St Paul's Cathedral on 3 June 1716.

Their son, Samuel, obtained his freedom of the Butchers' Company by Patrimony on 6 August 1746.

Jacob Marsh

24 April 1744
St Swithin's Lane,
Lombard Street

Removed to Lombard Street,
4 August 1749

Removed to Cornhill,
6 February 1761

He was the son of George Marsh (clerk) of Abbey Milton, Dorset and was apprenticed to William Lukin on 30 September 1726. He was turned over to Gabriel Sleath on 2 November 1731 and obtained his freedom on 6 November 1741.

Heal records him as a plate worker at St Swithin's Lane, 1744-48 and 78 Lombard Street, 1753-72.

John Matthew

13 September 1710
Ball Alley
Lombard Street

He was the son of Mary and William Matthew (No 1) (Citizen and Goldsmith) and was apprenticed to his father on 6 July 1704. Due to his father's death in 1707, he probably did not complete his apprenticeship. He obtained his freedom by Patrimony on 6 September 1710.

His brother was William Matthew (No 2).

Mary Matthew

28 May 1707
George Alley,
Lombard Street
Widow

She was the wife of William Matthew (No 1) and took over
the family business when her husband died in 1707.

Her two sons, William (No 2) and John, obtained their
freedom of the Goldsmiths' Company in 1711 and 1710
respectively.

William Matthew (No 1)

April 1697
Foster Lane

20 April 1700
George Alley,
Lombard Street

He was the son of Thomas Matthew (deceased) of Worcestershire and was apprenticed to John Smith on 28 July 1675.
He obtained his freedom on 27 June 1683. When he died in
1707, his wife, Mary, took over the business and entered her
own mark on 28 May.

His two sons, William (No 2) and John, were apprenticed
to him in 1701 and 1704 respectively.

William Matthew (No 2)

17 March 1711
N.S.
In the Minories

20 June 1720
O.S.
In the Minories

He was the son of Mary and William Matthew (No 1) (Citizen and Goldsmith) of London and was apprenticed to his father on 4 June 1701. Due to his father's death in 1707, he probably did not complete his apprenticeship. He obtained his freedom by Patrimony on 8 February 1711.

His brother was John Matthew.

Louis Mettayer

18 December 1700
N.S.
In Pall Mall

26 August 1720
O.S.
In Pall Mall

He was the son of Susanna and Samuel Mettayer (clerk) who was minister of La Patente Church, Spitalfields. Louis, together with his parents, brother Samuel and sisters Marie, Ann and Rachell, were all included in the Denization List of 12 December 1687 as an immigrate Huguenot family.

Louis was apprenticed to the Huguenot goldsmith, David Willaume (No 1), on 29 September 1693 and obtained his freedom on 17 December 1700. On 16 October 1706, he married Anne Hobbema at Spring Garden Chapel. He was made a Liveryman in October 1712 and died in 1740.

His sister, Marie, married David Willaume (No 1) in 1690 and his brother-in-law, Estienne Hobbema, married Anne Harache, sister of Pierre Harache (No 2).

Louis' daughter, Susanna, obtained her freedom by Patrimony on 5 December 1738.

Louis' son, Samuel, obtained his freedom by Patrimony on 3 December 1741.

Dorothy Mills

Circa 1746

(This mark is not recorded at Goldsmiths' Hall. Thought to be Dorothy Mills & Thomas Sarbitt and possibly entered in the missing volume of Small Workers marks 1739-58.)

6 April 1752
Saffron Hill

Presumably she was the wife of Hugh Mills and, following his death, entered into partnership with Thomas Sarbitt circa 1746.

Although she entered a mark under her own name in April 1752, by December 1753 she appears to have married Thomas Sarbitt and entered another mark under the name of Dorothy Sarbitt. (See under Sarbitt.)

Hugh Mills

 23 May 1739
At the Seive,
on Saffron Hill

 14 February 1746
Blue Court,
Saffron Hill

He was not apprenticed through the Goldsmiths' Company
nor was he a Freeman of the Company.

Following his death circa 1746, Dorothy Mills, who is
thought to have been his wife, entered into partnership with
Thomas Sarbitt.

Andrew Moore

 April 1697
Bridewell precinct

He was the son of Samuel Moore (Citizen and Goldsmith)
and obtained his freedom by Patrimony on 15 July 1664.

Thomas Morse

5 September 1720
N.S.
At the Spotted Dog,
in Lombard Street

5 September 1720
O.S.
At the Spotted Dog,
in Lombard Street

He was the son of Thomas Morse (gentleman deceased) of Coxen, Berkshire and was apprenticed to Isaac Maylin (Goldsmith) on 7 March 1711. He was turned over to Anthony Nelme (Goldsmith) on 13 October 1714 and obtained his freedom on 7 April 1720.

Anthony Nelme

 Prior to 1697 (Only recorded at
Goldsmiths' Hall in
1723 under Francis,
his son. Where found
on silverware prior
to 1697, it is presumed
to be an Anthony Nelme
mark which was entered
in the missing records.)

 April 1697
Ave Maria Lane

 April 1697
Ave Maria Lane

He was the son of John Nelme (yeoman) of Muchmerkle (?Marcle Much), Herefordshire and was apprenticed to Richard Rowley on 1 November 1672. At a later date he was turned over to Isaac Deighton, possibly due to the death of Richard Rowley. He obtained his freedom on 16 January 1680 and was made an Assistant in 1703. He was made 4th Warden in 1717 and 2nd Warden in 1722 but died on 23 January 1723 leaving his son, Francis, to carry on the business.

His son, Francis, was apprenticed to him in 1712 and obtained his freedom in 1719. Another son, called Younger, was apprenticed to Roger Hudson in 1713 but there is no record of his obtaining his freedom. A third son, John, was apprenticed to Anthony in 1718 and obtained his freedom by Patrimony in 1725.

Anthony Nelme continued

His daughter, Elizabeth, was born in 1690 and remained a spinster all her life. On 12 November 1760, when 70 years old, she obtained her freedom of the Goldsmiths' Company by Patrimony. The reason for this action was to enable her to qualify for charity from the Company. On 18 December 1760, she petitioned the Company's Court, 'that her father was many years a member of this Court and left her a comfortable Patrimony but she had unfortunately lost nigh all and the little which is left was insufficient to support her and her eyesight was greatly impaired by Needlework which she had long confined herself to and is now become unable to subsist herself and therefore praying the Favour of the Company.' Her petition was accepted and she was granted a pension of £15 per annum, payable half yearly. (*Court Minutes, Goldsmiths' Hall*.)

Francis Nelme

20 March 1723
Ave Maria Lane
Francis Nelme
the same marks
(as Anthony Nelme)

19 June 1739
Ave Maria Lane

He was the son of Anthony Nelme (Citizen and Goldsmith) of London and was apprenticed to his father on 6 March 1712. He obtained his freedom on 9 April 1719 and was made a Liveryman in October 1721. Following his father's death on 23 January 1723, Francis carried on the family business using the same marks as his father.

Hannah Northcote

6 June 1798
Plate worker
Berkeley Street,
Clerkenwell

3 December 1799
Berkeley Street,
Clerkenwell

Removed to 9 Cross Street,
Hatton Garden, 4 March 1800

She was the daughter of Simeon Coley (buckle maker) and married Thomas Northcote (Goldsmith) on 12 January 1788. When her husband died in 1798, she took over the family business. She died on 9 September 1831 at the age of seventy.

Thomas Northcote

20 August 1776
Spoon maker
Shoemaker's Row,
Blackfriars

29 October 1777
Shoemaker's Row,
Blackfriars

27 April 1779
Shoemaker's Row,
Blackfriars

Removed to Berkeley Street,
St John's Gate, 13 January 1781

16 May 1782
Spoon maker
Berkeley Street

19 November 1784
Plate worker
13 Berkeley Street,
Clerkenwell

27 November 1784
Plate worker
13 Berkeley Street,
Clerkenwell

Thomas Northcote continued

4 December 1786
Plate worker
13 Berkeley Street,
Clerkenwell

5 March 1789
Spoon maker
Berkeley Street

19 August 1789
Plate worker
13 Berkeley Street,
Clerkenwell

10 July 1792
Plate worker
13 Berkeley Street,
Clerkenwell

5 June 1794
with George Bourne
Plate workers
Berkeley Street,
Clerkenwell

11 July 1797
Berkeley Street,
Clerkenwell

He was the son of Richard Northcote (cooper) of Well Close Square, Middlesex and was apprenticed to Charles Hutton on 11 January 1764. He was turned over to Thomas Chawner on 23 June 1766, obtained his freedom on 3 July 1771 and was made a Liveryman in March 1781.

On 12 January 1788, he married Hannah Coley who, following his death on 22 May 1798 at the age of forty-nine, took over the business and entered her own mark.

Henry Nutting

9 April 1796
Plate worker
38 Noble Street,
Foster Lane

17 June 1808
with Robert Hennell (No 2)
Plate workers
38 Noble Street,
Foster Lane

3 October 1809
Plate worker
38 Noble Street,
Foster Lane

He was the son of William Nutting (maltster deceased) of Wormley, Hertfordshire and was apprenticed to Charles Wright (Goldsmith) on 3 July 1782. On 4 February 1784, he was turned over to Thomas Chawner and obtained his freedom on 6 January 1790.

His son, Henry, was apprenticed to him in 1808 and obtained his freedom in 1816.

Joseph Angell (No 1) was apprenticed to Henry senior in 1796.

Abraham Lopes De Oliveyra

(No date. Circa 1725)
Small worker
St Helen's,
Bishopsgate Street

3 July 1739
Houndsditch

He was not apprenticed through the Goldsmiths' Company nor was he a Freeman of the Company. He was born in Amsterdam in 1657 and emigrated to England where he married Rebecca de Abraham Morais in London in 1697. He died in 1750 at the age of ninety-three.

Charles Overing

April 1697
Carey Lane

He was the son of Thomas Overing (ironmonger deceased) of Leicester and was apprenticed to John Cruttall on 13 October 1680. He obtained his freedom on 8 June 1692.

His son, Thomas, obtained his freedom by Patrimony on 21 February 1716. Another son, John, was apprenticed to John East on 7 September 1715 but was turned over to Charles Overing on 22 February 1717 and obtained his freedom by Patrimony on 5 October 1721.

Richard Bayley was apprenticed to Charles Overing and John Gibbons in 1699.

James Overing

OV   7 October 1717
Carey Lane

He was a Freeman of the Turners' Company. Possibly he was a brother of Charles Overing.

His son, James, was apprenticed to Edward Holaday on 31 May 1717 and was turned over to Charles Overing on 8 December 1719 following Edward Holaday's death in June 1719. There is no record of James junior having obtained his freedom of the Goldsmiths' Company.

Mark Paillett

1698 (Between 22 April and 21 October)
Hemings Row,
near St Martin's Lane

He was the son of Daniel Paillet (gentleman deceased) of St Martin's in the Fields and was apprenticed to Thomas Symonds on 1 August 1688. He obtained his freedom on 10 January 1695. Heal records him as a plate worker until 1714.

Lewis Pantin (No 1)

21 March 1734
Castle Street,
near Leicester Fields

29 June 1739
Leicester Fields

He was the son of Mary and Simon Pantin (No 2) and probably took over the family business from his mother in 1734. He never became a Freeman of the Goldsmiths' Company.

Presumably Lewis Pantin (No 2) was his son.

Lewis Pantin (No 2)

 28 July 1768
45 Fleet Street

LP 19 October 1782
Gold worker
LP 36 Southampton Street,
Strand

LP 12 April 1792
Gold worker
8 Sloane Square,
Chelsea

Removed to 6 Crown Street,
Westminster, 30 October 1795

Removed to 17 Alfred Place,
Newington Causeway, 18 July 1800

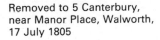 22 June 1802
Gold worker
30 Marsham Street,
Westminster

Removed to 5 Canterbury,
near Manor Place, Walworth,
17 July 1805

Lewis Pantin (No 2) continued

Presumably he was the son of Lewis Pantin (No 1). He obtained his freedom by Redemption on 11 March 1767 and was made a Liveryman in November 1776. He became bankrupt in 1787 (*The Gentleman's Magazine*) and applied for the lowly position of Beadle of the Goldsmiths' Company. On 2 November 1787, he was appointed Beadle but was dismissed on 4 December 1789 and died between 1802 and 1811.

His son was Lewis Pantin (No 3).

Lewis Pantin (No 3)

22 March 1788
Gold worker
36 Southampton Street,
Strand

20 December 1798
Small worker
62 St Martins-le-Grand

He was the son of Lewis Pantin (No 2) and obtained his freedom by Patrimony on 3 July 1799.

Apparently his first mark in March 1788 was entered from his father's premises. In both of his entries, March 1788 and December 1798, he signs himself as Lewis Pantin junior.

Mary Pantin

14 August 1733
Green Street,
Leicester Fields

She was the wife of Simon Pantin (No 2). When her husband
died in 1733, she took over the family business. It is probable
that, early in 1734, she handed over the business to her son,
Lewis Pantin (No 1).

Simon Pantin (No 1)

23 June 1701
St Martin's Lane

16 September 1717
In Castle Street

30 June 1720
O.S.
In Castle Street

He was apprenticed to Pierre Harache (No 1) and obtained
his freedom on 4 June 1701. He was made a Liveryman in
October 1712 and probably died early in 1729 when his son,
Simon (No 2), took over the business.

Simon (No 2) was apprenticed to him in 1717.

Augustin Courtauld was apprenticed to him in 1701 and
Peter Courtauld in 1705.

Simon Pantin (No 2)

4 February 1729
Castle Street,
near Leicester Fields,
St Martin's in the Fields

23 February 1731
Green Street,
Leicester Fields

He was the son of Simon Pantin (No 1) (Citizen and Goldsmith) and was apprenticed to his father on 22 May 1717. There is no record of his obtaining his freedom but this would not have been a requirement when working outside the city precincts. When he died in 1733 his wife, Mary, took over the business.

Their son was Lewis Pantin (No 1).

Sarah Parr

20 June 1728
Cheapside

She was the wife of Thomas Parr (No 1) and, upon his death in 1728, continued running the family business.

Their son, Thomas (No 2), appears to have taken over the firm when he entered his own mark in 1733.

Their daughter, Elizabeth, obtained her freedom of the Goldsmiths' Company by Patrimony on 27 July 1738 but did not enter a mark of her own.

Thomas Parr (No 1)

 April 1697
Wood Street

 19 August 1717
Cheapside

He was the son of Henry Parr (clerk deceased) of Cork, Ireland and was apprenticed to Simon Noy (Goldsmith) on 9 September 1687. He obtained his freedom on 8 August 1694 and was made a Liveryman in October 1712. Upon his death in 1728, his wife, Sarah, continued running the business, entering her own mark in June of that year.

One of their sons was Thomas Parr (No 2).

One of their daughters, Elizabeth, obtained her freedom of the Goldsmiths' Company by Patrimony on 27 July 1738.

Thomas Parr (No 2)

9 February 1733
Cheapside
Goldsmith

19 June 1739
Cheapside
Goldsmith

He was the son of Thomas Parr (No 1) and obtained his freedom of the Goldsmiths' Company by Patrimony on 5 March 1733. He was made a Liveryman in January 1750 and an Assistant in 1753. He became 4th Warden in 1771, 3rd Warden in 1772 and 2nd Warden in 1773.

In the Parlimentary Return of 1773, he is listed as a goldsmith at Whetstone. Presumably he had retired there.

Humphrey Payne

 3 December 1701
N.S.
Gutter Lane

 3 December 1701
N.S.
Gutter Lane

 1720
O.S.
Cheapside
(At the sign of the Hen and Chickens)

 15 June 1739
Cheapside
Goldsmith

He was the son of Nicholas Payne (tallow chandler) of Ludlow, Salop and was apprenticed to Roger Grainge on 15 August 1694. At a later date he was turned over to Thomas Parr (No 1). He obtained his freedom on 21 November 1701.

In 1708, he became a Liveryman and, in 1734, an Assistant of the Goldsmiths' Company. He was made 4th Warden in 1747, 3rd Warden in 1748 and 2nd Warden in 1749. Early in 1751, he handed his business over to his son, John, and retired to Daventry, Northamptonshire where he died on 1 August 1751.

His son, John, was apprenticed to him in 1732 and Robert Cox in 1744.

John Payne

 13 April 1751
Cheapside

 Circa 1761 (In the Goldsmiths' Company's own silver collection this mark is to be found on two items of plate which are known to have been commissioned from John Payne. Possibly the mark was entered in the missing volume of Large Workers marks 1759-73.)

He was the son of Humphrey Payne (Citizen and Goldsmith) of London and was apprenticed to his father on 1 January 1733. He obtained his freedom on 7 February 1740, was made a Liveryman in April 1740 and an Assistant in 1747.

On 13 February 1751, he married the only daughter of Mr Banks, Clerk to the Goldsmiths' Company. Also in 1751, he took over the family business, following his father's retirement, and entered his own mark in April of that year.

He became 4th Warden in 1760, 3rd Warden in 1761, 2nd Warden in 1762 and Prime Warden in 1765.

Edmond Pearce

1 February 1704
In the Strand
near the New Exchange

28 July 1720
O.S.
In the Strand,
near the New Exchange

He was the son of Edmond Pearce (hatter) of Tewkesbury, Gloucestershire and was apprenticed to Henry Beesley (Goldsmith) on 11 August 1693. Beesley originated from Twignorth, Gloucestershire.

On 10 November 1697, Edmond was turned over to Philip Rollos (No 1) and obtained his freedom on 24 January 1704.

Heal records him as a plate worker, New Exchange, Strand, 1704-22.

William Peaston

 8 January 1746
In New Rents,
St Martins-le-Grand

Removed to Deans Court,
8 August 1749

 12 July 1756
with Robert Peaston
St Martins-le-Grand

William and Robert Peaston were not apprenticed through the Goldsmiths' Company nor were they Freemen of the Company. Although they worked within the city boundaries, they would be exempt from becoming Freemen as their business address of St Martins-le-Grand was situated in a 'Liberty' area.

They may have been brothers although it is more probable that Robert was William's son. Records show that Robert was dead by 5 August 1778, the date when his son, William the Younger, was apprenticed to yet another William Peaston (Goldsmith) of Jewin Street who had become a Freeman of the Goldsmiths' Company on 7 December 1768. This second William was the son of George Peaston (husbandman) of Cranstoun, Midlothian and had been apprenticed to Nathaniel Appleton on 7 October 1761, turned over to William Shaw on 10 June 1763 and to William Skeen on 12 September 1768.

Heal records William as a working goldsmith, St Martins-le-Grand, 1745-60 and Jewin Street, 1778 although, in fact, these are two different William Peastons. Heal also records William and Robert Peaston as plate workers, St Martins-le-Grand, 1756-63.

Isabel Pero

1 May 1741
Orange Street,
near Leicester Fields

Born Isabella Yarnton, she married John Pero at St Benedict, Paul's Wharf on 16 December 1736. She was his second wife and took over the business in 1741, presumably because of his death.

She re-entered John's last mark as her own but with the lower portion removed.

John Pero

 24 August 1717
In the Strand

 23 November 1732
Suffolk Street

 22 June 1739
Orange Street
Free Goldsmith

He was the son of John Pero (Citizen and Stationer) of London and was apprenticed to Thomas Farren on 30 June 1709. He obtained his freedom on 12 July 1717 and was made a Liveryman in March 1739. He first married Mary Tomkins on 14 February 1721, then married Isabella Yarnton on 16 December 1736. Presumably, he died in 1741 when Isabella took over the business and re-entered his last mark as her own but with the lower portion removed.

His son, Edward, was apprenticed to Charles Gardner in 1740 but there is no record of his obtaining his freedom.

Jean Petry

21 November 1707
In the Pall Mall

Born in Heidelburg, he was the son of Mary and Bartholomew Petry (gentleman deceased) of Germany and was apprenticed to David Willaume (No 1) on 25 July 1700. He obtained his freedom on 21 November 1707.

Thomas Phipps

8 July 1783
with Edward Robinson
Small workers
40 Gutter Lane

8 August 1789
with Edward Robinson
40 Gutter Lane

With Edward Robinson
and James Phipps (No 2)
(No date or address. Presumably
entered between 22 June 1811 and
4 July 1811 being the dates of the
previous and following entries.)

Thomas Phipps continued

31 January 1816
with James Phipps (No 2)
Gutter Lane,
Cheapside

He was the son of James Phipps (No 1) (Citizen and Goldsmith) of Gutter Lane and was apprenticed to his father on 5 April 1769. He obtained his freedom on 7 May 1777, was made a Liveryman in February 1791 and died on 31 October 1823.

His son, James (No 2), was apprenticed to him on 5 February 1800 and obtained his freedom on 1 April 1807.

Another son, John, obtained his freedom by Patrimony in 1801 but appears to have become an attorney.

Edward Robinson was apprenticed to James Phipps (No 1) on 7 October 1772, obtained his freedom on 2 February 1780 and died on 10 January 1816.

Daniel Piers

3 November 1746
Spur Street

He was not apprenticed through the Goldsmiths' Company nor was he a Freeman of the Company.

Presumably he died in 1758 following which his widow, Mary, took over the business and entered her widow's mark in June 1758.

Mary Piers

2 June 1758
Spur Street,
Leicester Fields

She was the wife of Daniel Piers. Following his death, she took over the business and entered her widow's mark on 2 June 1758.

Alexis Pezé Pilleau

(No date. Presumably between
2 July 1724 and August 1724.)
N.S.
Chandos Street

(No date. Presumably between
2 July 1724 and August 1724.)
O.S.
Chandos Street
True Goldsmith

29 June 1739
Chandos Street
Goldsmith

His parents, Madeleine Pezé and Alexis Pilleau, a merchant goldsmith of Le Mans, France, were married in 1683. In 1688 they came to England as Huguenot refugees and, by 1697, Alexis senior was plying his trade of goldsmith and maker of artificial teeth in St Martin's Lane.

They had four sons and one daughter; Jean who remained in France and became a master goldsmith, Alexis Pierre who was born March 1692 and died July 1692, Alexis Pezé who was born 1696 and became a goldsmith, René who died young between April 1727 and September 1730 and daughter, Madeleine Louise, who was born December 1693 and was dead by 1730.

Alexis Pezé was born on 13 January 1696 and apprenticed to Jean Chartier on 27 April 1710 when fourteen years old. He obtained his freedom of the Goldsmiths' Company on 2 July 1724 and subsequently entered his first mark at some date prior to August 1724, this being the entry date of a following maker's mark.

On 25 December 1724, he married his master's daughter, Henrietta Chartier. They had six sons and two daughters.

In the autumn of 1730, his father, Alexis Pilleau, died leaving him his business.

Alexis Pezé made his will in 1762 by which time his wife, five sons and one daughter were already dead. He died on 2 January 1776.

Although Alexis Pezé is generally known as 'Pezé junior' or Pezé son of Pezé as entered in the records at Goldsmiths' Hall, this is not strictly correct. It seems that he dropped his first baptismal name of Alexis and used only Pezé which had been his mother's maiden name. Likewise, although his father's real name was Alexis, records at Goldsmiths' Hall describe him in one entry as Pezé father of Pezé who was apprenticed to Jean Chartier on 27 April 1710 and in another entry as Alexander Pillio, goldsmith of St Martins's in the Fields and father of René who was apprenticed to John Penkethman on 6 August 1712.

Philip Platel

25 November 1737
At Black Moor's Head,
at the corner of York Buildings,
in the Strand

He was not apprenticed through the Goldsmiths' Company
nor was he a Freeman of the Company.

Probably, he was related to Pierre Platel, the goldsmith,
possibly being the son of Pierre's brother, Claude Platel.

Pierre Platel

28 June 1699
Pall Mall

He was the son of Jean Baptiste Bertrand Platel du Plateau of
Ecrose St Dizier. In 1685, Pierre, with his father and brother,
Claude, fled to Flanders from the religious persecutions in
France. In 1688, they came to England, where, on 8 May 1697,
Pierre and his brother, Claude, took out letters of denization.
Pierre obtained his freedom by Redemption on 14 June 1699
by order of the Court of Aldermen.

On 16 April 1700, he married Elizabeth Peterson at St
James, Piccadilly. They had a son, Pierre, born 6 September
1701 and a daughter, Martha, born 4 February 1703. Pierre
junior became a vicar in 1732 and died in 1769.

Pierre senior was made a Liveryman in October 1708 and
was buried at St James, Piccadilly on 21 May 1719.

Philip Rainaud was apprenticed to him in 1700.

Paul De Lamerie was apprenticed to him in 1703. Note
the similarity of Paul's first mark of 1712 with that of his
master.

William Plummer

 8 April 1755
Foster Lane

Removed into Gutter Lane,
11 September 1757

 17 March 1774
Plate worker
47 Gutter Lane

 7 May 1789
Plate worker
47 Gutter Lane

He was the son of George Plummer (grasior) of Evington, Leicestershire and was apprenticed to the working goldsmith, Edward Aldridge (No 1) (Citizen and Clothworker) of Foster Lane, on 4 February 1746. He obtained his freedom of the Clothworkers' Company on 5 February 1755 and was buried at St Vedast, Foster Lane on 27 November 1791.

His son, William, was apprenticed to Thomas Whipham junior (Goldsmith) on 5 November 1777 but there is no record of his obtaining his freedom.

John Pollock

 16 October 1734
Over against the Bird in Hand,
in Long Acre

 26 June 1739
Long Acre

Removed to Belton Street,
Long Acre, 26 January 1744

He was not apprenticed through the Goldsmiths' Company
nor was he a Freeman of the Company.

Heal records him as a plate worker at Long Acre, 1734-
39; Old Belton Street, near Long Acre, 1748; and London,
1752-53.

William Priest

 12 October 1749
with William Shaw (No 2)
Maiden Lane

Removed to Wood Street,
2 January 1751

 27 June 1759
with William Shaw (No 2)

William Priest continued

Circa 1766 (This mark is not recorded at Goldsmiths' Hall. Presumed to be William and James Priest and entered in the missing volume of Large Workers marks 1759-73.)

He was the son of William Priest (Citizen and Armourer and Brazier) of London and was apprenticed to Richard Gurney on 30 July 1740. He obtained his freedom on 6 September 1749, was made a Liveryman in March 1758 and died between 1802 and 1811.

His brother, James, was apprenticed to him on 7 December 1750 and obtained his freedom on 4 July 1764. Heal records William Shaw and William Priest as working goldsmiths, Unicorn, Wood Street, near Maiden Lane, 1749-58; William Priest, goldsmith, corner of Lad Lane, Wood Street, 1763; and William and James Priest, goldsmiths, 30 Whitecross Street, 1764-73.

In the Parliamentary Return of 1773, William and James Priest are recorded as plateworkers, 30 Whitecross Street.

William Priest's marks are often found on coffee pots and tankards.

Benjamin Pyne

April 1697
St Martins-le-Grand

April 1697
St Martins-le-Grand

258

Benjamin Pyne continued

He was the son of Humfrey Pyne (gentleman deceased) of Ottery St Mary, Devon, was apprenticed to George Bowers on 23 October 1667 and obtained his freedom on 1 September 1676. On 25 December 1682, he married Susanna Salisbury of London at St Lawrence Jewry. He was made an Assistant of the Goldsmiths' Company in 1703, 4th Warden in 1715, 3rd Warden in 1720, 2nd Warden in 1721 and Prime Warden in 1725.

Following his bankruptcy, he resigned from the Goldsmiths' Company on 17 January 1728 and the same day applied for and obtained the lowly position of Beadle of the Goldsmiths' Company. He died, still in debt and was buried at Christchurch, Newgate on 9 April 1732 when about 78 years old.

On 23 June 1732, his daughters, Mary and Ann, petitioned the Company for a pension as they had been educated and maintained with hope of a decent provision and not brought up to any business and were now destitute. They were granted £5 each per annum. These payments ceased after 1734. On 7 February 1737, they both obtained their freedom of the Goldsmiths' Company by Patrimony.

His son, Benjamin, was apprenticed to him on 21 October 1708 and obtained his freedom on 18 May 1716. He became Assistant Assayer of the Goldsmiths' Company in 1720 but, in February 1736, he petitioned the Company to raise his salary to £70 a year since the work was very laborious, required constant attendance and was very prejudicial to his eyesight and health. Also, his salary was so small that he would find it hard to support himself in the case of sickness. The Court accepted his petition and raised his salary to the sum requested. However, he died in September 1737.

John Quantock

  (No date. After 3 July 1739, being the date of the preceding maker's entry.)
Facing Huggin Alley,
in Wood Street

 30 May 1754

He was the son of Thomas Quantock (yeoman) of Kingsbury Episcopi, Somerset and was apprenticed to James Gould on 14 January 1726. He obtained his freedom on 9 January 1739.

Heal records him as plate worker, Huggin Alley, 1734-54 and Wood Street, 1773. In the Parliamentary Return of 1773 he is recorded as plate worker in Wood Street.

He specialized in manufacturing candlesticks and tapersticks, as did his master, James Gould.

Philipe Rainaud

14 February 1708
At corner of Suffolk Street

26 October 1720
O.S.
At corner of Suffolk Street

He was the son of Ann and James Rainaud (gentleman deceased) of Rothsoire in Poictou Province, France and was apprenticed to Pierre Platel on 29 May 1700. He obtained his freedom on 13 February 1708 and was made a Liveryman in October 1721.

Heal records him as plate worker, Suffolk Street, 1707 until bankrupt in 1728.

Andrew Raven

April 1697
St Martins-le-Grand

April 1697
St Martins-le-Grand

He obtained his freedom by Redemption on 11 August 1697 by order of the Court of Aldermen. In October 1698, he was made a Liveryman of the Goldsmiths' Company.

Heal records him as plate worker, St Martins-le-Grand, 1697 and London, 1706-28.

Charles Rawlings

3 July 1817
Plate worker
12 Well Street

28 October 1819
Small worker
9 Brook Street,
Holborn

13 June 1822
Plate worker
12 Well Street

12 October 1826
Plate worker
12 Well Street

24 October 1826
Plate worker
12 Well Street

** 6 April 1829
with William Summers
Small workers
Brook Street,
Holborn

Removed to 10 Great Marlborough
Street, Regent Street, 9 January 1839

**2 December 1840
with William Summers
(No address. Presumably at
10 Great Marlborough Street.)

As the signature against each of the above entries in
the Company's records appears to be by the same Charles
Rawlings, it seems he occupied two separate premises at the
same time, one at Brook Street, for small works, the other at
Well Street for plate work.

He does not appear to have been apprenticed through
the Goldsmiths' Company nor become a Freeman of the
Company. He may be the Charles Rawlings, son of William
Rawlings (capillaire maker or wig maker deceased) of York,
who was apprenticed to Richard Coleman on 7 March 1810
to learn the trade of a watch finisher. There is no record of this
Charles obtaining the freedom of the Goldsmiths' Company.

Charles Rawlings specialized in manufacturing snuff boxes.

N.B. Syrup of Capillaire was a syrup or infusion of maiden
hair fern. Ben Johnson used to add it to his port wine.

** Mark entered in three sizes.

John Read

17 October 1701
with Daniel Sleamaker
Lawrence Pountney Lane

22 July 1704
Lawrence Pountney Lane

He was the son of John Read (yeoman) of Litchfield, Staffordshire and, having been apprenticed to John Archbold on 13 October 1686, he was turned over to Robert Timbrell at a later date. He obtained his freedom on 9 May 1694 and was made a Liveryman in October 1708.

Heal records him as plate worker, Lawrence Pountney Lane, 1701-04 and London, 1705-12.

Daniel Sleamaker was apprenticed to Robert Timbrell in 1690.

10 October 1815
* with David Reid
Plate workers
Dean Street,
Newcastle

*30 July 1817
Dean Street,
Newcastle

** Newcastle
By virtue of a Power of Attorney
I enter four marks (actually five)
of Christian Ker Reid of
Newcastle-upon-Tyne this ninth
day of July 1817.
(Signed) William Ker Reid,
Attorney to said Christian Ker Reid

** 16 May 1828
with David Reid
Dean Street,
Newcastle
(Entered) By virtue of above,
(Signed)   William Ker Reid,
           David Reid

N.B. These marks are to be found likewise
in the records of the Goldsmiths' Company of
Newcastle-upon-Tyne where they are imprinted
upon a copper plate.

He was a silversmith in Newcastle-upon-Tyne from 1778 until his death on 18 September 1834. Apparently, he moved to Newcastle from Edinburgh to work for the silversmith, John Langlands, with a view to an eventual partnership. However, Langlands took John Robertson into partnership instead, so Reid set up in business on his own and founded the present-day firm of Reid & Sons.

His two sons, William Ker and David, became silversmiths; William moved to London where he became a Freeman of the Goldsmiths' Company in 1814 while David remained in Newcastle and joined his father in partnership. Neither Christian Ker nor David ever became Freemen of the London or Newcastle Companies of Goldsmiths. After Christain Ker's death on 18 September 1834, his son, David, continued to run the family business in Newcastle.

Both William Ker and David married daughters of the silversmith, Edward Barnard (No 1). William Ker married Mary Barnard on 11 February 1812 and had thirteen children while David married Elizabeth Barnard on 26 August 1815 and produced ten children. When David died on 7 February 1868, C.J. Reid became senior partner of the Newcastle firm.

* Mark entered in two sizes.
** Mark entered in three sizes.

William Ker Reid

8 June 1812
with Joseph Cradock
Plate workers
67 Leather Lane

19 August 1819
with Joseph Cradock
3 Carey Street,
Lincoln's Inn Fields

24 September 1824
with Joseph Cradock
3 Carey Street,
Lincoln's Inn Fields

8 November 1825
Plate worker
5 Bream's Building,
Chancery Lane

21 February 1826
5 Bream's Building,
Chancery Lane

3 May 1828
5 Bream's Building,
Chancery Lane

William Ker Reid continued

His father was Christian Ker Reid, a silversmith of Newcastle-upon-Tyne, working from 1778 until his death in 1834. He was founder of the present day Newcastle firm of Reid & Sons.

William Ker's brother, David, followed by nephew, Christian John, continued to run the Newcastle firm after the death of Christian Ker Reid.

At some time William Ker Reid came to London where, on 11 February 1812, he married Mary, the daughter of the silversmith, Edward Barnard (No 1). They had thirteen children including Edward Ker and William Ker junior.

Edward Ker was apprenticed to his father in 1836 but obtained his freedom by Patrimony in 1842. He was made a Liveryman on 15 December 1848 and died on 10 February 1886.

William Ker junior was apprenticed to Edward Ker in 1846 but did not become a Freeman of the Goldsmiths' Company. He died in 1855 when 23 years old.

In 1812, William Ker senior entered into partnership with Joseph Cradock. They registered their first joint marks on 8 June of that year. On 2 November 1814, William Ker obtained his freedom of the Goldsmiths' Company by Redemption. He was made a Liveryman on 21 April 1818 and died on 1 February 1868.

It is interesting to note that in October 1815, July 1817 and May 1828, the Newcastle partnership marks of Christian Ker Reid and David Reid (William Ker's father and brother) were entered in the London records 'by virtue of a power of Attorney' signed by William Ker Reid.

John Charles Reilly

19 July 1818
Plate worker
12 Middle Row,
Holborn

He was not apprenticed through the Goldsmiths' Company nor was he a Freeman of the Company.

Charles Reily

31 May 1826
with Mary Ann Reily
Small workers
6 Carey Lane

*1 January 1829
with George Storer
Plate workers
6 Carey Lane

Removed to 3 Lovell's Court,
Paternoster Row, 26 June 1835

Removed to 6 Carey Lane,
16 February 1836

Charles Reily continued

 * 18 June 1840
with George Storer
(No address. Presumably
at 6 Carey Lane.)

He was not apprenticed through the Goldsmiths' Company
nor was he a Freeman of the Company. Presumably he was
the son of Mary and John Reily (goldsmith) of 6 Carey Lane.
John Reily appears to have married Mary Hyde at some
time between 28 November 1799, when he entered his first
mark in partnership with her, and 20 February 1801, when he
subsequently entered a solo mark. Presumably he was dead
by 31 May 1836 when Charles took over the business and
entered his first mark in partnership with his mother. Mary
subsequently retired or died by 1 January 1829 when Charles
entered a new mark in partnership with George Storer.

The firm specialized in manufacturing good quality snuff
boxes.

* Mark entered in two sizes.

John Reily

 * 28 November 1799
with Mary Hyde
Small workers
6 Carey Lane

 20 February 1801
Small worker
6 Carey Lane

 24 September 1802
6 Carey Lane

 *15 February 1805
6 Carey Lane

 9 April 1823
6 Carey Lane

13 June 1823
6 Carey Lane

He was not apprenticed through the Goldsmiths' Company nor was he a Freeman of the Company. He appears to have married Mary Hyde at some time between 28 November 1799, when he entered their partnership mark, and 20 February 1801, when he subsequently entered a mark of his own.

Presumably he was dead by 31 May 1826 when Charles, who is thought to have been his son, took over the business and entered a partnership mark with Mary.

* Mark entered in two sizes.

Isaac Ribouleau

16 July 1724
N.S.
In St Martin's Lane

(No date. Presumably 16 July 1724)
U.S.
In St Martin's Lane

He was the son of Stephen Ribouleau (distiller) of Hammersmith and was apprenticed to Augustin Courtauld (No 1) on 5 July 1716. He obtained his freedom on 2 July 1724.

Heal records him at Lombard Street when insolvent in 1729.

John Rich

13 June 1765
At the back of Tottenham Court Road,
near Whitfield Chapel in the Row

15 August 1780
Buckle maker
14 Tottenham Court Road

He was not apprenticed through the Goldsmiths' Company nor was he a Freeman of the Company.

John Robertson (No 1)

3 March 1780
with John Langlands (No 1)
Plate workers at
Newcastle-upon-Tyne
(These marks were entered at
Goldsmiths' Hall 'by virtue
of a Letter of Attorney')

He never became a Freeman of the Goldsmiths' Company of Newcastle-upon-Tyne. In 1778, he became a partner with John Langlands (No 1), a Newcastle silversmith. When Langlands (No 1) died in 1793, his widow continued the partnership with Robertson (No 1). Following its dissolution on 10 June 1795, Robertson (No 1) entered into partnership with David Darling.

In 1796, Robertson (No 1) commenced working on his own and continued to do so until his death on 6 July 1801. His wife, Ann, then took over the business and continued trading from July 1801 to September 1811, when she retired or died.

Their son, John Robertson (No 2), was apprenticed to Thomas Watson on 11 March 1799 and, in October 1811, went into partnership with John Walton. This partnership lasted until 1820. At the same time, Robertson (No 2) traded on his own account as a jeweller until about 1821.

N.B. Presumably the above three marks were entered in the London Goldsmiths' records for use on articles made for the London market. The firm's premises remained at Newcastle-upon-Tyne throughout this period. These three marks are to be found likewise in the records of the Goldsmiths' Company of Newcastle-upon-Tyne where they are imprinted upon a copper plate.

John Robins

20 October 1774
Plate worker
5 St John Street

(at) 67 Aldersgate Street,
18 July 1781

7 August 1787
(No address given)

Removed to 13 Clerkenwell Green,
5 February 1794

He was the son of John Robins (mason) of Brewton, Somerset and was apprenticed to Richard Wade on 3 October 1764.
On 27 January 1766 he was turned over to David Whyte. He
obtained his freedom on 6 November 1771 and was made a
Liveryman in March 1781. He died on 2 September 1831.

Thomas Robins, thought to be his cousin, was apprenticed
to him on 6 December 1786.

John Robins is known for manufacturing tea caddies and
globe inkstands.

Thomas Robins

 *10 June 1801
Plate worker
35 St John's Square

He was the son of Thomas Robins (mason) of Brewton, Somerset and was apprenticed to John Robins (Goldsmith) of Aldersgate Street, London on 6 December 1786. John Robins is thought to have been his cousin.

Thomas obtained his freedom on 6 August 1794, was made a Liveryman in June 1811 and died on 22 August 1859.

His mark is frequently found on entrée dishes.

* Mark entered in two sizes.

Edward Robinson

8 July 1783
with Thomas Phipps
Small workers
40 Gutter Lane

8 August 1789
with Thomas Phipps

40 Gutter Lane

With Thomas and James Phipps (No 2)
(No date or address. Presumably
entered between 22 June 1811
and 4 July 1811, being the dates
of the previous and following
entries of other makers)

He was the son of Edward Robinson (taylor) of London and was apprenticed to James Phipps (No 1), the father of Thomas Phipps, on 7 October 1772. He obtained his freedom on 2 February 1780, was made a Liveryman in February 1791 and died on 10 January 1816.

In July 1783, he entered into partnership with Thomas Phipps, his master's son.

In 1811, James (No 2), the son of Thomas Phipps, joined the partnership.

Elizabeth Roker

11 October 1776
Plate worker
96 Bishopsgate Without

It is probable that she was the wife of Philip Roker (No 3) in which case she presumably entered her mark in October 1776 following Philip's retirement or death.

John Roker

13 September 1743
Bishopsgate Street
Goldsmith

He was the son of Philip Roker (No 2) (Citizen and Goldsmith) of London and was apprenticed to his father on 25 May 1737. He obtained his freedom by Patrimony on 19 December 1743. He was dead by 3 August 1759 when his son, Thomas, was apprenticed to Beauchamp Warwick.

Heal records him as working goldsmith, Golden Cup, without Bishopsgate, 1740-45.

His brothers were Philip (No 3) and Matthew. Philip (No 3) was apprenticed to him in 1744.

Matthew Roker

29 April 1755
Greenwich, Kent

He was the son of Philip Roker (No 2) and obtained his freedom by Patrimony on 12 June 1754. Presumably he took over his father's business in April 1755.

Heal records him as plate worker, Greenwich, 1755-73.

In the Parliamentary Return of 1773, he is recorded as a spoon maker at Greenwich.

Philip Ludford Roker (No 1)

April 1697
Sherborne Lane

He was the son of Thomas Roker (bricklayer deceased) of Southwark, London and was apprenticed to Edward Gladwyn on 26 April 1676. There is no record of his obtaining his freedom. He married Ellenor Rooker and had four sons, including Philip (No 2), and five daughters.

Heal records him as silversmith, parish of St Mary Woolnoth, 1683-1701.

James Fraillon was apprenticed to him in 1699.

Philip Roker (No 2)

7 April 1720
N.S.
Long Acre

17 August 1720
O.S.
Long Acre

20 June 1739
King Street, Westminster
Goldsmith

Later moved to Greenwich

Baptized on 7 May 1693, he was the son of Philip Roker (No 1) and was apprenticed to Joseph Barbutt (spoonmaker, Citizen and Goldsmith) on 1 November 1707. He obtained his freedom on 7 April 1720. Presumably he retired or died in 1755 when his son, Matthew, took over the business and entered his own mark.

His sons were John, Philip (No 3) and Matthew.

Philip Roker (No 3)

28 June 1776
96 Bishopsgate Street Without
Spoonmaker

He was the son of Philip Roker (No 2) (Citizen and Goldsmith) of London and was apprenticed to his elder brother, John, on 10 January 1744. He eventually obtained his freedom by Patrimony on 1 December 1756. Probably he had continued working for his brother at Bishopsgate Street and may have taken over the firm in 1756 as a result of his brother's death, following which he obtained his freedom by Patrimony. It is known that John Roker was dead by August 1759.

In the Parliamentary Return of 1773, he was listed as a spoonmaker of Bishopsgate Street, therefore an earlier mark to the one illustrated must have been entered in one of the missing volumes of makers' marks. It is probable that Elizabeth Roker was his wife, in which case Philip presumably retired or died in October 1776, this being the date when she entered her own mark.

Heal records John and Philip Roker (No 3), goldsmiths, Golden Cup, Bishopsgate Without, 1743-73.

Philip Rollos (No 1)

April 1697
Over against Bull Inn Court,
in the Strand

He was the son of John Rollos and obtained his freedom
of the Goldsmiths' Company by Redemption on 11 August
1697. He was made a Liveryman in October 1698.

His son was Philip Rollos (No 2).

Edmond Pearce was turned over to him in 1697.

Philip Rollos (No 2)

20 August 1705
In Heath Cock Court,
in the Strand

28 September 1720
In Heath Cock Court,
in the Strand

He was the son of Philip Rollos (No 1) (goldsmith) of
St Martin's in the Fields and was apprenticed to Dallington
Ayres (Citizen and Goldsmith) on 2 December 1692. At a later
date, prior to April 1699, he was turned over to his father and
eventually obtained his freedom on 26 July 1705. Probably the
'later date' was when his father obtained his own freedom of
the Goldsmiths' Company. In October 1712, he was made a
Liveryman of the Company.

Richard Rugg (No 1)

 30 May 1754
Carolina Court,
Saffron Hill

Removed to Clerkenwell Green,
15 July 1754

He was the son of Richard Rugg (husbandman deceased) of
Cimington, Somerset and was apprenticed to James Gould
on 10 January 1738. He obtained his freedom on 3 September 1746.

His son, Richard (No 2), was apprenticed to him in 1763.
John Crouch (No 1) was apprenticed to him in 1758.

Richard Rugg (No 2)

18 March 1775
Plate worker
St John's Square

(The above mark may be Richard Rugg
(No 1) but more likely it is Richard
Rugg (No 2) since Richard (No 1) was
at least 50 years old at this time
whereas Richard (No 2) had obtained
his freedom only five years
previously)

He was the son of Richard Rugg (No 1) (Citizen and Goldsmith) of London and was apprenticed to his father on 2 November 1763. He obtained his freedom on 7 November 1770, was made a Liveryman in December 1771 and died between 1795 and 1801.

He was listed in the Parliamentary Return of 1773 as a plate worker of St John's Square, Clerkenwell.

Philip Rundell

PR PR PR PR	4 March 1819 Plate worker 16 Dean Street, Soho
PR PR PR	25 May 1819 16 Dean Street, Soho
PR PR PR	31 October 1822 16 Dean Street, Soho

Born in 1746, he was the son of Thomas Rundell (doctor) of Widcombe, Bath, Somerset and was apprenticed to William Rogers (jeweller) of Bath in 1760.

He came to London circa 1767-69 where he joined the firm of Theed & Pickett of Ludgate Hill as a shopman. About 1772, he became a junior partner with Pickett and eventually acquired the firm in 1785. He took John Bridge into partnership in 1788 and his own nephew, Edmund Waller Rundell, by 1805. Like Philip Rundell, John Bridge had been an apprentice under William Rogers in Bath.

Philip Rundell continued

From 1788, the firm was known as Rundell & Bridge then, from 1805, as Rundell, Bridge & Rundell. About 1802, Philip Rundell engaged Benjamin Smith (No 1) and Digby Scott of Greenwich as manufacturing silversmiths to the firm. This continued until January 1814 when Benjamin Smith (No 1) moved to Camberwell and set up on his own. In 1807, Rundell entered into a working partnership with Paul Storr. Storr ran the manufacturing side of the firm while Rundell, Bridge & Rundell of Ludgate Hill remained the retail outlet. When Storr left to set up on his own in March 1819, Philip Rundell retained the manufacturing side of the firm and entered his own mark at Goldsmiths' Hall on 4 March 1819. This situation continued until he retired from the firm in 1823, leaving John Bridge to take over as senior partner.

Apparently Philip Rundell was very difficult to work with, being of violent disposition, sly, cunning and very suspicious. His employees nicknamed him 'vinegar' while his placid partner, John Bridge, was called 'oil'.

Philip Rundell died on 13 February 1827, leaving a fortune of over £1.25 million.

Meanwhile, the firm continued until its closure at the end of 1843.

John Hugh Le Sage

11 October 1718
Little St Martin's Lane,
near Long Acre

26 July 1722
Old Street,
at corner of Great Suffolk Street
Free Goldsmith

25 June 1739
Great Suffolk Street,
near the Haymarket
Free Goldsmith

He was the son of Hugh Le Sage (gentleman deceased) of St Martin's in the Fields and was apprenticed to Louis Cuny on 7 May 1708. He obtained his freedom on 25 September 1718 and was made a Liveryman in April 1740.

He married Judith Decharmes at Hungerford Market Church on 10 April 1725. Their son, Simon, was apprenticed to him in 1742.

Edward Wakelin was apprenticed to him in 1730.

Richard Beale was turned over to him in 1725 having previously been apprenticed to Jonathan Newton in 1722.

Heal records him at the above addresses on the dates stated and at Great Suffolk Street until 1743.

Simon Le Sage

5 April 1754
Great Suffolk Street,
Charing Cross

He was the son of John Hugh Le Sage (Citizen and Goldsmith) and was apprenticed to his father on 6 May 1742. On the same day he was turned over to Peter Meure (Freeman of the Butchers' Company) but did not obtain his freedom of the Goldsmiths' Company until 5 June 1755.

It is possible that his father continued working until early in 1754, following which Simon took over the business and entered his own mark on 5 April 1754.

Heal indicates that he left off business in 1761.

William Sampel

27 January 1755
with George Baskerville
New Inn Passage,
Clare Market

29 August 1755
Baldwin's Gardens

He was not apprenticed through the Goldsmiths' Company nor was he a Freeman of the Company.

Heal records him as plate worker, Baldwin's Gardens, 1755; and London, 1763.

Dorothy Sarbitt

 13 December 1753
Saffron Hill

She was not apprenticed through the Goldsmiths' Company nor was she a Freeman of the Company.

She was formerly Dorothy Mills (see under Mills) and entered into partnership with Thomas Sarbitt circa 1746. Presumably their partnership mark was entered at Goldsmiths' Hall in the missing volume of Small Workers marks 1739-58.

In April 1752, she entered her own mark as Dorothy Mills.

At some unknown date she became the wife of Thomas Sarbitt and subsequently entered her own mark as Dorothy Sarbitt in December 1753, possibly due to Thomas's death.

Adey Bellamy Savory

 14 February 1826
Plate worker
54 Cornhill

 13 October 1826
54 Cornhill

 11 November 1829
54 Cornhill

 11 November 1826
54 Cornhill

3 April 1830
54 Cornhill

290

26 January 1832
54 Cornhill

7 September 1833
with Joseph (No 2) and Albert Savory
Plate workers and spoon makers
14 Cornhill
Factories at 15 Gee Street,
Goswell Street and at
6 Finsbury Place South

5 July 1834
with Joseph (No 2) and Albert Savory
14 Cornhill
Factories at 15 Gee Street,
Goswell Street and at
5 Finsbury Place South

He was the son of Joseph Savory (No 1) who had been apprenticed to James Hunt (Goldsmith) on 2 July 1760 and had obtained his freedom of the Goldsmiths' Company by Service on 3 February 1768. When Adey Bellamy obtained his freedom by Patrimony on 6 October 1802, he was trading as a coal merchant but by 1826, when he entered his first mark, he was trading as a goldsmith.

He had four sons; Thomas Cox, Albert, Joseph (No 2), and Adey Bellamy who became a bookseller. The other three sons obtained their freedom by Patrimony; Thomas on 2 December 1829 and Albert and Joseph (No 2) both on 4 December 1833.

Thomas Cox Savory

T·C·S   13 September 1827
Plate worker
54 Cornhill

T·C·S   2 November 1827
54 Cornhill

T·C·S   27 January 1832
54 Cornhill

He was the son of Adey Bellamy Savory and obtained his freedom by Patrimony on 2 December 1829, more than two years after he entered his first mark.

Presumably he worked with his father, since both gave their address as 54 Cornhill.

Thomas had three brothers; Adey Bellamy junior who became a bookseller and Joseph (No 2) and Albert, both of whom obtained their freedom of the Goldsmiths' Company and joined their father in partnership.

Richard Scarlett

24 September 1719
N.S.
Foster Lane
Free Broderer

24 June 1720
O.S.
Foster Lane

11 September 1723
O.S.

He was the son of William Scarlett (Citizen and Broderer) and was apprenticed to his father on 12 December 1710 to learn the trade of silversmith. When Richard obtained his freedom by Service on 5 February 1718, he likewise became a Freeman of the Broderers' Company.

He married Dorothy Arnold at Christchurch, Newgate on 28 March 1719. She was buried there on 3 December 1736.

William Scarlett

April 1697
Foster Lane
Free Broderer

29 June 1720
O.S.
Foster Lane

25 September 1722
O.S.
Foster Lane

18 October 1725
O.S.
Foster Lane

He was the son of Thomas Scarlett (cooper deceased) of Dereham, Norfolk and was apprenticed to Simon Scott (Citizen and Goldsmith) on 27 April 1687. Although there is no record of his having obtained his freedom of the Goldsmiths' Company, he did become a Freeman of the Broderers' Company at some date prior to July 1694, this being the date from when the Broderers' Company freedom records have been preserved. At some later date, he became a member of the Company's Court and eventually became its Master in 1726.

His son Richard, who also became a silversmith by trade, was apprenticed to him in 1710 and obtained his freedom of the Broderers' Company in 1718.

John Schofield

 10 February 1776
with Robert Jones
Plate workers
40 Bartholomew Close

 13 January 1778
Plate worker
29 Bell Yard, Temple Bar

 1 October 1787
29 Bell Yard

He was not apprenticed through the Goldsmiths' Company
nor was he a Freeman of the Company.

He is known for manufacturing candlesticks and cande-
labra. Heal records Robert and John Schofield, goldsmiths,
London, 1772-76.

Digby Scott

4 October 1802
with Benjamin Smith (No 1)
Plate workers
Lime Kiln Lane,
Greenwich

21 March 1803
with Benjamin Smith (No 1)
Lime Kiln Lane,
Greenwich

He was not apprenticed through the Goldsmiths' Company nor was he a Freeman of the Company.

He worked in partnership with Benjamin Smith (No 1) for the firm of Rundell and Bridge at their Greenwich workshops. Scott appears to have supplied the financial backing for Smith (No 1).

Robert Sharp

Circa 1763

Circa 1767

(These five marks are not recorded at Goldsmiths' Hall. They are presumed to be Daniel Smith and Robert Sharp and were probably entered in the missing volume of Large Workers marks, 1759-73)

Circa 1769

9 December 1778
with Richard Carter
and Daniel Smith
Plate workers
14 Westmoreland Buildings

7 February 1780
with Daniel Smith
14 Westmoreland Buildings
(Note that two of the previous marks have been reused with the letters 'RC' removed, presumably due to Richard Carter's death)

7 January 1788
Plate worker
14 Westmoreland Buildings,
Aldersgate

(Note that two of the previous marks
have been reused with the letters 'DS'
removed)

He was the son of Robert Sharp (yeoman) of Newcastle-upon-Tyne and, having been apprenticed to Gawen Nash (Citizen and Goldsmith) on 4 February 1747, he was turned over on the same day to Thomas Gladwin (Citizen and Merchant Taylor).

He obtained his freedom of the Goldsmiths' Company on 4 May 1757, was made a Liveryman in December 1771 and died in 1803.

In the Parliamentary Return of 1773, he and his partner, Daniel Smith, are recorded as plate workers of Aldermanbury. Also, they were fellow apprentices under Thomas Gladwin from 1747 until 1753 when Smith obtained his freedom.

Another Robert Sharp, son of one John Sharp (brewer deceased) of Newcastle-upon-Tyne, was apprenticed to Robert Sharp in 1770 but there is no record of his having obtained his freedom. Possibly he was a nephew of Robert.

Richard Sibley (No 1) was apprenticed to Daniel Smith and Fendall Rushford in 1785 and turned over to Robert Sharp in 1791.

Daniel Smith's son, George, was apprenticed to Robert Sharp in 1765 and obtained his freedom in 1772.

The firm of Smith & Sharp supplied plate for Parker & Wakelin from circa 1765 to 1774.

William Shaw (No 1)

16 January 1729
O.S.
Gerrard Street,
Soho

16 January 1729
N.S.
Gerrard Street,
Soho

24 June 1739
Gerrard Street

24 April 1745
Gerrard Street

He was the son of Thomas Shaw (clerk deceased) of Atherstone, Warwickshire and was apprenticed to Edward Holliday on 9 March 1715. He obtained his freedom on 12 November 1724.

The Gentleman's Magazine records him as bankrupt in July 1745.

William Shaw (No 2)

 3 January 1749
Maiden Lane

 12 October 1749
with William Priest
Maiden Lane

Removed to Wood Street,
2 January 1751

 27 June 1759
with William Priest

He was the son of Thomas Shaw (dry cooper) of London
and was apprenticed to John Swift on 11 November 1736.
He obtained his freedom on 6 April 1748 and was made a
Liveryman in April 1751.

In the Parliamentary Return of 1773, he is recorded as a
plate worker of Bishopsgate Street.

His mark is frequently found on coffee pots and tankards.

Alice Sheene

29 April 1700
Ball Alley,
in Lombard Street

She was the wife of Joseph Sheene. When he died in 1700, she took over the family business.

Heal records her as plate worker of Lombard Street, 1700-15.

Joseph Sheene

April 1697
Ball Alley,
in Lombard Street

He was the son of Joseph Sheene (mercer) of Tewkesbury, Gloucestershire and was apprenticed to Benjamin Bradford on 10 April 1677. For some reason his date of freedom does not appear to have been entered in the records and yet he was made a Liveryman in October 1698.

When he died in 1700, his widow, Alice, continued the family business.

Richard Sibley (No 1)

 14 November 1803
with Thomas Ellerton
Plate workers
14 Bartholomew Close

 11 March 1805
Plate worker
14 Bartholomew Close

 7 October 1805
with William Burwash
Plate worker
14 Bartholomew Close

13 July 1812
Plate worker
30 Red Lion Street,
Clerkenwell

He was the son of John Sibley (goldsmith deceased) of Bath, Somerset and was apprenticed to Fendall Rushforh (Citizen and Goldsmith) on 2 November 1785. By consent, he was turned over on the same day to Daniel Smith (Citizen and Merchant Taylor). On 2 March 1791, he was turned over to Robert Sharp (Citizen and Goldsmith).

He obtained his freedom on 2 October 1793, was made a Liveryman in June 1811 and died in 1836.

His sons, Richard (No 2) and Arthur, were apprenticed to him in 1821 and 1831 respectively.

Daniel Sleamaker

17 October 1701
with John Read
Laurence Pountney Lane

15 August 1704
St Swithins Lane

He was the son of Thomas Sleamaker (husbandman deceased) of Brinley, Warwickshire and was apprenticed to Robert Timbrell on 14 January 1691. He obtained his freedom on 29 July 1698 and was made a Liveryman in April 1705.

His partner, John Read, was also apprenticed to Robert Timbrell in 1686.

Gabriel Sleath

14 March 1707
N.S.
Gutter Lane

17 June 1720
O.S.
Gutter Lane

18 June 1739
Gutter Lane

22 November 1753
with Francis Crump (No 1)
Gutter Lane

Born on 11 January 1674 at Friern Barnet, he was the son of
Gabriel Sleath (Citizen and Tallow Chandler) of London and
was apprenticed to Thomas Cooper on 27 November 1691.
He obtained his freedom on 22 October 1701 and was made
a Liveryman in October 1712.

By his first wife, Anne, he had a son, Thomas, baptized on
27 July 1704 and buried on 18 August 1704. Anne was buried
at Friern Barnet on 14 April 1729. He married his second wife,
Jane Crane, on 17 August 1729. Gabriel Sleath was buried at
Friern Barnet on 21 March 1756.

Francis Crump (No 1) was apprenticed to him in 1726 as was
Francis Crump (No 2) in 1752.

Benjamin Smith (No 1)

 4 October 1802
with Digby Scott
Plate workers
Lime Kiln Lane,
Greenwich

 21 March 1803
with Digby Scott
Lime Kiln Lane,
Greenwich

 11 May 1807
Plate worker
 Lime Kiln Lane,
Greenwich

 25 June 1807
Lime Kiln Lane,
Greenwich

 23 February 1809
with James Smith
 Plate workers
Lime Kiln Lane,
Greenwich

14 October 1812
Plate worker
Lime Kiln Lane,
Greenwich

Removed to Camberwell Terrace,
15 January 1814

5 July 1816
with Benjamin Smith (No 2)
Plate workers
Camberwell

25 June 1818
Plate worker
Camberwell

Born on 15 December 1764, he was the son of Ralph Smith of Edgbaston near Birmingham, Warwickshire. His first marriage was to Mary Adams on 8 October 1788 at Edgbaston parish church. They had four sons, including Benjamin (No 2), and three daughters. His wife, Mary, died about 1800.

In May 1790, when he was recommended by letter to Matthew Bolton, he was already known as a metal chaser. By September 1792, both he and his brother, James, were working with Bolton, having set up the firm of Bolton & Smith, latchet manufacturers. (Latchets were thongs for fastening shoes.)

Benjamin Smith (No 1) continued

In 1794, they were joined by a John Lander (jeweller) who had invented an elastic shoe latchet. Benjamin and James, at this time, were described as button makers.

In 1801, Benjamin threatened to withdraw and move to London, a threat which he carried out since, on 1 February 1802, he married Mary Shiers at Greenwich church. They had one daughter who was born in 1803.

Meanwhile, Matthew Bolton and James Smith formed a new partnership in 1802, while Benjamin Smith set up his own firm at Greenwich with the financial backing of Digby Scott. This new firm of Benjamin's, which entered its first mark at Goldsmiths' Hall on 4 October 1802, manufactured almost entirely for Rundell & Bridge, later Rundell, Bridge & Rundell. On 2 December 1807, Benjamin obtained his freedom of the Goldsmiths' Company by Redemption and, in 1809, his brother, James, joined him at the Greenwich factory. Then, in 1814, Benjamin left Rundell's employment and moved to Camberwell where he continued producing work for Rundell's amongst his other commissions. In 1816, he entered marks in partnership with his son, Benjamin (No 2), who had been apprenticed to him in 1808.

Benjamin (No 1) died on 28 August 1823 after a long illness of over a year, by which time his son had already taken over the business.

Benjamin Smith (No 2)

5 July 1816
with Benjamin Smith (No 1)
Plate workers
Camberwell

15 July 1818
Camberwell

24 May 1822
Removed to 12 Duke Street,
Lincoln Inn Fields

1 December 1837
12 Duke Street,
Lincoln Inn Fields

Born on 6 October 1793, the eldest son of Mary (née Adams) and Benjamin Smith (No 1), he was apprenticed to his father on 6 July 1808.

In 1817, he married Susannah, the daughter of Apsley Pellatt (glass manufacturer).

He obtained his freedom of the Goldsmiths' Company on 3 January 1821, was made a Liveryman in April 1842 and died in May 1850.

His son, Apsley, married Emma, the daughter of G.R. Elkington of Birmingham, who was famed for his electro-plating process and manufacture of Elkington Plateware.

Daniel Smith

Circa
1763

Circa
1767

(These five marks are not
recorded at Goldsmiths' Hall.
They are presumed to be
Daniel Smith and Robert Sharp
and were probably entered in
the missing volume of Large
Workers marks, 1759-73)

Circa
1769

9 December 1778
with Richard Carter
and Robert Sharp
Plate workers
14 Westmoreland Buildings

7 February 1780
with Robert Sharp
14 Westmoreland Buildings
(Note that two of the previous marks
have been reused with the letters 'RC'
removed, presumably due to Richard
Carter's death)

Daniel Smith continued

He never became a Freeman of the Goldsmiths' Company. He was the son of William Smith (gentleman deceased) of Hawick, Cumberland and was apprenticed to Thomas Gladwin (Freeman of the Merchant Taylors' Company) on 6 November 1740. He obtained his freedom of that Company on 7 February 1753 and was made a Liveryman on 25 November 1766. In the Parliamentary Return of 1773, he and his partner, Robert Sharp, are recorded as plate workers of Aldermanbury. Robert Sharp had been a fellow apprentice under Thomas Gladwin from 1747 to 1757.

Daniel Smith probably retired at the beginning of January 1788, this being when an old partnership mark was re-entered by Robert Sharp but with Daniel Smith's initials removed.

His son, George Smith, was apprenticed to Robert Sharp on 8 May 1765, obtained his freedom on 7 October 1772 and probably remained working with the firm.

William Fountain and Richard Sibley (No 1) were both turned over to Daniel Smith (Merchant Taylor) in 1777 and 1785 respectively.

George Smith (No 1)

28 February 1732
Gutter Lane
Free Goldsmith

4 September 1739
Gutter Lane
Goldsmith

He was the son of George Smith (victualler) of St Martin's in the Fields and was apprenticed to Edmund Pearce on 3 March 1705. At a later date he was turned over to John Smith.
  He obtained his freedom on 23 May 1718.

George Smith (No 2)

13 December 1750
with Samuel Smith
Foster Lane

He was the son of George Smith (No 1) (Citizen and Goldsmith) and was apprenticed to Gabriel Sleath on 31 December 1728. He obtained his freedom on 7 December 1750.

George Smith (No 3)

1 February 1774
Spoon maker
110 Wood Street

12 August 1775
110 Wood Street

23 July 1776
110 Wood Street

22 October 1776
110 Wood Street

20 October 1778
Spoon maker
60 Paternoster Row

17 July 1780
60 Paternoster Row

10 August 1782
60 Paternoster Row

3 November 1786
with William Fearn
Plate workers
60 Paternoster Row

312

Removed to 1 Lovell's Court,
Paternoster Row, 29 June 1790

From the Goldsmiths' Company records it seems most probable that he was the son of Thomas Smith (butcher) of Wolverhampton, Staffordshire, in which case he was apprenticed to Thomas Chawner on 4 December 1765 for a period of seven years to learn the trade of a spoon maker. At a later date he was turned over to Pierce Tempest but there is no record of his having obtained his freedom of the Goldsmiths' Company. However, there was a George Smith who was apprenticed about this time to Thomas Chawner's partner, William Chawner (No 1). As William Chawner (No 1) was a member of the Pewterers' Company, this George Smith became free of the same Company when he obtained his freedom on 17 March 1768.

Although this was only 2 years 3 months after George Smith (No 3) was apprenticed to Thomas Chawner, it may well be that these two Smiths were one and the same person, having been transferred from one master to another during the apprenticeship. This would explain why no freedom date was recorded in the Goldsmiths' records. Unfortunately, the Pewterers' apprenticeship records no longer exist to verify the supposition.

In the Parliamentary Return of 1773, George Smith is listed as a spoon maker of 110 Wood Street, so presumably there was an earlier mark than that of 1 February 1774 as illustrated. Probably it was entered in the missing volume of Large Workers marks, 1759-73.

In 1778, he changed his premises, taking over those of his old master, Thomas Chawner, at 60 Paternoster Row.

During 1786, he entered a mark in partnership with William Fearn, who had been a fellow apprentice with him under Thomas Chawner.

William Fearn entered into partnership with William Eley in 1797 and George Smith (No 3) appears to have retired in 1799 when his son, George Smith (No 4), entering his own mark from his father's premises, signing himself as 'Geo Smith junior'.

George Smith (No 3) appears to have died between 16 February 1804, when Smith (No 4) last signed an entry as 'junior', and 9 April 1807 when Smith (No 4) entered a partnership mark with Richard Crossley without the word 'junior'.

George Smith (No 4)

20 June 1799
Spoon maker
1 Lovell Court,
Paternoster Row

8 November 1803
Spoon maker
31 St John's Square,
Clerkenwell

Removed to 16 Hosier Lane,
Smithfield, 16 February 1804

9 April 1807
with Richard Crossley
Spoon makers
Giltspur Street

20 January 1812
Spoon maker
16 Hosier Lane

He was the son of George Smith (No 3) and was apprenticed to William Fearn to learn the trade of goldsmith on 5 August 1789. He obtained his freedom on 5 October 1796.

His brother, John, was apprenticed to William Fearn in 1791, turned over to George Smith (No 4) in 1797 and obtained his freedom in 1798.

George Smith (No 5)

GS 21 November 1767
Huggin Alley,
Wood Street

G·S 9 August 1771
Huggin Alley
Wood Street

GS 8 April 1775
Buckle maker
4 Huggin Lane

G.S 21 September 1776
4 Huggin Lane

G·S 14 May 1778
4 Huggin Lane

GS 27 April 1779
4 Huggin Lane

G·S 17 January 1782
4 Huggin Lane

GS 25 January 1782
4 Huggin Lane

G★S
G★S 21 December 1782
G·S Huggin Lane

GS	25 May 1784	
GS	Huggin Lane	

GS	5 August 1786	
	4 Huggin Lane	

GS	20 March 1787	
GS	Huggin Lane	

G·S	24 September 1789	
G·S	Buckle maker	
	Huggin Lane	

GS TH	7 January 1792	
GS TH	with Thomas Hayter	
	Plate workers	
	4 Huggin Lane	

He was the son of George Smith (yeoman) of Witney, Oxfordshire and was apprenticed to John Eaton (Citizen and Goldsmith) on 2 August 1753. On the same day he was turned over to Samuel Eaton (leatherseller) of Huggin Court. He obtained his freedom on 14 January 1761, was made a Liveryman in December 1771 and died on 1 May 1805 aged 66 years.

Heal records him as goldsmith and buckle maker, 4 Huggin Lane, Wood Street, 1769-93 and as Smith & Hayter, goldsmiths, Huggin Lane, Wood Streeet, 1792-96.

Thomas Hayter, his son-in-law, was apprenticed to him in 1782 and obtained his freedom in 1790.

George Smith (No 6)

August 1758
Red Cross Street

He was the son of John Smith (waterman) and was apprenticed to William Aldridge on 2 May 1750. He obtained his freedom on 3 May 1758.

James Smith (No 1)

22 April 1718
N.S.
Foster Lane

25 August 1720
O.S.
Foster Lane

He was the son of Thomas Smith (yeoman) of Hampstead, Herefordshire and was apprenticed to Peter White on 20 March 1710. He obtained his freedom on 3 April 1718 and was made a Liveryman in May 1731. He died in 1737.

John Bayley was apprenticed to him in 1732.

James Smith (No 2)

14 September 1744
Winchester Court,
Monkwell Street

25 September 1746
Now of Old Bailey

He was the son of James Smith (Citizen and Tinplate worker deceased) of London and was apprenticed to John Ferris on 4 September 1735. He was turned over to John Montgomery on 5 December 1738 and obtained his freedom on 5 July 1743.

Samuel Smith

13 December 1750
with George Smith (No 2)
Foster Lane

4 February 1754
Foster Lane

He was the son of Samuel Smith (Citizen and Goldsmith deceased) of London and was apprenticed to Samuel Wood on 6 December 1743. He obtained his freedom on 11 January 1750.

John Spackman (No 1)

April 1697
At Charing Cross

He was the son of Thomas Spackman of Marlborough, Wiltshire and was apprenticed to Roger Stephens on 15 April 1668. He obtained his freedom of the Goldsmiths' Company on 1 September 1676 and was made a Liveryman in November 1687.

His son, John Spackman (No 3), obtained his freedom by Patrimony on 16 June 1720 and was made a Liveryman in August 1720.

His brother, Thomas Spackman (No 1), was turned over to him in June 1696 and obtained his freedom in May 1700.

A John Spackman (No 4) and a Thomas Spackman (No 2), who may have been his nephews, were apprenticed to him in 1693 and 1701 respectively. Neither appears to have obtained his freedom.

11 September 1741
Foster Lane
Goldsmith

24 November 1742
Removed into Gutter Lane
The above mark being lost,
the other mark was entered
at the time of removal.
(The 'above mark' refers to
the previous one entered on
11 September 1741)

He was the son of Thomas Spackman (No 1) (Citizen and Goldsmith deceased) of London and was apprenticed to Elizabeth Goodwin (widow of James Goodwin deceased) on 21 October 1730. He was turned over to William Justice on 29 November 1734 and obtained his freedom of the Goldsmiths' Company on 6 December 1737.

Thomas Spackman (No 1)

25 May 1700
Foster Lane

15 January 1707
Foster Lane

1 November 1725
Marlborough

He was the son of Thomas Spackman (grocer) of Marlborough, Wiltshire and was apprenticed to William Swadling on 19 November 1690. He was turned over to his brother, John Spackman (No 1), on 16 June 1696, obtained his freedom of the Goldsmiths' Company on 17 May 1700 and was made a Liveryman in October 1708.

Heal records him as bankrupt in 1719 which perhaps could account for the return to Marlborough before setting up in business again with a new mark in 1725.

He was dead by October 1730 when his son, John Spackman (No 2), was apprenticed to Elizabeth Goodwin.

William Spackman (No 1)

1 November 1714
Lilypot Lane

14 July 1720
O.S.
Lilypot Lane

N.S. (No date or address.
Marks were entered
between September

O.S. 1723 and May 1725)

He was the son of Joseph Spackman (chapman deceased) of Marlborough, Wiltshire and was apprenticed to William Andrews on 27 July 1703. He was turned over to Nathaniel Lock on 30 April 1706 and obtained his freedom of the Goldsmiths' Company on 4 November 1712.

Heal records him as plate worker, Lilypot Lane, 1714-26.

His two brothers, John Spackman (No 4) and Thomas Spackman (No 2), were apprenticed to John Spackman (No 1) in 1693 and 1701 respectively but neither appears to have obtained his freedom. It is possible that John Spackman (No 1) was their uncle.

William Spackman (No 1) was dead by 7 June 1737 when his son, William (No 2), was apprenticed to Robert Jenkes (Goldsmith). William (No 2) was turned over to Peter Archambo (No 1) (Butcher and goldsmith) on 27 July 1737 and obtained his freedom of the Goldsmiths' Company on 1 December 1745.

Francis Spilsbury (No 1)

24 July 1729
Foster Lane
Free Goldsmith

15 June 1739
O.S.
Foster Lane

12 December 1739
N.S.
Foster Lane

He was the son of Edward Spilsbury (Citizen and Cook deceased) of London and was apprenticed to Richard Green on 2 November 1708. He obtained his freedom on 12 July 1717 and was made a Liveryman in March 1737.

Heal records him as plate worker, Black Spread Eagle, Foster Lane, 1729-39.

His son, Francis (No 2), was made a Liveryman in 1763 and died on 6 August 1793.

Nicholas Sprimont

25 January 1743
Compton Street

Born on 23 January 1716 at Liège, France, the son of Peter Sprimont and Gertrude Goffin, he was apprenticed to his uncle, Nicholas Joseph Sprimont, to become a silversmith.

Later, he travelled to England where he married Ann Protin at Knightsbridge Chapel on 13 November 1742. His working period as a silversmith in London spanned only from 1742 to 1747. Pieces bearing his mark are very rare.

About 1745, he entered into partnership with Charles Gouyn (jeweller) as part manager of the Chelsea Porcelain Factory. The partnership was dissolved in 1749 and Gouyn left, taking some of the workers with him. Sprimont remained as manager under the patronage of the Duke of Cumberland's secretary, Sir Edward Fawkener, until about 1756. Sprimont then took over as proprietor but, in 1757, became very ill and had to close the factory for about a year.

Eventually, he decided to retire due to gout and general poor health and, in 1763, he put the factory up for auction. However, its sale was not completed until August 1769 when a James Cox bought it for £600. On 17 August, 1769, William Duesbury of Derby agreed to buy the factory from Cox and this sale was completed on 5 February 1770.

Sprimont remained living at Chelsea and Richmond until his death in late 1770. His collection of pictures was sold by Christie's on 26-27 March 1771 in 173 lots for £1,239.

2 May 1792
With William Frisbee
Plate workers
5 Cock Lane,
Snowhill

12 January 1793
Plate worker
30 Church Street,
Soho

27 April 1793
30 Church Street,
Soho

8 August 1794
30 Church Street,
Soho

Removed to 20 Air Street,
St James, 8 October 1796

29 November 1799
20 Air Street,
Piccadilly

21 August 1807
Plate worker
53 Dean Street,
Soho

18 February 1808
Plate worker
53 Dean Street,
Soho

15 December 1808
53 Dean Street,
Soho

21 October 1813
53 Dean Street,
Soho

12 September 1817
Plate worker
53 Dean Street,
Soho

Removed to Harrison Street,
Grays Inn Road, 4 March 1819

2 September 1833
Plate worker
17 Harrison Street,
Grays Inn Road

17 December 1834
17 Harrison Street

Born in 1771, he was the son of Thomas Storr, a silver chaser who became an innkeeper. On 7 July 1784, Paul, the son of Thomas Storr (victualler) of Union Street, New Palace Yard, Westminster, was apprenticed to William Rock (Citizen and Vintner) of Parliament Square. Paul obtained his freedom of the Vintners' Company in October 1791. Between April 1794 and June 1809 he accepted seven apprentices through the Vintners' Company.

On 2 May 1792, he entered his first mark in partnership with William Frisbee. This partnership did not last long, for Storr entered his own mark on 12 January 1793, having apparently taken over Andrew Fogelberg's premises in Church Street. By October 1796 he had moved to 20 Air Street, Piccadilly, previously occupied by the goldsmith, Thomas Pitts, from circa 1767 to 1793.

In 1801, he married Elizabeth Susanna Beyer, the daughter of a family of pianoforte and organ builders in Compton Street. She was a year older than Paul.

They had ten children; seven girls and three boys. Elizabeth born in 1802, Harriet in 1804, Paul in 1805, Emma in 1806, Francis in 1808, Mary Anne in 1809, Eleanor in 1811, Sophia in 1812, John Bridge in 1814, and Anna Maria in 1815. In spite of Storr's large family there was no son to carry on the business when he retired.

Paul junior joined the Merchant Service when about 14 years old and became a sailor while Francis, having spent about 5 years working with his father from 1824 to 1829, decided to take holy orders. He entered Queens College, Oxford in 1829 where he took his BA degree in 1833 and his MA degree in 1836. His third son, John Bridge, so named after one of Storr's partners in Rundell, Bridge & Rundell, unfortunately died while still an infant.

In 1807, Storr was persuaded to take over the manufacturing side of Rundell, Bridge & Rundell. This branch of the firm was called 'Storr and Co' with workshops at 53 Dean Street, while the parent company, run by Philip Rundell and John

Bridge, was the retail outlet for the workshop's products.

Although Storr always stamped his own mark on his silverware, the firm of Rundell, Bridge & Rundell often added its mark elsewhere on the article. This mark was not entered at Goldsmiths' Hall.

By 1811, Storr was a partner in the firm, the other partners being Philip Rundell, John Bridge, Edmund Rundell and William Theed. Storr had difficulty in working with quarrelsome Philip Rundell, the senior partner and eventually left the firm to open his own workshop at 17 Harrison Street, off Grays Inn Road in March 1819.

In 1822, Storr took over a shop at 13 New Bond Street as a retail outlet for his goods. It was run for him by John Mortimer who had been an assistant of Mr Gray, the previous owner. Meanwhile Storr continued running the workshop in Harrison Street. The firm was called 'Storr and Mortimer, Goldsmiths and Silversmiths'.

By 1826 trade had dwindled and Mortimer had so overstocked the shop that the firm of Storr and Mortimer was nearly bankrupt. Storr then appealed to John Samuel Hunt, his nephew by marriage, for assistance. The result was that Hunt became a partner and injected £5,000 into the business. The firm thus continued until 1838 when it moved to 156 New Bond Street.

However, Storr and Mortimer were constantly having disputes and eventually, in 1838, Storr retired with his wife to Hill House, Tooting where she died on 4 November 1843 and he on 18 March 1844. In his will, proved on 3 April 1844, he left an estate of some £3,000.

Mary Sumner

 18 March 1807
Spoon maker
1 Clerkenwell Close

 31 August 1809
with Elizabeth Sumner
Spoon makers
1 Clerkenwell Close

 21 August 1810
with Elizabeth Sumner
1 Clerkenwell Close

Presumably she was the wife of William Sumner (No 1) and took over the family business when William died in 1807.
Elizabeth Sumner was probably their daughter.

William Sumner (No 1)

1 May 1775
with Richard Crossley
Plate workers
1 Clerkenwell Close

27 January 1776
with Richard Crossley
1 Clerkenwell Close

10 May 1777
with Richard Crossley
1 Clerkenwell Close

27 January 1780
with Richard Crossley
1 Clerkenwell Close

6 April 1782
Plate worker
1 Clerkenwell Close

14 December 1784
Spoon maker
1 Clerkenwell Close

9 May 1787
Spoon maker
1 Clerkenwell Close

7 June 1788
1 Clerkenwell Close

 30 September 1799
1 Clerkenwell Close

 15 October 1802
Spoon maker
1 Clerkenwell Close

 31 March 1803
1 Clerkenwell Close

He was the son of Gilbert Sumner (farmer deceased) of Hadley, Essex and was apprenticed to Thomas Chawner on 5 October 1763. He obtained his freedom on 7 November 1770, was made a Liveryman in February 1791 and presumably died in 1807, following which his widow, Mary Sumner, entered her own mark.

William Sumner (No 2)

12 May 1787
Small worker
9 Albion Buildings,
Bartholomew Close

He was not apprenticed through the Goldsmiths' Company nor was he a Freeman of the Company.

Possibly he was a relative of William Sumner (No 1).

John Sutton

15 April 1697
Lombard Street
Present Touchwarden

He was the son of Thomas Sutton (gentleman) of Brignall, Yorkshire and was apprenticed to John Winterton on 8 February 1661. At a later date he was turned over to Arthur Manwaring. He obtained his freedom on 19 February 1668 and was made a Liveryman in September 1674.

In 1697 he was the Company's Touch Warden. He became 4th Warden in 1696, 3rd Warden in 1701, 2nd Warden in 1703 and Prime Warden in 1707.

Heal records him as plate worker, parish of St Mary Woolnoth, 1674-1707.

Between 1679 and 1693, he is known to have had two sons, John and Thomas, three daughters named Ann and three daughters named Sarah.

His brother, Leonard, was apprenticed to him on 26 August 1668 and obtained his freedom on 27 October 1675.

Thomas Sutton

 7 January 1712
Monkwell Street

He was the son of Charles Sutton (Citizen and Butcher) of London and was apprenticed to John Ladyman (Goldsmith) on 29 September 1702. He obtained his freedom on 5 December 1711.

Heal records him as plate worker, Monkwell Street, 1711.

John Swift

 (No date. Entered between May and October 1728)
Staining Lane
Goldsmith

 29 June 1739
Noble Street
Goldsmith

 18 July 1757
Noble Street

 22 August 1757
Noble Street

John Swift continued

He was the son of Anthony Swift (merchant taylor deceased) of St Olave's, Southwark and was apprenticed to Thomas Langford (Citizen and Goldsmith) on 6 March 1718. He was turned over to William Paradise (goldsmith) of Lad Lane on 6 April 1719 and then turned over to Thomas Serle of Gutter Lane on 9 May 1723. He obtained his freedom of the Goldsmiths' Company on 10 June 1725 and was made a Liveryman in March 1758.

His son, John, was apprenticed to him in 1750 and obtained his freedom in 1758.

Pierre Maingy of Guernsey was apprenticed to him in 1732 and John de Gruchy of Jersey in 1758.

John Swift's mark is frequently found on coffee pots, tea pots and tankards.

Richard Syng

April 1697
In Carey Lane

April 1697
In Carey Lane

He was the son of George Syng (gentleman) of London and was apprenticed to Abraham Hinde on 2 April 1679. He obtained his freedom on 23 November 1687 and was made a Liveryman in April 1705.

His two sons, Benjamin and Joseph, were apprenticed to him in 1709 and 1711 respectively. There is no record of Benjamin obtaining his freedom, but Joseph obtained his by Patrimony in 1734.

Ann Tanqueray

 Circa 1726   (No date given)
O.S.
(No address given. Presumed to be Pall Mall)

 Circa 1726   (No date given)
N.S.
(No address given. Presumed to be Pall Mall)

Baptized on 14 July 1691, she was the daughter of David Willaume (No 1). In 1717, she married David Tanqueray who had been one of her father's apprentices. When her husband died, circa 1726, she took over the business and entered her own mark.

She was buried on 25 July 1733 at Tingrith, Bedfordshire and her will was proved on 21 November 1733.

David Tanqueray

23 December 1713
N.S.
Green Street,
near Leicester Fields

12 August 1720
O.S.
In the Pall Mall

He was the son of David Tanqueray (deceased) of St Lô in the Province of Normandy, France and was apprenticed to David Willaume (No 1) on 16 September 1708.

He entered his first mark in December 1713 after only five years apprenticeship. Eventually he took up his freedom of the Goldsmiths' Company on 4 October 1722.

In 1717 he married Ann, the daughter of David Willaume (No 1). They had two sons, both of whom became rectors. David, born 1721, became rector of Cranley and Bow Brickhill, Buckinghamshire while Thomas, born 1724, became rector of Tingrith, Bedfordshire.

David Tanqueray was dead by January 1727 when one of his apprentices was turned over to his widow.

Samuel Taylor

3 May 1744
Maiden Lane,
Wood Street

27 January 1757
Maiden Lane,
Wood Street

He was the son of Thomas Taylor (Citizen and Weaver) of London and was apprenticed to John Newton on 3 March 1737. He obtained his freedom on 3 April 1744 and was made a Liveryman in May 1751.

In the Parliamentary Return of 1773 he was recorded as a plate worker of Maiden Lane.

He specialized in manufacturing tea caddies and sugar bowls.

James Tookey

 11 May 1750
Noble Street,
Foster Lane

 25 January 1762
Silver Street

He was the son of Charles Tookey (baker deceased) of
St Giles without Cripplegate and was apprenticed to Henry
Green on 5 April 1733. He obtained his freedom on 2 July
1741 and was made a Liveryman in March 1758.

He was not recorded in the Parliamentary Return of 1773
but an Elizabeth Tookey was recorded therein as spoon maker
of Silver Street. Presumably she was James' widow and had
taken over the business following his recent death.

Heal records him as plate worker, Noble Street, 1750.

His son, Thomas, was apprenticed to him in 1766 and
obtained his freedom 1773.

Elizabeth Tuite

 7 January 1741
George Street,
York Buildings

Presumably she was the widow of John Tuite and entered
her mark in January 1741 following her husband's death.

John Tuite

(No date. Entered between
September 1721 and July 1725)
Irelands Yard in Blackfriars

Removed to Litchfield Street
near Newport Market

Circa
1732

Circa
1733

(These two marks are not
recorded at Goldsmiths' Hall.
Possibly John Tuite did
not enter them as they are
similar to his first entry.)

27 June 1739
Litchfield Street,
St Anns, Westminster

He was the son of James Tuite (merchant) of Drogheda,
Ireland and was apprenticed to John Matthews, a goldsmith
in Dublin, in 1703. He obtained his freedom in 1710 and came
to London about 1720.

He may have died in December 1740 since Elizabeth Tuite,
who was probably his wife, entered a mark of her own in
January 1741.

Heal records him as goldsmith, Irelands Yard, Blackfriars,
1721; Green Door, Litchfield Street, near Newport Market,
1721-39; and George Street, York Buildings, Strand, 1745.
However, the last address is probably that of his widow
trading under his name.

He specialized in manufacturing salvers.

William Tuite

 (No date. Entered between
December 1755 and March 1758)
King Street,
Golden Square

He was not apprenticed through the Goldsmiths' Company
nor was he a Freeman of the Company. Possibly he was the
son of John and Elizabeth Tuite.

On 24 March 1761, he married Catherine Reddan at St
Paul's, Covent Garden.

The Gentleman's Magazine recorded him as bankrupt in
February 1770.

In the Parliamentary Return of 1773, he was recorded as
plate worker of Great Queen Street, Lincoln's Inn.

Heal records him as goldsmith, King Street, Golden
Square, 1756; and 41 Great Queen Street, Lincoln's Inn
Fields, 1761-75.

7 December 1775
Spoon maker
Holywell Street,
Strand

 25 September 1779
Plate worker
 5 Holywell Street,
Strand

 29 October 1781
Holywell Street,
Strand

He was not apprenticed through the Goldsmiths' Company nor was he a Freeman of the Company.

In the Parliamentary Return of 1773, he was recorded as spoon maker of Holywell Street so presumably an earlier mark was entered in the missing volume of Large Workers marks, 1759-73.

Heal records him as plate worker, Holywell Street, 1775-86.

Aymé Vedeau

18 June 1739
Green Street,
Leicester Fields

He was the son of John Vedeau (gentleman) of St Martin's in the Fields and was apprenticed to David Willaume (No 2) on 3 May 1723. He obtained his freedom on 8 January 1733 and was made a Liveryman in September 1746.

Presumably an earlier mark, circa 1733, was entered at Goldsmiths' Hall but unfortunately all makers' marks under 'V' in the Large Workers records for this period are missing.

In July 1742, he and five other members resigned from the Goldsmiths' Company in order to be independent witnesses for the prosecution at the trial of six goldsmiths charged with counterfeiting assay marks on wrought plate to avoid paying duty and assay charges. The six accused were: Richard Gosling, Edward Aldridge, James Smith, David Mowden, Louis Laroche and Matthias Standfast. Of these six, it seems that only Edward Aldridge was acquitted, the others being fined or jailed. On 5 August 1742, following the completion of his evidence, Aymé Vedeau was re-elected into the Goldsmiths' Company.

Heal records him as plate worker, Green Street, Leicester Fields, 1739-73.

In the Parliamentary Return of 1773, he was recorded as plate worker of Green Street, Leicester Fields.

Edward Vincent

25 June 1739
Dean Street,
Fetter Lane

It is likely that he was the son of Robert Vincent (Citizen and Goldsmith) of London and was apprenticed to William Parker (Citizen and Goldsmith) on 17 December 1711. On 3 December 1716 he was turned over to George Wanley and obtained his freedom on 3 December 1719.

Presumably he entered marks at Goldsmiths' Hall prior to 1739 but unfortunately the page of makers' marks under 'V' in the Large Workers records for this period is missing. He is known to have accepted apprentices through the Goldsmiths' Company from 1721 onwards.

Another possibility is that he was Edward Vincent, son of William Vincent (yeoman) of Hendon, Middlesex and was apprenticed to Robert Cooper (Citizen and Goldsmith) on 20 December 1699. He obtained his freedom on 23 July 1712 but, here again, all of his marks are missing from the records although he is known to have accepted four apprentices through the Goldsmiths' Company between 1712 and 1716.

Edward Wakelin

 17 November 1747
Panton Street,
near Haymarket

 Circa (This mark is not recorded at
1759 Goldsmiths' Hall. Presumed to
be John Parker and Edward
Wakelin and entered in the
missing volume of Large
Workers marks, 1759-73)

He was the son of Edward Wakelin (baker deceased) of
Uttoxeter, Staffordshire and was apprenticed to John Le
Sage on 3 June 1730. He eventually took up his freedom
on 7 September 1748. In 1747, he became senior partner in
George Wickes' firm in Panton Street.

About 1759, he entered into partnership with John Parker.
John was the son of Thomas Parker (gentleman) of Longdon,
Worcestershire and had been apprenticed to George Wickes
on 5 July 1751. He obtained his freedom on 5 May 1762.

By the end of 1761, the firm was known as Parker and
Wakelin. This partnership lasted until 1776 when Edward
Wakelin's son, John, together with William Taylor, entered
their own partnership mark. Edward Wakelin probably retired
in 1776. He died on 7 February 1784 at Mitcham, Surrey.

John Wakelin

25 September 1776
with William Taylor
Plate worker
Panton Street

9 May 1777
with William Taylor
Panton Street

20 October 1792
with Robert Garrard (No 1)
Plate workers
Panton Street

He was the son of Edward Wakelin (Goldsmith) of Panton Street and was apprenticed to his father on 5 March 1766. He eventually took up his freedom by Patrimony on 6 January 1779.

By September 1776 he appears to have taken over his father's business, this being when he entered his own mark in partnership with William Taylor. Following Taylor's death on 29 July 1792, John Wakelin entered a new mark in partnership with Robert Garrard (No 1) in October 1792.

John Wakelin appears to have retired or died in 1802, this being when Robert Garrard (No 1) entered his own mark.

Thomas Wallis (No 1)

 8 March 1758
Little Britain

 22 January 1763
Little Britain

Moved to Aldersgate Street,
13 September 1764

 **7 November 1778
Plate worker
Monkwell Street

He was the son of John Wallis (butcher) of Coventry and was apprenticed to William Jones on 7 June 1749. He obtained his freedom on 1 December 1756 and was made a Liveryman in December 1771.

In the Parliamentary Return of 1773 he was recorded as a plate worker of 37 Monkwell Street. Heal records him as plate worker, Little Britain, 1758; goldsmith, Aldersgate Street, 1765; and plate worker, 37 Monkwell Street, 1767-84.

He appears to have vacated 37 Monkwell Street by 2 March 1786, this being when a John Harris, plate worker, entered his own mark from the same address.

Thomas Wallis (No 1) died in either 1820 or 1821.

** Mark entered in three sizes.

Thomas Wallis (No 2)

**6 January 1780
Buckle maker
54 Red Lion Street,
Clerkenwell

*26 October 1786
(Address as above)

16 July 1787
(Address as above)

*26 June 1789
(Address as above)

*15 September 1792
Plate worker
(Address as above)

*16 August 1796
(Address as above)

*14 September 1801
(Address as above)

22 February 1810
with Jonathan Hayne
Plate workers
16 Red Lion Street,
Clerkenwell

Thomas Wallis (No 2) continued

**3 December 1817
with Jonathan Hayne
(Address as above)

17 February 1820
with Jonathan Hayne
(Address as above)

He was the son of Billers Wallis (victualler, deceased) of Shadwell, Middlesex and was apprenticed to Thomas Wallis (No 1) (Goldsmith) of Monkwell Street on 2 October 1771. He obtained his freedom on 3 February 1779 and was made a Liveryman in April 1791.

Jonathan Hayne was apprenticed to him in 1796 and obtained his freedom in 1804. Wallis (No 2) subsequently took him into partnership and entered their joint mark in February 1810. He appears to have retired by 3 July 1821 when Hayne entered his own mark at Goldsmiths' Hall.

Wallis (No 2) continued to give 16 Red Lion Street as his address until some date between 1829 and 1835, when he retired to Broxburn, Hertordshire where he died on 10 June 1836.

Heal records him as working goldsmith & spoon maker, 54 Red Lion Street, Clerkenwell, 1777-1814.

* Mark entered in two sizes
** Mark entered in three sizes

Joseph Ward

April 1697
Water Lane
near Fleet Street

19 September 1717
St Paul's Churchyard

He was the son of Aron Ward (shoemaker deceased) of Eckenton, Worcestershire and was apprenticed to Jospeh Slicer on 4 October 1672. He obtained his freedom on 4 January 1689, was made a Liveryman in April 1705 and an Assistant in October 1714.

He became bankrupt in 1723 and resigned from the Court of the Goldsmiths' Company in January 1726.

Richard Watts

10 February 1710
N.S.
Maiden Lane

24 June 1720
O.S.
Gutter Lane

He was the son of William Watts (Citizen and Lorimer) of London and was apprenticed to Christopher Canner (No 1) on 8 December 1698. He obtained his freedom on 17 March 1707.

He was dead by 6 May 1736 when his son, Joseph, was apprenticed to John Fessey. Joseph obtained his freedom of the Goldsmiths' Company on 7 June 1743.

Samuel Wheat

11 May 1756
Maiden Lane,
Wood Street

20 April 1757
Maiden Lane,
Wood Street

He was the son of William Wheat (Citizen and Turner deceased) of London and was apprenticed to Henry Bickerton on 3 September 1746. He obtained his freedom on 7 April 1756.

In the Parliamentary Return of 1773, he was recorded as a goldsmith of Maiden Lane. Heal records him as goldsmith, Maiden Lane, 1756-73.

Samuel Wheatley

27 April 1810
with John Evans
Plate workers
3 Old Street,
Goswell Street

23 August 1811
Plate worker
3 Old Street,
St Lukes

He was the son of James Wheatley (Citizen and Gold and Silver Wire Drawer) of Whitefriars and was apprenticed to Ann Chesterman (widow) on 5 April 1777.

On 5 April 1780, he was turned over to Charles Chesterman (No 2) by consent of Sarah Chesterman, the executor of Ann's will.

He obtained his freedom on 5 May 1784.

Thomas Whipham

20 June 1737
Foster Lane
Free Goldsmith

18 June 1739
Foster Lane

1 May 1740
with William Williams
Foster Lane

Removed to Ave Maria Lane,
25 July 1753

24 October 1757
with Charles Wright
Ave Maria Lane

Circa
1759

(This mark is not recorded at
Goldsmiths' Hall. Possibly
Thomas Whipham and Charles
Wright. It may have been
entered in the missing volume
of Large Workers marks 1759-73)

He was the son of William Whipham (innkeeper) of Layton,
Bedfordshire and was apprenticed to Thomas Farren on 3
July 1728.

He obtained his freedom on 7 June 1737, was made a
Liveryman in September 1746 and an Assistant in 1752. He

became 4th Warden in 1765, 3rd Warden in 1766, 2nd Warden in 1767 and Prime Warden in 1771. He died at St Albans on 27 August 1785.

In the Parliamentary Return of 1773, he was listed as a goldsmith of Fleet Street. Heal records him as working silversmith, Foster Lane, 1737-39; Ave Mary Lane, 1751-56; and Grasshopper, (61) Fleet Street, 1760-84. Also, with William Williams as plate workers (Spread Eagle), Foster Lane, 1740-46; and with Charles Wright as plate workers, 9 Ave Mary Lane, 1757-75.

Charles Wright was apprenticed to him in 1747.

His son, Thomas, obtained his freedom by Patrimony in 1768 and eventually became Prime Warden in 1790. This is one of the rare cases where both father and son became Prime Warden of the Goldsmiths' Company. It seems that Thomas junior continued working in his father's firm and eventually took over the business, although he never entered a mark at Goldsmiths' Hall. He died in 1815.

It is possible that the unrecorded mark of circa 1759, illustrated as being Whipham & Wright, may be that of Thomas and William Chawner. However, Thomas Chawner was apprenticed to Ebenezer Coker in December 1754 and did not obtain his freedom until January 1762, whereas this mark was taken from an article assayed in 1759, only five years after Thomas Chawner commenced his apprenticeship. Therefore, it seems unlikely to be that of Thomas and William Chawner.

Fuller White

 31 December 1744
Golden Ball & Pearl,
Noble Street

 4 March 1745
with John Fray
Golden Ball & Pearl,
Noble Street

 9 January 1750
Golden Ball & Pearl,
Noble Street

 5 July 1758
Golden Ball & Pearl,
Noble Street

He was the son of Fuller White (deceased) of Great Hallenbury, Essex and was apprenticed to Edward Feline on 8 January 1734. He obtained his freedom on 5 December 1744, was made a Liveryman in March 1750 and died on 2 July 1775.

In the Parliamentary Return of 1773, he was recorded as a plate worker of Noble Street. Heal records him as plate worker, Golden Ball & Pearl, Noble Street, 1742-73.

His mark is frequently found on coffee pots and tankards.

John White

10 December 1719
N.S.
At the corner of Arundel Street,
in the Strand

4 January 1725
O.S.
At the corner of Arundel Street,
in the Strand

26 June 1739
At corner of Green Street,
near Leicester Fields

He was the son of Christopher White (apothecary) of Wareham, Dorset and was apprenticed to Robert Cooper on 8 September 1711. He obtained his freedom on 3 December 1719.

Heal records him as plate worker, Golden Cup, Arundel Street, Strand, 1719-24; as goldsmith, London, 1720-33; and as plate worker, Green Street, 1739.

George Wickes

3 February 1722
N.S.
Threadneedle Street

3 February 1722
O.S.
Threadneedle Street

30 June 1735
Panton Street, St James,
Haymarket

6 July 1739
Kings Arms, Panton Street,
near Haymarket

George Wickes was baptized on 7 July 1698 at St Mary's Church, Bury St Edmunds. He was the son of James Wickes (upholsterer deceased) of Bury St Edmunds, Suffolk and was apprenticed to Samuel Wastell on 2 December 1712. He obtained his freedom of the Goldsmiths' Company on 16 June 1720 and was made a Liveryman on 13 March 1740.

On 9 January 1722 he married Alder Phelpes, the youngest of three daughters of Samuel and Mary Phelpes. Alder, who was at least seven years his senior, was an heiress, which may account for Wickes being able to set up in business with his own mark within a month of marrying her.

Heal records him as plate worker, Leadenhall Street, before 1721; Threadneedle Street, 1721; and in partnership with John Craig as goldsmiths & jewellers, corner of Norris Street, Haymarket, c1730-35. Wickes partnership with Craig appears to have been terminated by June 1735 when Wickes entered his own mark at Goldsmiths' Hall. Craig died on 14 December 1736. Meanwhile, Wickes continued working on his own until Edward Wakelin joined him and entered his own mark in November 1747.

In September 1748, Wickes apparently retired or became a sleeping partner, allowing Wakelin to carry on the silversmithing side of the business.

Heal further records Wickes as plate worker, King's Arms, Panton Street, two doors from Haymarket, 1735-61; and in partnership with Samuel Netherton as goldsmiths & jewellers, King's Arms, Panton Street, 1751-(left off business) 1759. Presumably Netherton dealt with the jewellery side of the business.

Following Wickes' probable severing of financial interest in the firm in 1759, Wakelin entered into partnership with John Parker. Wickes died on 31 August 1761 aged 63 years and was buried at St Peter's church, Thurston, Suffolk. Alder, his widow, died on 4 June 1774 and was buried with him.

Wickes' clientele from 1735 to 1747 included Frederick, Prince of Wales, the Dukes of Devonshire, Chandos, Kingston, Roxburgh, Montrose and Bridgewater, the Earls of Inchiquin, Scarborough and Kildare, the Dowager Duchess of Norfolk, the Marquess of Caernarvon and Viscount Leinster.

David Willaume (No 1)

April 1697
St James Street

29 January 1719
St James Street

27 July 1720
O.S.
St James Street

He was the son of Anne and Adam Willaume (goldsmith) of Metz, France which is where he trained to be a silversmith. He came to England in 1686 as a Huguenot refugee and took out papers of denization in December 1687.

On 19 October 1690, he married Marie Mettayer, the daughter of Samuel Mettayer (minister) and sister of Louis Mettayer. Louis Mettayer was apprenticed to him in 1693.

On 27 September 1693, by order of the Court of Aldermen of the City of London, he was made a Freeman of the Goldsmiths' Company by Redemption. He was made a Liveryman in 1698 and an Assistant in 1724.

In 1700, both Pierre Le Cheaube and Jean Petry were apprenticed to him as was his own son, David (No 2), in 1706. In 1708, David Tanqueray was apprenticed to him and eventually married his daughter, Ann, in 1717.

Both David Willaume (No 1) and (No 2) kept 'running cashes' which was a system of lending money on security.

Willaume (No 1) probably retired at some date prior to April 1728, this being when his son, David (No 2), entered his own mark.

In 1730, Willaume (No 1) purchased the Manor of Tingrith, Bedfordshire where his descendants, named Tanqueray-Willaume, survived into the twentieth century. He is known to have died at some date prior to 22 January 1741.

His work was of the highest standard in both design and craftsmanship. His clientele included the Dukes of Devonshire, Portland, Abercorn, Buccleuch and Brunswick, Lord Brownlow and Earl Fitzwilliam.

David Willaume (No 2)

2 April 1728
N.S.
In St James of St George,
Hanover Square

2 April 1728
O.S.
In St James of St George,
Hanover Square

19 June 1739
(No address given)

Born on 5 March 1693, he was the son of Marie and David Willaume (No 1) (Citizen and Goldsmith) of London and was apprenticed to his father on 6 March 1707. He eventually took up his freedom by Patrimony on 2 May 1723 and was made a Liveryman in March 1726.

His sister, Ann, married David Tanqueray in 1717 and died in 1733.

Willaume (No 2) married Marianne, daughter of Samuel Le Febure, on 17 April 1721. In 1733, he married again. This time it was to Elizabeth, daughter of Charles Dymoke of Ampthill, Bedfordshire. They had four sons and two daughters including Mary who married her cousin, the Rev Thomas Tanqueray, rector of Tingrith. Willaume's wife, Elizabeth, was buried at Tingrith on 20 June 1746 but he did not die until 26 January 1761.

Aymé Vedeau was apprenticed to him on 3 May 1723, the day after Willaume (No 2) obtained his own freedom.

William Cripps was apprenticed to him in 1730.

William Williams

1 May 1740
with Thomas Whipham
Foster Lane
Goldsmiths

10 September 1742
Spread Eagle,
Foster Lane

He was the son of William Williams (shopkeeper) of Hitchin, Hertfordshire and was apprenticed to Thomas Farren on 9 September 1731. He obtained his freedom on 5 December 1738 and was made a Liveryman in September 1746.

Joseph Willmore

21 February 1805
Small worker
14 Bouverie Street,
Fleet Street

Removed to 11 Thavies Inn,
Holborn, 6 March 1823

14 March 1840
(No address given)

He was not apprenticed through the Goldsmiths' Company
nor was he a Freeman of the Company.

Possibly he was the well-known Birmingham silversmith
of that name and these marks were entered in the London
Goldsmiths' records for use on articles made for the London
market.

Edward Wood

N.S. 18 August 1722
On Puddledock Hill,
at the end of
O.S. Great Carter Lane

26 August 1735
Carey Lane

30 September 1740
Carey Lane

He was the son of John Wood (Citizen and Turner) of London and was apprenticed to James Roode (Goldsmith) on 6 July 1715. He obtained his freedom on 2 August 1722 and was made a Liveryman in March 1737.

Heal records him as plate worker, Puddle Dock (Upper Thames Street), 1722; and at Carey Lane from 1735 until his death in 1752.

Both Wood and his master, Roode, specialized in manufacturing salt cellars.

David Hennell (No 1) was apprenticed to him in 1728 and likewise specialized in manufacturing salt cellars.

Samuel Wood

 3 July 1733
Gutter Lane,
by Cheapside

 29 September 1737
Gutter Lane,
by Cheapside
Free Goldsmith

 15 June 1739
Gutter Lane

Removed to Foster Lane,
15 July 1754

 2 October 1756
Foster Lane

Born circa 1704, he was the son of George Wood (gentleman deceased) of Carswell, Staffordshire and was apprenticed to Thomas Bamford on 7 June 1721. He obtained his freedom on 5 March 1731, was made a Liveryman in April 1737 and an Assistant in 1745. He became 4th Warden in 1758, 3rd Warden in 1759, 2nd Warden in 1760 and Prime Warden in 1763.

He and his wife, Elizabeth, had a daughter, Elizabeth, born in May 1738.

In the Parliamentary Return of 1773, he was recorded as a plate worker of Southgate. Heal records him as plate worker, Gutter Lane, 1733-40; and at Southgate, 1773.

The Gentleman's Magazine, 6 October 1794, states that he had died at Southgate, aged ninety, of a second paralytic stroke. For the last two years of his life, he used to ride to town every week to transact business at Goldsmiths' Hall, being the father and oldest member of that company.

Both he and his master, Bamford, specialized in manufacturing casters and Wood is particularly well known for his cruets.

Charles Wright

24 October 1757
with Thomas Whipham
Ave Maria Lane

Circa 1759 (This mark is not recorded at Goldsmiths' Hall. Possibly Thomas Whipham and Charles Wright. It may have been entered in the missing volume of Large Workers marks 1759-73)

22 July 1775
Plate worker
9 Ave Maria Lane

3 February 1780
9 Ave Maria Lane

25 August 1780
9 Ave Maria Lane

Charles Wright continued

He was the son of Thomas Wright (carrier) of Sheffield and was apprenticed to Thomas Whipham on 3 June 1747. He obtained his freedom on 3 July 1754, was made a Liveryman in 1758 and an Assistant in 1777. He became 4th Warden in 1783, 3rd Warden in 1784 and 2nd Warden in 1785. In 1790, he resigned from the Goldsmiths' Company and died in 1815.

In the Parliamentary Return of 1773, he was recorded as a plate worker of Ave Mary Lane. Heal records him as goldsmith, 9 Ave Mary Lane, Paternoster Row, from 1764 (when he married) until 1780; 76 Strand, 1784-88; and 94 Watling Street, 1790. The Goldsmiths' Company records state that from 31 May 1783, the premises at 9 Ave Maria Lane were occupied by Thomas Chawner.

Edward Barnard (No 1) and Henry Nutting were apprenticed to him in 1781 and 1782 respectively.

It is possible that the unrecorded mark of circa 1759, illustrated as being Whipham and Wright, may be that of Thomas and William Chawner. However, Thomas Chawner was apprenticed to Ebenezer Coker in December 1754 and did not obtain his freedom until January 1762, whereas this mark was taken from an article assayed in 1759, only five years after Thomas Chawner commenced his apprenticeship. Therefore, it seems unlikely to be that of Thomas and William Chawner.

Thomas Wright (No 1)

6 September 1721
O.S.
Maiden Lane

9 November 1722
In Maiden Lane
Free Goldsmith
Small old standard mark
witness my hand, Tho. Wright

He was the son of John Wright and obtained his freedom
by Patrimony on 3 December 1719.

Thomas Wright (No 2)

12 August 1774
Buckle maker
Jewin Court,
Jewin Street

27 April 1778
Jewin Court,
Jewin Street

Later removed to 10 Great Turnstile,
Holborn

Removed to 30 Little Bell Alley,
Coleman Street, 17 February 1802

He was not apprenticed through the Goldsmiths' Company
nor was he a Freeman of the Company.

ADDENDUM

The Aldridge Family

Edward (No 1) was the son of William Aldridge and obtained his freedom of the Clothworkers' Company by Patrimony on 4 February 1724. The following day he entered his first mark at Goldsmiths' Hall, giving his address as St Leonards Court, Foster Lane.

On 19 October 1723, he married Elizabeth Parker at Christchurch, Newgate. They had three daughters, born 1724, 1725 and 1733 respectively and a son, John, born 1737.

On 29 June 1739, he entered his second mark, giving his address as Lillypot Lane. Heal records him as being at the Golden Ewer, Lillypot Lane in Noble Street from 1739 to 1743.

In June 1742, he and five other goldsmiths were charged with counterfeiting assay marks on wrought plate to avoid paying duty and assay charges. By August 1742 he had been prosecuted, tried and acquitted of the charge against him. The other five were Richard Gosling, James Smith, David Mowden, Louis Laroche and Matthias Standfast, all of whom were either fined or jailed.

On 20 April 1743, he moved to new premises in Foster Lane. Heal records him at the Golden Ewer, Foster Lane from 1743 onwards.

On 8 March 1751, Edward Aldridge (No 2), who is thought to have been his nephew, was apprenticed to Starling Willford (Citizen and Goldsmith) and the same day turned over to Edward Aldridge (No 1) (Citizen and Clothworker). Edward (No 2) was the son of Charles Aldridge (staymaker) of Cambridge, Gloucestershire. It seems that his apprenticeship to Starling Willford was one of convenience enabling him to become a Freeman of the Goldsmiths' Company. His actual training was with the experienced Edward (No 1) who, although being a working goldsmith, was not a Freeman of the Goldsmiths' Company.

On 20 July 1753, Edward (No 1) entered his third mark, this time in partnership with John Stamper. Heal records this partnership as existing from 1753 to 1757 after which Stamper appears to have set up on his own at the corner of Hind Court opposite Water Lane in Fleet Street.

On 5 April 1758, Edward (No 2) obtained his freedom of the Goldsmiths' Company. Apparently he remained working with Edward (No 1) and was taken into partnership by him. Heal notes their partnership as being dissolved in 1762 with Edward (No 1) remaining at the Golden Ewer, Foster Lane while Edward (No 2) moved to George Street, St Martins-le-Grand.

In July 1763, Edward (No 2) became a Liveryman of the Goldsmiths' Company. In the Parliamentary Return of 1773 he was recorded as still being in business at the George Street address. Presumably his mark while at these premises and his earlier partnership mark with Edward (No 1) at Foster Lane were both entered at Goldsmiths' Hall in the now missing volume of Large Workers marks, 1759-73. Heal then records

Edward (No 2) as being at Bishopsgate in 1781. He died at some time between 1802 and 1811.

Meanwhile, on 5 July 1758, Charles the son of Charles Aldridge (staymaker) of Slimbridge, Gloucestershire was apprenticed to his brother, Edward (No 2) (Citizen and Goldsmith) and on the same day turned over to Edward (No 1) (Citizen and Clothworker). This appears to have been another apprenticeship of convenience whereby Charles became a Freeman of the Goldsmiths' Company and not of the Clothworkers' Company when he obtained his freedom on 5 February 1766.

Charles' freedom record includes the statement that it was with the 'consent of Elizabeth Aldridge widow and one of the executors of said Edward Aldridge deceased'. Edward (No 1) had only recently died. His will was signed on 3 December 1765 and proved on 8 January 1766, therefore, it seems most likely that he died in December 1765, probably after a short illness.

In his will he left all his personal estate, goods, utensils, stock in trade, etc in trust for his wife for her sole use and benefit for the rest of her life. The trust was to be administered by his two executors. After her death, the executors were to dispose of the residue 'to such person or persons as my said wife shall leave by her last will and testament'. He also bequeathed a mourning ring of one guinea value to each of his two executors. (Public Record Office PROB/11/915 Will No 1.) Since there is no mention of his children in the will, it is possible that they were all dead at this time.

Following his death, Elizabeth Aldridge apparently kept the business going, possibly with the help of Charles Aldridge, since he seems to have remained working with the firm. Presumably her mark was entered at Goldsmiths' Hall in the now missing volume of Large Workers marks, 1759-73. Grimwade in his book 'London Goldsmiths 1697-1837', page 252, illustrates an unascribed widow's lozenge as probably being her mark.

On 6 October 1768, Elizabeth, widow and late acting executor of Edward Alridge, turned over John Seede, her deceased husband's apprentice, to Charles Aldridge (gold-smith, Citizen and Goldsmith) of Foster Lane. This John Seede, who originated from Bristol, had been apprenticed to Joseph Bridges (Citizen and Goldsmith) on 3 March 1765 and the same day turned over to Edward Alridge (No 1) (Citizen and Clothworker). The fact that Seede had remained with Elizabeth for nearly two years following his master's death is a further indication that the business had continued to op-erate. However, his being turned over to Charles Aldridge of Foster Lane in October 1768 may indicate that Elizabeth had retired by then or even sold the business to Charles.

The next documentation of Charles Aldridge is made by Heal who records him as a plateworker at a new address of Aldersgate Street, 1772-86 and as a goldsmith at Falcon Street, Aldersgate Street, 1790-93. However, he also records him as being in partnership with Henry Green both at Aldersgate Street, 1773-77 and at 62 St Martins-le-Grand, 1775-84.

In the Parliamentary Return of 1773, he is recorded with Henry Green at Aldersgate Street which means that his part-nership mark and possibly an earlier solo mark would have been entered at Goldsmiths' Hall, presumably in the missing volume of Large Workers' marks, 1759-73. The reason for apparently operating from two premises concurrently could be that one was a workshop and the other a retail outlet.

On 19 August 1775 he and Henry Green entered a further partnership mark at Goldsmiths' Hall giving their address as 62 St Martins-le-Grand. In 1786 the partnership appears to have been dissolved with Green entering his own mark on 9 September from 62 St Martins-le-Grand and Aldridge on 20 September from 18 Aldersgate Street.

Charles Aldridge's final recorded mark was entered on 25 September 1789 from 18 Aldersgate Street and, as previously stated, Heal records his continuing in business until 1793.

Will of Peter Archambo (No 1)

In his will, dated 20 May 1759 and proved on 7 August 1767, he appoints his son, Peter Archambo (No 2), his brother, John Archambo, and his nephew, Peter Meure, as his executors.

He is described as a gentleman of Twickenham, Middlesex which would indicate that he had already retired when his will was drawn up in 1759. Possibly he retired at the end of 1749 following which Peter (No 2) took over the business and entered his first mark from his father's address in January 1750.

In his will, Peter Archambo (No 1) makes the following bequests:

1. £400 consolidated bank securities in trust to his executors to administer as follows:

a) Interest and dividends from these securities to be paid to his sister, Margaret Archambo, for the rest of her life.

b) Following her death, the £400 to be shared equally between his daughters, Ann, Elizabeth and Esther.

2. £400 consolidated bank securities, together with all accrued interest and dividends, to be transferred to Elizabeth Greenhow (grand daughter) on her twenty-first birthday or day of marriage, whichever occurs first. If she should die before gaining her inheritance, then it is to be divided equally between his four children, Peter, Ann, Elizabeth and Esther.

3. £10 each (for mourning) to Peter (son), Ann, Elizabeth and Esther (three daughters), Elizabeth Greenhow (grand daughter), John Archambo (brother), Peter Marchant (brother-in-law) and Mary his wife, Margaret Archambo (sister) and Peter Meure (nephew).

4. £400 consolidated bank securities to Peter Archambo (son).

5. Under the will of his late wife's father, Peter Troubee, he received £186 for each of his five children, Peter, Martha, Ann, Elizabeth and Esther which he was to hold and use for their benefit. Also, from the estate of his late wife's brother, Peter Troubee, he received £314 for each of his five children.

He had already paid out Martha's share totalling £500 (£186 + £314) to her husband, Michael Greenhow. (Note: In his will, the £314 is incorrectly written as £340).

Likewise, he had already paid out Esther's share totalling

£500 to her husband, Thomas Argles. He now directs his executors to pay similar sums of £500 to his daughters, Ann and Elizabeth.

(Note: His daughter, Martha, was already dead when he drew up his will and signed it on 20 May 1759).

6. The residue of his estate to be divided into four equal parts as follows:

a) One part to Peter Archambo (son).

b) One part to Ann Archambo (daughter).

c) One part to Elizabeth Archambo (daughter).

d) Remaining part to be sub-divided, one half to Thomas Argles (son-in-law), the other half in trust to his executors for the use of Esther (daughter) during her lifetime and after her death for any children she may produce.

In a codicil which Peter Archambo (No 1) had drawn up and signed on 12 January 1766, he makes the following amendments:

1. He appoints Thomas Argles (son-in-law and husband of Esther) to be the sole executor of Esther's and her children's inheritance.

2. As both Peter and Mary Marchant are dead, he directs that their £20 for mourning is to be used for funeral expenses.

3. To Elizabeth Greenhow (grand daughter) he bequeaths as much of his household plate as she desires amounting to £10 intrinsic value.

4. £5 for mourning to Ann Newman (servant) if she is still in his service at the time of his death.

Peter's will was proved on 7 August 1767 by Peter Archambo (No 2) with power reserved for John Archambo and Peter Meure.

On 5 February 1768 a second probate was granted to Peter Meure, probably as a result of the death of Peter Archambo (No 2).

(Public Record Office. PROB/11/931. Will No. 294)

George Baskerville's Will

His will, dated 16 June 1781 and proved in March 1782, names his wife, Sarah Baskerville, as his sole executor.

He is described as a silversmith of London and he bequeaths all his stock in trade, china, glass, etc and property, including freehold houses, gardens, etc in Castle Street in the city of New Sarum, Wiltshire to his wife, Sarah Baskerville.

Probably there were no surviving children since none are mentioned in his will. However, it is possible that he had a sister, Sarah, and two brothers, Richard and Thomas as indicated by a Thomas Baskerville's will dated 27 February 1781 and proved in June 1781.

In this will, Thomas Baskerville (gentleman) of New Sarum, Wiltshire appoints his two brothers, George and Richard Baskerville and his sister, Sarah, to be his joint executors. He bequeaths his late wife's wearing apparel and gold sleeve buttons to his sister, Sarah, and his best diamond ring to Susannah Thompson, daughter of his sister, Sarah. His silver watch and gold mourning ring of his late wife to Simon Baskerville, son of his sister, Sarah.

Finally, he bequeaths the residue of his goods, chattels and real and personal estate to his two brothers, George and Richard Baskerville and his sister, Sarah.

(Public Record Office.
George Baskerville's Will: PROB/11/1088. Will No. 111
Thomas Baskerville's Will: PROB/11/1078. Will No. 283)

Hester Bateman's Will

In her will, dated 23 July 1792 and proved on 9 March 1795, she appoints Peter Bateman (son), Letisia Clarke (daughter) and Ann Bateman (daughter-in-law) to be her executors.

She makes three main bequests, two of which are sub-divided into various clauses.
1. She bequeaths all her linen and wearing apparel to

be shared equally between Letisia Clarke and Ann Corkerill, her daughters.

2. She bequeaths £730 on trust to her executors, Peter and Ann Bateman, for them to dispose of as follows:

a) During the lifetime of Ann Corkerill, they are to hold £600 and pay Ann the interest from this sum at the minimum rate of 5% per annum. It is to be for her own use for the rest of her natural life. The interest is not to be subject to any control by her husband or any future husband or liable to any debt, insolvency, bankruptcy, etc that he may incur.

b) Following Ann Corkerill's death, the interest on £200 of the £600 is to be paid to Ann's son, Richard Corkerill. When Richard reaches the age of 21 years, Peter and Ann Bateman may pay him the £200 if they think it prudent. Otherwise, they are to wait until he is 24 years old before paying him this money.

c) The remaining £400 of the £600 is to be divided equally between her executors, Peter Bateman, Letisia Clarke and Ann Bateman.

d) The remaining £130 of the £730 is for Richard Corkerill (Hester's son-in-law and husband of Ann Corkerill). The money is to be advanced to him in amounts and on occasions at the discretion of the executors. Meanwhile, they must pay him the interest on any part of the money still outstanding.

3. She bequeaths £512 in trust to her executors for them to dispose of as follows:

a) Pay £170 to Alice Bateman (daughter-in-law).

b) Pay £114 to Alice's son, Thomas Bateman.

c) Pay £114 to Alice's daughter, Hester Marshall or her representative.

d) Pay £114 to Alice's son, Peter Bateman, when he is 24 years old or before, if the executors think it prudent.

e) If any of the other three die, their share is to be divided between the above family.

Hester's will was witnessed by John Clarke and Elizabeth Clarke.

(Will at Goldsmiths' Hall Library, London)

Note: Whereas in Hester's will her daughter is named as Letisia, under the proving of her will it is spelt in three different ways, Letticia, Lettitia and Letitia.

John Cafe's Will

It seems that he suspected his death was imminent since he began his will with the words, 'being weak in body but of a sound and disposing mind, memory and understanding'. He signed it on 28 April 1757 and was dead by 27 August 1757 when probate was proved.

Among his bequests he left his Somerset properties 'Messuages, Tenements, Lands and Hereditaments with the Appurtenants' at both Blackford and the adjoining village of North Cadbury to his wife during her lifetime and then to his five children. If all his children were to die before reaching the age of twenty-one and were without issue, then these properties were to pass to his two brothers, Michael and William and his sister Mary, the wife of William Foot.

The unexpired lease of his dwelling house, outbuildings and land in Gutter Lane, London, he left to his brother, William, together with, 'all my furnaces, utensils and patterns now in my workshop and used in my trade or business'. His business seems to have consisted entirely of manufacturing candlesticks and tapersticks for both trade and retail sale.

John Cafe also left £7,500 in cash from which his executors, Marmaduke Daintry (goldsmith) and John Winning, were 'to permit and suffer my brother William Cafe to have and make use of £500 part thereof in order to enable him to carry on his business without paying any interest for the same space for seven years'. Nevertheless, the executors were to take in the £500 loan at any time during the seven years if there was any danger of it being 'lost' and, in the case of nonpayment, they were to sue and recover the money by any lawful means possible. It would seem from this clause that John was somewhat doubtful of his brother's capabilities to continue running his own business and remain solvent.

The remaining £7,000 was to be held in trust by the executors and the interest thereof used to pay a pension to his mother and father and to maintain, educate and pay the apprenticeships of his children as the trustees should think fit. When each child reached the age of twenty-one, he or she was to be paid an equal share of the £7,500.

Other small bequests followed including £10 apiece to his relations to buy themselves mourning.

(Public Record Office. PROB/11/832. Will No. 243)

William Cafe

He was apprenticed to his brother, John, on 11 March 1742 but for some reason was turned over to Simon Jouet (Goldsmith) on 19 March 1747. Why he had himself turned over is open to conjecture. Maybe he and John had conflicting opinions which led to eventual parting since it would seem from John's will and subsequent events that William did not have the business acumen of his brother.

It is possible that William remained with Jouet for some years after completing his apprenticeship or he may have returned to work with his brother where he remained until John's death in 1757.

Under John Cafe's will, William inherited his brother's silversmithing business and premises in Gutter Lane. Probate on John's will was proved on 27 August 1757 but William had already entered his first two marks at Goldsmiths' Hall on 16 August 1757, giving his business address as Gutter Lane.

Presumably John had died at the end of July or early August and William, having inherited the business in Gutter Lane, found it necessary to register his own mark as the new owner as soon as possible. Likewise, because of his new status, he applied for freedom of the Goldsmiths' Company and this was granted to him on 5 October 1757.

He continued running the business, manufacturing candlesticks and tadapersticks, but its output gradually declined during the 1760s.

In 1772, he became bankrupt, which seems to confirm the doubts implied within John Cafe's will, yet he continued to take on apprentices through the Goldsmiths' Company, there being three between 1773 and 1777.

On 1 December 1784, his son, Thomas, was apprenticed to him 'to learn his art of goldsmith'. Thomas obtained his freedom as a silver turner on 7 November 1792.

William's last apprentice was a Deliverance Smith who was apprenticed to him in 1790 'to learn his art of shopkeeper'. In the records of these last two apprenticeships, William's address is given as High Street, Marylebone and it would seem that he was running a shop at this address, perhaps as a retailer of silverware thereby enabling him to remain within the trade. All told, he had nineteen apprentices between 1757 and 1790.

William died early in 1802, his will being proved on 17 March of that year. He had very little to bequeath. His household goods and chattels he left to Jane, his second wife, together with property at 31 Paddington Street for the duration of her life and thereafter in trust, with the profits being paid to his daughter, Mrs Elizabeth Upstone.

(Public Record Office. PROB/11/1371. Will No. 179)

Robert Albion Cox's Family

To date, no record has been found of Robert Albion Cox having had a wife and children. He is known to have had three brothers; Edward, Albin and William.

Edward was apprenticed to his brother, William, in 1761 and Albin was apprenticed to Robert Albion in 1763 but there is no record of either obtaining his freedom of the Goldsmiths' Company.

William was apprenticed to his brother, Robert Albion, on 11 January 1753 and obtained his freedom of the Goldsmiths' Company on 6 February 1760. He entered a mark at Goldsmiths' Hall as a small worker on 20 March 1771 giving his address as Little Britain. On 18 October 1784, he entered new marks from 11 Aldersgate Street. Heal records him as a goldsmith and jeweller at 70 Cox's Court, Little Britain, 1768-72; at St Paul's Churchyard, 1773-74; in partnership with Thomas Watson at 23 Aldersgate Street, 1774-84 and alone at 11 Aldersgate Street in 1784.

William died a widower in January 1802 at Piddletrenthide, Dorset. In his will, dated 4 April 1801 and proved on 17 December 1802, he left all his property and possessions to his sons, Robert Albion, Theodore Emanuel, John, Rev George Edward, Charles James and grandson, William. (Public Record Office, PROB/11/1383, Will No. 880). In fact, William had a sixth son, William, but only the other five are mentioned in his will.

William's son, Robert Albion, and nephew of Robert Albion, was a refiner at Little Britain. He obtained his freedom by Patrimony on 5 April 1786, was made a Liveryman in 1791 and an Assistant in 1813. He became 4th Warden in 1815, 3rd Warden in 1816, 2nd Warden in 1817 and Prime Warden in 1818. He died on 20 June 1826.

Theodore Emanuel (gentleman) obtained his freedom by Patrimony on 3 March 1801, was made a Liveryman in October 1801 and died circa 1802-11.

John (gentleman) obtained his freedom on 1 December 1802, was made a Liveryman in 1806 and died on 20 January 1814.

The Rev George Edward (clerk) obtained his freedom by Patrimony on 2 December 1812.

William's son, William (stockbroker), obtained his freedom by Patrimony on 7 June 1815, was made a Liveryman in 1816 and an Assistant in 1827. He became Prime Warden in 1833 and again in 1846. In 1851, he resigned from the Goldsmiths' Company and died in 1867.

Robert Albion Cox's Will

In his will, dated 25 November 1789 and proved on 10 June 1790, he appoints William Cox (brother), Peter Barfoot (friend) and Thomas Horne (friend) as his executors. He is recorded as Robert Albion Cox of Little Britain, London and of Piddletrenthide, Dorset. This is the same village where John

Bridge of Rundell & Bridge, goldsmiths, was born in 1755. At All Saints church, Piddletrenthide there is a memorial tablet to Robert Albion Cox and another to his brother, William Cox, who died in 1802.

In his will, Robert Albion makes numerous bequests as follows:

1. £3,500 to William Marle, clerk and nominal partner in his banking and refining business at Little Britain. William Marle was at the time on a salary of £300 per annum.

2. £3,000 to Robert Albion Cox, junior, nephew and clerk in his banking and refining business.

3. £3,000 to Robert Pattison, clerk in his banking and refining business.

4. £200 to Thomas Parsons, clerk in his business at Little Britain.

5. £100 to John Smith, clerk in his business at Little Britain.

6. The above five legacies to be paid within twelve months of his death.

7. To James Jeffery, clerk at Bill Quay, Durham, an annuity of twelve pounds payable by quarterly instalments for the rest of his life provided he is still in Cox's service at the time of Cox's death. First payment to be £5 paid within three months of Cox's death. If Jeffery sells or mortgages the annuity then all payments will cease forever.

8. To Ann Powell, his servant, for honest and faithful service and constant attendance during his illness, an annuity of twenty pounds payable by quarterly instalments for the rest of her life provided she is still in Cox's service at the time of his death. First payment to be £5 paid within three months of Cox's death. If she sells or mortgages the annuity then all payments will cease forever.

9. £500 to his executors on trust that they make Francis Newman pay the dividends from trust money in stocks, etc in his name to the previously agreed charitable use of the poor and other inhabitants of Piddletrenthide, Dorset.

10. £50 each to Peter Barfoot and Thomas Horne for executing his will.

11. To William Cox (brother), his share in the banking busi-

ness at Dorchester, Dorset with partner, Henry Marder. The business to be carried on for the term previously agreed between Robert Albion Cox and Henry Marder. William Cox is to receive all profits, etc from this business that would have been due to Robert Albion Cox.

12. To William Cox (brother) to carry on and manage upon trust, his banking and refining business at Little Britain, London. Future profits to be shared as follows:

1/3rd to William Cox (brother)
1/3rd to William Marle
1/6th to Robert Albion Cox (nephew)
1/6th to Robert Pattison

Likewise these four legacies to put money into the firm in the same proportion whenever necessary to carry on the running of the firm.

13. That William Marle, Robert Albion Cox (nephew) and Robert Pattison continue to assist William Cox (brother) in carrying on his banking and refining business for two years after Cox's death. Likewise Thomas Parsons and John Smith for two years at their present salaries.

14. That William Marle, Robert Albion Cox (nephew), Robert Pattison, Thomas Parsons and John Smith shall produce within twelve months of Cox's death, an up to date account of Cox's estates and effects for his executors and residuary legatee.

15. If any one of the following, William Marle, Robert Albion Cox, Robert Pattison, Thomas Parsons or John Smith, fails to carry out or comply with any of the instructions, etc, in this will or is not in Cox's employment at the time of his death, then he will not receive any legacy, etc, from this will.

16. His executors shall, within twelve months of his death, produce an up to date valuation of all his estate, etc.

17. If the nett value of his estate after payment of debts and legacies in his will does not amount to £60,000 then the legacies to William Marle, Robert Albion Cox, Robert Pattison, Thomas Parsons and John Smith are to be proportionally reduced until a nett value of estate of £60,000 remains for the residuary legatee.

18. £10 each to his servants, Eleanor Carter and Susanna Powell at London and Charity Troke at Piddletrenthide, provided they are in his employment at the time of his death.
19. To William Cox (brother and residuary legatee) the residue of his estate, etc (approximately £60,000) after payment of all legacies, debts, funeral expenses, etc.

(Public Record Office. PROB/11/1192. Will No. 282)

The Crespel Family

Heal records Sebastian and James Crespel as being at Whitcomb Street, Leicester Fields, 1762-73; and James on his own at Panton Street, Haymarket, 1779.

However, from 1769 onwards the Crespels (Sebastian (No 1) and James (No 1), were supplying plates and dishes to the firm of Edward Wakelin, as revealed in the Wakelin general workmen's ledger of 1766 onwards (*Garrard MSS*, Victoria and Albert Museum).

Also, other ledgers, kept by the Crespels and the firm of Wakelin and Taylor (John Wakelin and William Taylor) and their successors from 1778 to 1806, record raw metal being issued to the Crespels and completed articles being supplied in return to either 'Shop' or clients of Wakelin and Taylor. Presumably 'Shop' refers to Wakelin and Taylor's premises in Panton Street (see Will of Robert Garrard (No 1)).

From 1782 it seems that the Crespels were virtually owned by Wakelin and Taylor and operated solely as manufacturers to the firm. From 1788 onwards the Wakelin and Taylor ledger is headed 'James Crespel', which may indicate that Sebastian (No 1) had retired or died.

The ledgers finish in October 1806 without any apparent successor to the Crespel business. This may be due to the death of James Crespel's son, Honorius or Honore, in the spring of 1806, he being the last Crespel to work as a freeman for Robert Garrard (No 1).

James Crespel (No 1) had at least four sons and one daughter. They were Honorius, Andrew (No 1), Sebastian

(No 2), James (No 2) and Mary who was a beneficiary under Honorius's will.

Honorius was apprenticed to John Wakelin on 3 February 1779 and obtained his freedom on 1 November 1786. In his will, dated 30 January 1806 and proved on 16 April 1806, he left to his sister, Mary Crespel, 'all few household furniture of every description that shall belong to me' and 'what may be in the drawers that I have at present in Panton Street'.

He also made bequests to his brother, Sebastian (No 2) and to his father, James (No 1), who was the executor of his will. (Public Record Office, PROB/11.1441, Will No. 282).

Andrew (No 1) was apprenticed to John Wakelin on 2 February 1785 and obtained his freedom on 4 July 1792.

Sebastian (No 2) was apprenticed to his brother, Honorius (flatter and Goldsmith) on 3 June 1801 but, following Honorius's death, was turned over to Robert Garrard (No 1) (silversmith and Grocer) on 7 May 1806. At the time, Robert Garrard was in control of the Wakelin firm, having taken over from John Wakelin. Also he was related to the Crespel family, having married Sarah Crespel who is thought to have been the daughter of either James (No 1) or Sebastian (No 1).

Sarah was born in 1767, married Robert Garrard at some date prior to 1793 and died in 1824.

Sebastian (No 2) obtained his freedom on 3 May 1809 but did not enter his own mark until 3 August 1820 from 11 James Street, Haymarket. On 12 October 1836, he is recorded as having moved to premises in Castle Street, Leicester Square.

James (No 2) was apprenticed to Thomas Gardner on 5 January 1803 and obtained his freedom on 4 July 1810.

Catherine Fox's Will (wife of Charles Fox (No 2))

Her will is dated 20 October 1860 and was proved on 27 August 1862, her executors being two of her sons, Frederick Fox and George Fox.

In it she bequeathed her personal wardrobe to her daughter, Mary, the wife of Thomas Fisk, her pair of silver candlesticks to her son, Charles Thomas, and her silver mug to her nephew, Joseph Goodson.

All her furniture, plate, china and other household effects she stipulated should be shared equally between her sons, Frederick and George, and her daughter, Mary.

Also, she bequeathed £50 to Hannah, the daughter of her son, Frederick.

The remainder of her estate she bequeathed to her sons, Frederick and George, to divide into four equal trusts as follows:
a) For Frederick's benefit.
b) For George's benefit.
c) For the benefit of the five daughters of her late son, Yonge William.
d) For the benefit of her daughter, Mary Fisk.
The five daughters of Yonge William are listed as: Caroline Richards wife of Jospeh Richards, Mary Ann Cooper wife of Alfred Cooper, Hannah Fox, Ellen Jenkins widow and Louisa Fox.

(Somerset House)

Will of Robert Garrard (No 1)

In his will, dated 6 January 1817, he appoints James Lee (nurseryman) and Sarah (wife) to be his executors.

In a codicil, which he added on 25 March 1818, he appoints Robert (son) to be his third executor.

His will, with codicil, was proved on 4 April 1818 as follows:
1. To Sarah, his wife, £200 to be paid within one month of his death, 'to enable her to commence housekeeping'.
2. To Sarah, his wife, his leasehold house in the High Road, Kensington together with its furniture, household goods, etc.
3. To his two executors, James Lee, nurseryman and Sarah, his wife, £4,000 in trust to invest in government stocks, shares or securities. All dividends and interest from this investment to be for Sarah's personal use for the rest

of her life. After his wife's death, the £4,000 investment is to be shared equally between his younger sons, Stephen and Henry, and his daughters, Sarah, Miriam and Caroline. Sarah is to receive her share within 6 months, Stephen and Henry when they are 21 years old and Miriam and Caroline when they marry or reach the age of 21 years. Should any one of them die before inheriting, his or her share is to be divided equally between the remainder. If all but Sarah should die, then the investment is to be shared equally between Sarah and her other three brothers, Robert, James and Sebastian.

4. To Sarah, his daughter, £3,000 to be paid in instalments. £1,000 within 12 months, £1,000 within 2 years and the remaining £1,000 within 3 years, including all interest. This legacy can be paid sooner provided 'my said Trustees can conveniently raise the Money for that purpose without injury to the business to be carried out by my sons Robert, James and Sebastian'.

5. To his two executors, James Lee and Sarah, his wife, £13,000 in trust to invest in government stocks and shares and administer on behalf of his children, Stephen, Henry, Miriam and Caroline. Each of them is to receive their portion (£3,000) upon reaching the age of 21 years. The remaining £1,000 is to be paid out in equal shares on behalf of Stephen and Henry for their apprenticeship 'and place out in the world for their advancement'. Should any of these four children die unmarried or under the age of 21 years, their share is to be divided equally between the remainder and his daughter, Sarah. Should all four children die, their shares are to be divided equally between his daughter, Sarah and sons, Robert, James and Sebastian.

All dividends and interest from the invested £13,000 are to be paid to his wife, Sarah, for her to use in educating and maintaining the four children, Stephen, Henry, Miriam and Caroline. Should his wife die or remarry, James Lee as the other executor is to receive the money and be responsible for educating and maintaining the children.

6. To his two executors, James Lee and Sarah (wife), 'all that Messuage or Dwelling House and Premises in Panton Street

aforesaid with the Shop and Appurtenant thereto belonging wherein I now carry on business and also the Room and Yard behind the Shop together with the Messuage thereto adjoining formerly in the occupation of Mr John Wakelin deceased and now of Mr Valle as my undertenant'. All these premises are to be held in trust by his executors for his sons, Robert, James and Sebastian.

(Note: At the commencement of his will he refers to some of his premises as being located in the Haymarket and being occupied by Mr Godfrey Hosier. Presumably this property was included in the above bequest to his three sons.)

7. To Robert, his son, all household goods and furniture in the above premises in Panton Street (see item 6).

8. To Robert, James and Sebastian, his sons, 'all that Messuage or Tenement (dwelling house) in Panton Street aforesaid now in the occupation of Mr James Crespell wherein I carry on a Manufactory'.

(Note: This is additional property to that referred to in item 6.)

9. He instructs that a full valuation be carried out by his executors of all his, 'Stock in Trade Patterns Models the fitting use of the Shop the Fixtures Tools and other things as they shall be found valued in the annual Stock Book taken next immediately proceeding my demise'.

10. To Robert, his son, £8,000 of the above valued stock, etc (see item 9).

11. To James and Sebastian, his sons, £6,000 each of the above valued stock, etc (see item 9).

12. All remaining stock, etc is to be bought from the trustees at valuation figures plus interest by Robert, James and Sebastian in three equal instalments at three, four and five year periods after his death.

13. To Robert, James and Sebastian, his sons, he directed that they immediately become 'Copartners' in his 'Trade and business' by entering into a proper deed of copartnership, with Robert holding 40%, James 30% and Sebastian 30%. He also recommends that they adopt 'Articles of Copartnership similar to those which subsisted between my late Partner Mr John Wakelin and myself'.

14. He empowers his trustees to lend £5,000 for a period of five years to Robert, James and Sebastian, 'to enable them to commence business as Copartners'. Once the loan is repaid, the £5,000 is to be invested in Government stocks or shares. The interest from the £5,000, whether on loan or invested, is to be paid to Sarah, his wife, 'so long as she shall remain my Widow'. After her remarriage or death, the £5,000 loan or investment is to become part of the residue of his estate.

15. To his niece, Julia Garrard who was living with him, £500 to be paid within 12 months.

16. To Thomas Netherton Parker, his much valued friend of Sweeney Hill, Salop, he bequeaths £20 with the warmest feelings of esteem as a small tribute of his gratitude and respect for him.

(Note: Thomas Netherton Parker was the son of John Parker who was in partnership with Edward Wakelin at the Panton Street premises circa 1759-76. Also, as his second Christian name was Netherton, it may be that his godfather was Samuel Netherton who was in partnership with George Wickes at these premises circa 1751-59.)

17. To James Taylor (jeweller) of Margaret Street, Cavendish Square he bequeaths £50.

(Note: Possibly a relative of William Taylor who was in partnership with John Wakelin at the Panton Street premises circa 1776-92.)

18. To each of his servants in the Shop and living with him at the time of his death, £10 for mourning.

19. To James Lee (executor), £100 as compensation for having to execute his will.

20. The residue of his estate, goods, chattels, etc is to be divided equally between his children Stephen, Henry, Sarah, Miriam and Caroline and to be held in trust until they reach the age of 21 years or marry. Should any one of them die before receiving his or her legacy then that share is to be divided as previously described for the £13,000 held in trust (see item 5).

21. He vests the guardianship of all his children who are under age with his executor, James Lee, in conjunction with his wife, Sarah, 'so long as she remains unmarried'.

His will was signed on 6 January 1817, but on 25 March 1818 he added a codicil appointing his son, Robert, to be his third executor and bequeathing £100 to him for his trouble.

He died on 26 March 1818 and his will, with codicil, was proved on 4 April 1818.

(Public Record Office. PROB/11/1603. Will No. 172)

From his will it seems his leasehold premises in Panton Street were quite extensive, consisting of a dwelling house with adjoining shop, back room and yard, all formerly occupied by John Wakelin. Another adjoining dwelling house was occupied by James Crespel and used by Robert Garrard as a manufactory while further premises in the Haymarket were occupied by Godfrey Hosier.

James Gould

According to the inscription on his vault in the churchyard at Kingsbury Episcopi, Somerset, James Gould died on 25 February 1750 aged 51 years. Therefore, it is probable that he was born during 1698. The inscription also states, 'Here lyeth inter'd the Body of Mrs Mary Gould wife of James Gould citizen and Goldsmith of London, and daughter of ------ Dampier of Blackford Gent. Who departed this Life ye 10 day of Feb. 17-- in ye 54 year of her age'. (For a complete record of the vault's inscription see, '*An Inventory of Church Plate in Somerset, Part 111*' by Rev. E.H. Bates and Rev. F. Hancock. Somerset Arch. Soc. Transactions Vol. XLV, 1899, page 144). In 1899, Dampier's Christian name and Mary's year of death were already indecipherable on the vault.

However, in the parish records of births, held at the Taunton Records Office, Somerset, is an entry that Mary, eldest child of William Dampier and Mary his wife of Blackford, was born on 1 November 1703. (William and Mary Dampier eventually had a total of ten children born between 1703 and 1718). Since Mrs Mary Gould, née Dampier, was in her 54th year at the time of her death, it seems, therefore, that she died on 10 February 1757.

James and Mary Gould had four sons and three daughters, none of whom appear to have survived their father's death in 1750. The eldest son, James, was born on 22 February 1730 and baptized at St Vedast, Foster Lane, London. He was apprenticed to his father on 3 October 1744 but died prior to 1750 without obtaining his freedom of the Goldsmiths' Company. He was buried in the family vault at Kingsbury Episcopi. His father in his will dated 23 January 1750, bequeathed all of James' pictures and drawings to his nephew, James, the son of William Gould (Goldsmith).

The other six children were William, Henry, Mary, John, Mary and Mary.

William was baptized in 1731 at St Vedast, London, but died while less than two years old (Kingsbury vault inscription). He was re-interred at Kingsbury Episcopi on 16 February 1736 (Taunton Records Office).

Henry was baptized in 1732 at St Vedast, died while less than two years old and was buried at Kingsbury Episcopi (vault inscription).

Mary (No 1) was baptized in 1734 at St Vedast, died while less than two years old and was re-interred at Kingsbury Episcopi on 16 February 1736.

John was baptized in 1735 at St Vedast, died while less than a year old and was re-interred at Kingsbury Episcopi on 16 February 1736.

Mary (No 2) was baptized in 1736 at St Vedast and buried at Kingsbury Episcopi on 16 February 1736.

Mary (No 3) was baptized in 1737 at St Vedast and presumably died prior to 1750 since she was not mentioned in her father's will. She was buried in the family vault at Kingsbury Episcopi.

Another Mary, wife of James Gould Gent., was also buried at Kingsbury Episcopi on 23 July 1731 and re-interred on 16 February 1736 (Taunton Records Office). Probably this was the mother of James Gould (Goldsmith) whose father was recorded at Goldsmiths' Hall as James Gould (gentleman).

Besides being a wealthy goldsmith, James Gould seems to have been a considerate person who cared for his fellow beings. According to the inscription on his vault he 'acquired a handsome fortune with a Good Character. He gave fifty pounds to five poor widows of this parish and ye like sum to five poor widdowes of Ilminster. A worthy example'. He also gave a silver flagon with round topped lid to Kingsbury parish church in 1749. The flagon was made by Richard Gurney and Thomas Cooke of London and assayed in 1749. On the flagon was an inscription, 'The gift of James Gould Gent. to the Parish Church of Kingsbury in the County of Somersett Whose Family lyes Enter'd in a Vault the South side of the Churchyard neare the Church 1749'. (from '*An Inventory of Church Plate in Somerset, Part 111*', page 143-144).

James' final mark was entered at Goldsmiths' Hall on 27 August 1747 by his wife, Mrs Mary Gould. Presumably James was unable to attend personally, probably due to ill health.

When he signed his will in 1750, James made no bequest to, nor mention of, his wife although she was still alive. Also, he made no mention of his business or premises in London, nor of his stock in trade, tools, patterns, etc. Presumably he had already wound up or disposed of the business as a going concern since he no longer had a son to follow in his footsteps. In fact, his last apprentice, William Pragnell, was turned over in October 1749 to John Priest to complete his apprenticeship. The reason why his wife was not included in his will is open to conjecture. Perhaps he had already given her money from the sale of his business or maybe she had wealth of her own, inherited from the Dampier family.

Over a working period of twenty-six years James took on nine apprentices, including his brother, William, in 1724 and his son, James, in 1744. Of the other seven apprentices, six hailed from Somerset within an eighteen mile radius of Kingsbury Episcopi. They were John Quantock, John Cafe, John Hyatt who later went into partnership with Charles Semore, John Paget, Richard Rugg and John Laver. The odd-man-out was the previously mentioned William Pragnell of London who was turned over to John Priest. Obviously John Priest was known to James Gould, having served his apprenticeship under James' younger brother, William.

James Gould's Will

In his will, dated 23 January 1750 and proved on 2 March 1750, he appoints Hannah Baker (widowed sister), Robert Willy (gentleman) of East Sambrooke, Somerset and Robert Elliott (gentleman) of Gutter Lane, Cheapside, London to be his executors. Robert Elliott had been a bucklemaker and small plate worker trading in London during the 1720s.

James Gould describes himself as a gentleman of Islington, London and commences with the words, 'being in good and perfect mind, memory and understanding, but considering the uncertainty of human life, do make this my last will and testament'. He stipulates that he is to be buried in his vault in Kingsbury Episcopi churchyard, Somerset and desires that his three first cousins and their sons, if living, shall support his pall to the place of internment.

In his will he makes the following bequests:

1. To his widowed sister, Hannah Baker, all his properties both at Kingsbury Episcopi and Chard in Somerset for her lifetime and then to be passed on to his nephew, James, the son of his silversmithing brother, William.

Out of the rents and profits from these properties, Hannah Baker must pay £15 per annum to kinsman, John Gould, the son of Nicholas Gould (mercer) late of Crewkerne, Somerset. After her death the £15 annual payment is to be continued by his nephew, James, until such time as John Gould dies.

2. To Hannah Baker, 'one room of goods entire which was my fathers at Burrow Hill, Kingsbury'. This is an area on the west side of the village and now called 'One Tree Hill'. Presumably their father's house was located there.

3. To his nephew, James, the son of William Gould, his silver tankard and all his dead son's pictures and drawings. Presumably these had been the possessions of his own son, James, who had been apprenticed to him in 1744.

4. To his nieces, Jane Baker and Mary Gould Baker, £1,000 to each of them to be paid out of the sale of his Stocks in Public Funds. Should either of them die unmarried or before reaching the age of twenty-one, then £800 is to go to their

brother, Thomas Baker, if still living and £100 each to Robert and Mary Willy, the children of Robert Willy (executor).

If all three of the Baker children, Jane, Mary and Thomas, die unmarried or before reaching the age of twenty-one, then £800 is to go to his godson, James Gould.

5. To his niece, Jane Baker, his gold watch.

6. To his brother, John Gould, he releases him from his Debt of Bond together with all interest due on it provided he makes no claims on James' estate.

7. To his brother, William Gould, £20 for mourning plus mourning rings to both he and his wife.

8. To each of his servants living with him at the time of his death, £5 for mourning.

9. To Mrs Mary Barnard, a mourning ring valued at ten guineas.

Also mourning rings to the Rev Bonoyer, the Rev Arthur of Sudgate, Mrs Davies, Mrs Nicholas, Mrs Rideout the younger, Mrs Collins of Ilminster and her son and Mrs Bonner.

10. To each of his pall bearers, gloves, scarves, hatbands and mourning rings.

11. To Robert Willy and Robert Elliott (executors), £20 each plus mourning rings.

12. To cousin, Sarah Gould, a mourning ring.

13. To five poor widows from the parish of Kingsbury Episcopi, £50 from his personal estate to be divided equally between them. The list of widows to be approved by his sister, Hannah Baker, or, in the event of her death, by his brother, William Gould.

14. To five poor widows of Ilminster, Somerset, £50 from his personal estate to be divided equally between them. The list of widows to be approved by Mrs Collins of Ilminster.

15. To his nieces, Jane Baker and Mary Gould Baker, the residue of his estate.

16. His funeral expenses, including all mourning rings, are not to exceed £80.

(Public Record Office. PROB/11/786. Will No. 80)

William Gould

William Gould was a candlestick and taperstick manufacturer, a craft he had learnt while apprenticed to his brother, James. Possibly his greatest work was the original Knesworth chandelier made for the Fishmongers' Company, although it was this same chandelier which led to his conviction for fraud.

It was in February 1750 that the Fishmongers' Company commissioned a chandelier in memory of Sir Thomas Knesworth from a Joseph Dyer of Lombard Street. Since Dyer was only a retail goldsmith and, as such, had no mark of his own registered at Goldsmiths' Hall, he employed William Gould to manufacture the piece.

The chandelier was to be in two tiers, one of eight nozzles and the other of six nozzles. It was to cost not more than £250 and be delivered in April 1750. By October 1750, when the Prince of Wales visited the Fishmongers' Hall, it had been completed and hung at a total cost of £484-1s-3d, considerably more than the previously agreed estimate.

In January 1752, the Court of the Fishmongers' Company was informed that the chandelier had been fraudulently manufactured. Apparently it had been sent for repair to the workshop of a William Alexander of Wood Street. He was a founder, brazier and plate worker with his own mark registered at Goldsmiths' Hall. Chiefly he was a manufacturer of brass chandeliers and a general ironmonger who supplied the Fishmongers' Company with brass lanterns and kitchenware. While repairing the chandelier, one of his workmen overheated a silver branch causing it to open and disclose a quantity of copper. Other parts were checked and found to be concealing a great quantity of copper.

Further investigations followed and two of William Gould's workmen, who assisted in making the chandelier, testified that the fraudulent work must have been done 'before they came to work in the morning'. When William Gould was confronted, he confessed and subsequently was indicted and convicted of fraud.

On 6 February 1752, presumably following his conviction,

his three current apprentices were turned over to other masters. Walter Barry and John Butcher transferred to John Cafe who had been an apprentice of James Gould, while John Monk transferred to John Priest who had been an apprentice of William Gould.

In March 1752, the chandelier was fully assayed by the Goldsmiths' Company. This would confirm which parts were sub-standard. As a result, it was decided to completely replace the chandelier and Dyer was asked by the Fishmongers' Company to provide a new one in collaboration with Alexander. Alexander, however, refused to work with Dyer since Dyer was outside the trade. Eventually a compromise was agreed whereby Alexander paid the Fishmongers' Company £279-6s-0d, this being the melt-down value of the silver in Gould's chandelier while Dyer repaid the remaining £204-15s-3d to make up the total amount originally paid to Dyer by the Fishmongers' Company.

Meanwhile Alexander, who had now hired Gould's two workmen, submitted various designs of chandelier to the Fishmongers' Company for consideration. His Dolphin pattern of one tier with twelve branches was accepted with an agreed delivery in June 1752. This is the chandelier that now hangs in the company's court dining room. It is in parcel-gilt silver, weighs 1,330 oz and bears the mark of William Alexander who charged some £650 for it, complete with chain and case.

Following his conviction for fraud, William Gould surprisingly took on three more apprentices, the first being his son, James, on 15 November 1753, then Richard Cannon in 1755 and Mordecai Lloyd in 1761. Of these three, only James Gould obtained his freedom, it being on 14 January 1761. Why William should have been permitted to accept a new apprentice within twenty-one months of turning over his three previous apprentices is open to conjecture. Could he have been working with another manufacturing silversmith at the time? According to the Goldsmiths' Company records, he was working in Old Street from September 1753 but apparently moved back to Foster Lane in May 1756.

The next record of William Gould is in 1763 when he

petitioned the Goldsmiths' Company for the vacant post of Junior Weigher in the Assay Office, but at the meeting of the Court of Assistants on 9 December 1763, it was minuted that he had 'some years ago been guilty of a fraud in concealing a great quantity of copper in a silver chandelier made for the Fishmongers' Company and that the same was a fact well known to many of the gentlemen of this Court and therefore it was moved and seconded that the said William Gould's petition be rejected and returned to him'.

Gould was apparently desperate for money for he presented a further petition to the Court of Assistants on 14 December 1763, pointing out that he was now a poor Liveryman and that 'through divers losses and misfortunes I am now strained in my circumstances and in a great want of some charitable assistance and therefore praying for a return of my said Livery fine'.

This was originally paid to the Company as a fee when he was made a Liveryman in 1746. As the Company's affairs were 'in a prosperous condition', it was decided to return his Livery fine of £20 on his 'executing a release of all his privilages as a Liveryman'. This is the last known record of William Gould, the date of his death not having been traced.

In the Parliamentary Return of 1773, his son, James Gould, candlestick maker of Ave Maria Lane, is recorded as being in business. He had obtained his freedom on 14 January 1761 after serving under his father. Therefore his mark would have been registered at Goldsmiths' Hall sometime between 1761 and 1773, in the now missing volume of Large Workers marks.

This James Gould had a son, William, born 1787, died 1874, who likewise became a silversmith. He in his turn is known to have had a son, William James, born 1814, died 1891, who joined the original Carla Rosa opera company under Carla Rosa himself.

LONDON ASSAY OFFICE HALLMARKS

 Standard Mark (Lion Passant)

Denotes a minimum silver content of 92.5%. This mark (for Sterling Standard silver) is used by all Assay Offices in England. It has been struck on English silverware since 1544.

 Britannia Mark

Denotes a minimum silver content of 95.84%. This mark (for Britannia Standard silver) was introduced in 1697 and remained in compulsory use until 1720 when the Sterling Standard was restored. The Britannia Standard continues as an optional alternative and is still used occasionally.

 Assay Office Mark (or Town Mark)

This indicates the Assay Office at which the assaying and hallmarking were carried out. The Leopard's Head mark illustrated here represents the London Assay Office and appears on articles of gold and Sterling Standard silver.

The mark is often found on provincial silver where it appears in addition to the provincial town mark.

In May 1822, the London Assay Office introduced the uncrowned Leopard's Head for use on all articles of gold and silver. However, for some unknown reason, this mark is occasionally found on spoons bearing the date letter for 1821, whereas all other articles of 1821 apparently bear the crowned Leopard's Head.

Lion's Head Erased

This is an Assay Office mark used in conjunction with the Britannia mark on articles of Britannia Standard. In the London Assay Office, it replaced the Leopard's Head as Town mark when the Britannia Standard was introduced in 1697, but in other English Assay Offices, it was used together with the appropriate Town mark.

 Sovereign's Head (or Duty Mark)

This indicates that excise duty was paid on the article of gold or silverware bearing it. The duty was collected by the Assay Office on behalf of the Commissioners of Stamps (later the Inland Revenue).

The mark was introduced in 1784 and remained in use until 1890 when the duty was abolished. When first introduced on 1 December 1784, the mark was an incuse Sovereign's Head. Subsequently, it was changed to a raised Sovereign's Head in May 1786. This means that articles bearing the letter 'i' for 1784 will only have the incuse Sovereign's Head if they were assayed during the period from December 1784 to May 1785 inclusive.

 Date Letter Mark

This indicates the year in which the article was hallmarked. At the London Assay Office, this mark was changed during May of each year up until the end of 1974. Thus each Date Letter covered a portion of two calendar years. On 1 January 1975 the changeover was standardised for all the Assay Offices whereby it occurs on 1 January of each year.

Prior to 1974, a twenty letter alphabet was always used by the London Assay Office.

'Drawback' Mark

This mark was in use for less than eight months, from 1 December 1784 to 24 July 1785. The mark constitutes an incuse figure depicting Britannia and was stamped by the Assay Office on articles intended for export.

Normally a manufacturer paid excise duty to the Assay Office on all articles as they were assayed, at a rate of 8 shillings per ounce on gold and 6 pence per ounce on silver. When a manufacturer later specified that an article was to be exported, the duty was 'drawn back' and repaid to him, this transaction being indicated on the finished article by the incuse Britannia mark.

The actual stamping of the mark on finished articles was abandoned after such a short period because of the damage it could cause to the finished article. However, the manufacturer continued to be reimbursed for the duty he had paid on the article that was to be exported.

a 1678

 l 1688
William
Mary

  b 1679

 m 1689

c 1680

n 1690

d 1681

o 1691

e 1682

p 1692

f 1683

q 1693

g 1684
James II

r 1694
William III

h 1685

s 1695

i 1686

t 1696
To
26 March
1697

k 1687

399

1697 27 March to 29 May

 1697

 1698

 1699

 1700

 1701 Anne

 1702

 1703

 1704

1705

 1706

1707

1708

 1709

1710

1711

 1712

 1713 George I

 1714

1715

400

 A 1716 L 1726
George II

B 1717 M 1727

C 1718 N 1728

 D 1719 O 1729

E 1720 P 1730

F 1721 Q 1731

G 1722 R 1732

H 1723 S 1733

I 1724 T 1734

 K 1725 V 1735

		a	1736	l 1746
		b	1737	m 1747
		C	1738	n 1748
		d	1739	o 1749
		d	1739	p 1750
		e	1740	q 1751
		f	1741	r 1752
		g	1742	ſ 1753
		h	1743	t 1754
		i	1744	u 1755
		k	1745	

A	1756	**L**	1766
B	1757	**M**	1767
C	1758	**N**	1768
D	1759	**O**	1769
	George III		
E	1760	**P**	1770
F	1761	**Q**	1771
G	1762	**R**	1772
H	1763	**S**	1773
J	1764	**T**	1774
K	1765	**U**	1775

a 1776

b 1777

  l 1786

c 1778

m 1787

d 1779

n 1788

e 1780

o 1789

f 1781

p 1790

g 1782

q 1791

h 1783

r 1792

  i 1784

s 1793

k 1785

t 1794

u 1795

 1796

B 1797	**L** 1806
C 1798	**M** 1807
D 1799	**N** 1808
E 1800	**O** 1809
F 1801	**P** 1810
G 1802	**Q** 1811
H 1803	**R** 1812
I 1804	**S** 1813
K 1805	**T** 1814
	U 1815

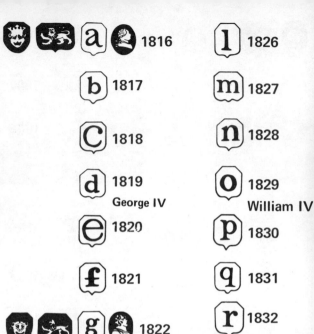

a 1816	**l** 1826
b 1817	**m** 1827
C 1818	**n** 1828
d 1819 George IV	**o** 1829 William IV
e 1820	**p** 1830
f 1821	**q** 1831
g 1822	**r** 1832
h 1823	**s** 1833
i 1824	**t** 1834
k 1825	**u** 1835

406

1836

Victoria

 1846

 1837

 1847

    1838

 1848

 1839

 1849

 1840

 1850

 1841

 1851

 1842

 1852

 1843

 1853

 1844

 1854

 1845

 1855

407

  1856

 1866

 1857

 1867

 1858

 1868

 1859

 1869

 1860

 1870

 1861

 1871

 1862

 1872

 1863

 1873

 1864

 1874

1865

1875

 1876

 1886

 1877

 1887

 1878

 1888

 1879

 1889

 1880

 1890
Queen's head
not used after
1890

 1881

 1891

 1882

 1892

 1883

 1893

 1884

 1894

 1885

 1895

 **a** 1896

b 1897

c 1898

d 1899

e 1900

Edward VII
f 1901

g 1902

h 1903

i 1904

k 1905

l 1906

m 1907

n 1908

o 1909
George V

p 1910

q 1911

r 1912

s 1913

t 1914

u 1915

1916

 1926

 1917

 1927

 1918

 1928

 1919

 1929

 1920

 1930

 1921

 1931

 1922

 1932

  1923

 1933

 1924

 1934

 1925

 1935

Edward VIII

A 1936 **L** 1946

George VI

B 1937 **M** 1947

C 1938 **N** 1948

D 1939 **O** 1949

E 1940 **P** 1950

F 1941 **Q** 1951

Elizabeth II

G 1942 **R** 1952

H 1943 **S** 1953

I 1944 **T** 1954

K 1945 **U** 1955

1956

 1957

 1958

 1959

 1960

 1961

 1962

 1963

 1964

 1965

 1966

m 1967

n 1968

o 1969

p 1970

q 1971

r 1972

s 1973

t 1974

413

Ⓐ	1975	Ⓛ	1985
Ⓑ	1976	Ⓜ	1986
Ⓒ	1977	Ⓝ	1987
Ⓓ	1978	Ⓞ	1988
Ⓔ	1979		
Ⓕ	1980		
Ⓖ	1981		
Ⓗ	1982		
Ⓙ	1983		
Ⓚ	1984		

INDEX OF MAKERS MARKS

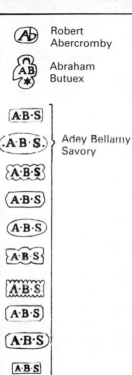 Robert Abercromby

Abraham Butuex

Adey Bellamy Savory

 Ann Chesterman

 Augustin Courtauld

 Ann Farren

 Andrew Fogelberg & Stephen Gilbert

 Ann Kersill

 Anthony Nelme

 Francis Nelme

415

Mary Bainbridge

Abraham L.
De Oliveyra

 William Bainbridge

 Peter Archambo (No 1)

 Thomas Bamford

 Adey Bellamy Savory, Joseph Savory (No 2) & Albert Savory

 John Bache

 Benjamin Cartwright (No 1)

  Richard Bayley

 Benjamin Cartwright (No 1)

 Ann Smith & Nathaniel Appleton

 Ann Tanqueray

 Aymé Videau

Benjamin Cartwright (No 2)

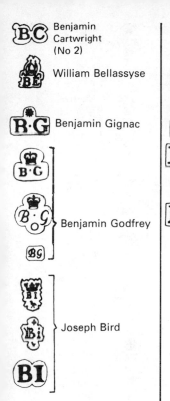

Benjamin Cartwright (No 2)

William Bellassyse

Benjamin Gignac

Benjamin Godfrey

Joseph Bird

John Boddington

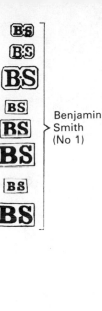

Benjamin Smith (No 1)

Benjamin Smith (No 2)

Benjamin Smith (No 1) & Benjamin Smith (No 2)

Benjamin Smith (No 1) & James Smith

 Abraham Buteux

 Charles Aldridge & Henry Green

 Charles Aldridge

 Christopher Canner (No 1)

Christopher Canner (No 2)

 Charles Bellassyse

Christopher Canner (No 2)

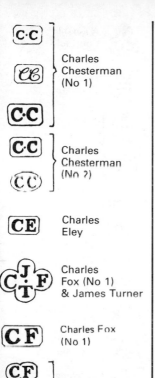

C·C	Charles Chesterman (No 1)
CC	
C·C	
C·C	Charles Chesterman (No 2)
CC	
CE	Charles Eley
CJTF	Charles Fox (No 1) & James Turner
CF	Charles Fox (No 1)
CF	Charles Fox (No 2)
C·F	
CF	

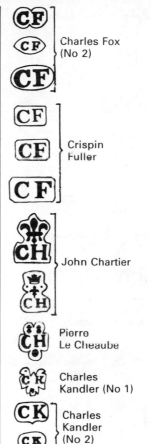

CF	Charles Fox (No 2)
CF	
CF	
CF	Crispin Fuller
CF	
CF	
CH	John Chartier
CH	
CH	Pierre Le Cheaube
CK	Charles Kandler (No 1)
CK	Charles Kandler (No 2)
CK	

Joseph Clare (No 1)

 Joseph Clare (No 2)

 Nicholas Clausen

 Lawrence Coles

Matthew Cooper (No 1)

 Matthew Cooper (No 2)

 Robert Cooper

 Isaac Cornasseau

 Edward Cornock

 Augustin Courtauld

 Peter Courtauld

 Paul Crespin

 Charles Rawlings

 Charles Rawlings & William Summers

 Christian Ker Reid

Christian Ker Reid & David Reid

   Charles Reily & George Storer

Louis Cuny

 Charles Wright

 Daniel Chartier

 John Bache & William Denny

   David Hennell (No 1)

 David Hennell (No 1) & Robert Hennell (No 1)

 Isaac Dighton

 Dorothy Mills

 Possibly Dorothy Mills & Thomas Sarbitt

   Daniel Piers

421

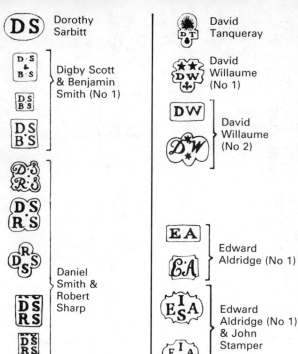

DS Dorothy Sarbitt

Digby Scott & Benjamin Smith (No 1)

Daniel Smith & Robert Sharp

David Tanqueray

David Willaume (No 1)

David Willaume (No 2)

EA Edward Aldridge (No 1)

Edward Aldridge (No 1) & John Stamper

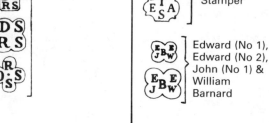

Edward (No 1), Edward (No 2), John (No 1) & William Barnard

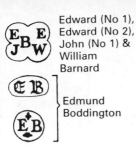 Edward (No 1), Edward (No 2), John (No 1) & William Barnard

 Edmund Boddington

 Elizabeth Buteux

 Ebenezer Coker

 Edward Cornock

 John Eckford (No 1)

 John Eckford (No 2)

 Edward Edwards (No 1)

 Edward Edwards (No 2)

 Edward Farrell

 Edward Feline

 Elizabeth Godfrey

 Edmund Pearce

423

Elizabeth Roker

 Elizabeth Tuite

 Edward Vincent

  Edward Wakelin

   Edward Wood

 Hester Fawdery

William Fawdery

Thomas Farren

 John Fawdery (No 1)

  William Fawdery

     Francis Crump (No 1)

 Edward Feline

 Francis Harache

 Charles Frederick Kandler

424

Charles Frederick Kandler

 William Fleming

 Francis Nelme

 Thomas Folkingham

 William Fordham

 James Fraillon

 Francis Spilsbury

  Fuller White

 Fuller White

 Daniel Garnier

 Francis Garthorne

 George Garthorne

    George Baskerville

 George Baskerville & William Sampel

425

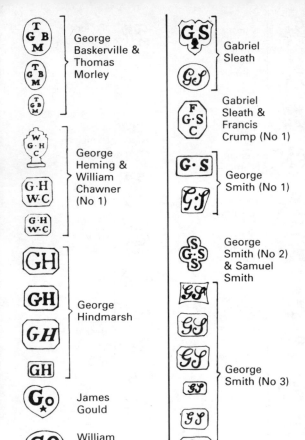

George Baskerville & Thomas Morley

Gabriel Sleath

Gabriel Sleath & Francis Crump (No 1)

George Heming & William Chawner (No 1)

George Smith (No 1)

George Hindmarsh

George Smith (No 2) & Samuel Smith

James Gould

William Gould

George Smith (No 3)

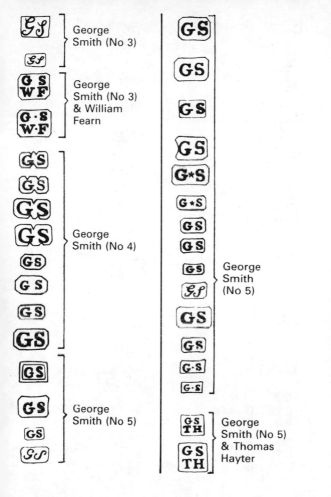

427

George Smith (No 6)

 John P. Guerier

    George Wickes

 Paul Hanet

 Pierre Harache (No 1)

 Pierre Harache (No 2)

 Pierre Harache (No 2)

         Hester Bateman

 Henry Brind

  Henry Chawner

428

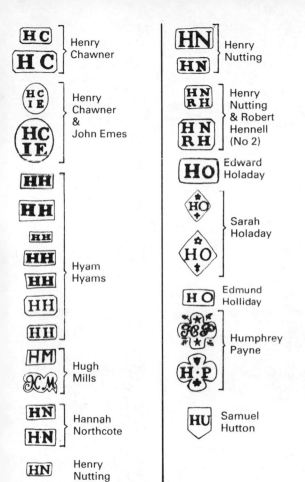

HC / HC	Henry Chawner
HC IE / HC IE	Henry Chawner & John Emes
HH / HH / HH / HH / HH / HH / HII	Hyam Hyams
HM / HM	Hugh Mills
HN / HN	Hannah Northcote
HN	Henry Nutting
HN / HN	Henry Nutting
HN RH / HN RH	Henry Nutting & Robert Hennell (No 2)
HO	Edward Holaday
HO / HO	Sarah Holaday
HO	Edmund Holliday
HP / HP	Humphrey Payne
HU	Samuel Hutton

Joseph Allen & Mordecai Fox

John Bache

 John Bayley

 Joseph Bird

   John Bridge

 John Cafe

  John Carter

 John Chartier

  Joseph Clare (No 1)

  Joseph Clare (No 2)

 Isaac Cornasseau

  Joseph Cradock & William Ker Reid

430

	Joseph Cradock & William Ker Reid		
	Joseph Cradock		James Gould
	John Crouch (No 1) & Thomas Hannam		
	John Eckford (No 1		Jean Harache
	John Eckford (No 2)		John Hyatt
	John Edwards & Edward Edwards (No 1)		John Hyatt & Charles Semore
	John Edwards & William Frisbee		John Jacob
	John Fawdery (No 2)		
	James Fraillon		Jeremiah King
	John Fray & Fuller White		

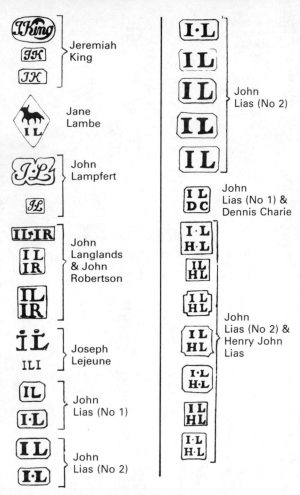

Jeremiah King

Jane Lambe

John Lampfert

John Langlands & John Robertson

Joseph Lejeune

John Lias (No 1)

John Lias (No 2)

John Lias (No 2)

John Lias (No 1) & Dennis Charie

John Lias (No 2) & Henry John Lias

John Lias (No 2), Henry John Lias & Charles Lias

Isaac Liger

John Liger

Jacob Margas

Jacob Marsh

James Murray & Charles Kandler (No 1)

Simon Jouet

John Parker & Edward Wakelin

John Payne

Isobel Pero

John Pero

John Pollock

John Quantock

433

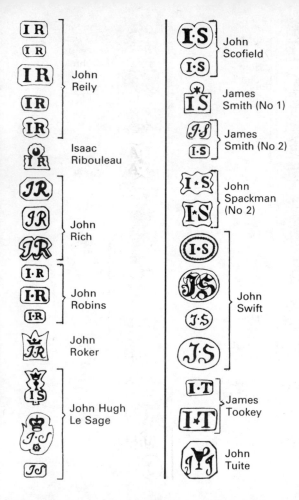

John Reily

Isaac Ribouleau

John Rich

John Robins

John Roker

John Hugh Le Sage

John Scofield

James Smith (No 1)

James Smith (No 2)

John Spackman (No 2)

John Swift

James Tookey

John Tuite

John Tuite

John Wakelin & William Taylor

John Wakelin & Robert Garrard (No 1)

John White

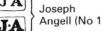

Joseph Allen

Joseph Angell (No 1)

Joseph Angell (No 1) & John Angell (No 1)

Joseph Angell (No 1) & John Angell (No 2)

John Jackson

John Cafe

John Crouch (No 2)

John Charles Reilly

John Denziloe

John Eckford (No 2)

John Emes

John Emes

  James Gould

       Jonathan Hayne

  Joseph Willmore

 Charles Kandler (No 1) & James Murray

 Charles Kandler (No 1)

Charles Frederick Kandler

Jeremiah King

John Ladyman

George Lambe

Jane Lambe

Jonathan Lambe

Paul De Lamerie

Louisa P. Courtauld

 Louisa P. Courtauld & George Cowles

 Louisa P. Courtauld & Samuel Courtauld (No 2)

 Samuel Lea

 John Leach

 Ralph Leake

 Samuel Lee

 Lewis Hamon

 Isaac Liger

 Louis Laroche

 Louis Laroche

 Lewis Mettayer

 Nathaniel Lock

 Matthew Lofthouse (No 1)

 Seth Lofthouse

437

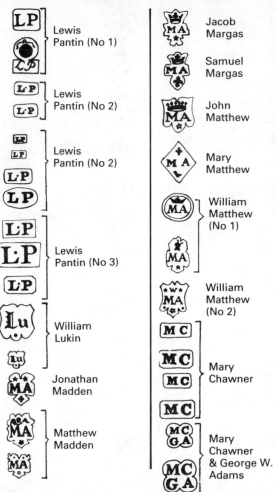

Lewis Pantin (No 1)

Lewis Pantin (No 2)

Lewis Pantin (No 2)

Lewis Pantin (No 3)

William Lukin

Jonathan Madden

Matthew Madden

Jacob Margas

Samuel Margas

John Matthew

Mary Matthew

William Matthew (No 1)

William Matthew (No 2)

Mary Chawner

Mary Chawner & George W. Adams

438

Matthew Cooper (No 1)

 Matthew Cooper (No 2)

 Lewis Mettayer

 Magdalen Feline

 Mordecai Fox

 Mary Hyde & John Reily

 Mary Lofthouse

 Matthew Lofthouse (No 1)

 Andrew Moore

 Thomas Morse

 Mary Pantin

 Mary Piers

 Matthew Roker

 Mary & Charles Reily

 Mary Sumner

 Mary & Elizabeth Sumner

 Nicholas Clausen

 Antony Nelme

Antony Nelme

 Francis Nelme

 Nicholas Sprimont

 Charles Overing

James Overing

 Peter Archambo (No 1)

Peter Archambo (No 2) & Peter Meure

 Mark Paillet

 Simon Pantin (No 1)

 Thomas Parr (No 1)

 Humphrey Payne

      Peter & Jonathan Bateman

440

Peter &
Ann
Bateman

 Peter, Ann
 & William
Bateman

 Peter &
William
Bateman

 Pierre
Bouteiller

 Pierre
Le Cheaube

 Peter
Courtauld

 Paul
 Crespin

  Paul Crespin

 Edmund
Pearce

 John Pero

 Jean Petry

 Philip
 Garden

441

Pierre Gillois

 Paul Hanet

 Pezé Pilleau

 Peter Jouet

  Paul De Lamerie

 Pierre Platel

 Pezé Pilleau

 Philip Platel

 Philip Rainaud

   Philip Roker (No 2)

 Philip Roker (No 3)

 Philip Rollos (No 2)

   Philip Rundell

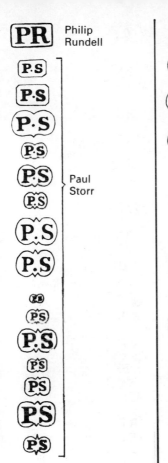

PR Philip Rundell

P·S
P·S
P·S
P·S
P·S
P·S
P·S
P·S

P·S
P·S
P·S
P·S
P·S
P·S

Paul
Storr

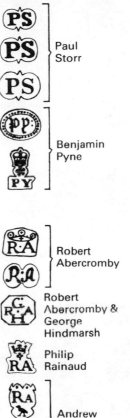

PS
PS
PS
} Paul Storr

PP
PY
} Benjamin Pyne

R·A
R·A
} Robert Abercromby

R·G·A·H Robert Abercromby & George Hindmarsh

RA Philip Rainaud

R·A
Ra
} Andrew Raven

443

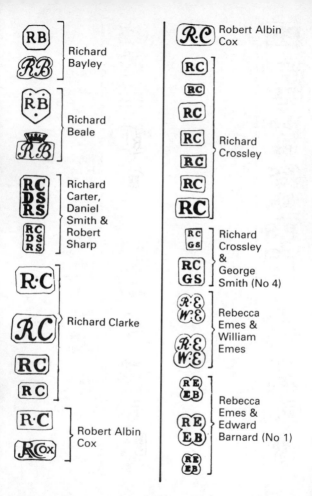

Richard Bayley

Richard Beale

Richard Carter, Daniel Smith & Robert Sharp

Richard Clarke

Robert Albin Cox

Robert Albin Cox

Richard Crossley

Richard Crossley & George Smith (No 4)

Rebecca Emes & William Emes

Rebecca Emes & Edward Barnard (No 1)

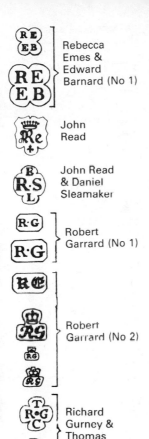

Rebecca
Emes &
Edward
Barnard (No 1)

John
Read

John Read
& Daniel
Sleamaker

Robert
Garrard (No 1)

Robert
Garrard (No 2)

Richard
Gurney &
Thomas
Cooke

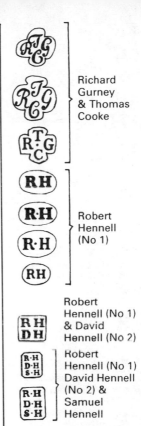

Richard
Gurney
& Thomas
Cooke

Robert
Hennell
(No 1)

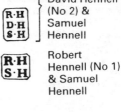

Robert
Hennell (No 1)
& David
Hennell (No 2)

Robert
Hennell (No 1)
David Hennell
(No 2) &
Samuel
Hennell

Robert
Hennell (No 1)
& Samuel
Hennell

445

R·H	
RH	
RH	Robert Hennell (No 2)
RH	
RH	
R·I I·S	Robert Jones & John Schofield
RI	Isaac Ribouleau
R·K	Richard Kersill
RM RC	Robert Makepeace (No 1) & Richard Carter
RM RC	
RM	Robert Makepeace (No 2)
RM TM	Robert Makepeace (No 2) & Thomas Makepeace
Ro	Philip Roker (No 1)
RO	Philip Roker (No 2)

 Philip Rollos (No 1)

 Philip Rollos (No 2)

R·R Richard Rugg (No 1)

R·R Richard Rugg (No 2)

 Richard Scarlett

RS Robert Sharp

R·S Richard Sibley (No 1)

 Richard Watts

Richard Watts

S·A	
SA	
S A	
SA	
SA	Stephen Adams (No 1)
S·A	
S·A	
S·A	
S·A	
SA	
SA	
SA	
SA	
S·A	

SA
SA
SA
SA
SA
SA } Stephen Adams (No 2)

 John Hugh Le Sage

S·C
SC } Samuel Courtauld (No 1)

SC Sebastian Crespel (No 2)

S·C
I·C Sebastian Crespel (No 1) & James Crespel (No 1)

S·C Richard Scarlett

S·C William Scarlett

Samuel Godbehere

       Samuel Godbehere & Edward Wigan

 Samuel Godbehere, Edward Wigan & James Bult

 Samuel Godbehere & James Bult

 Samuel Hennell

   Samuel Hennell

 Samuel Hennell & John Terry

 Sarah Holaday

  Samuel Hutton

 Sarah Hutton

William Shaw (No 1)

Alice
Sheene

 Joseph
Sheene

 Simon
Jouet

 Samuel
Lea

 Samuel
Lee

 Simon
Le Sage

 Daniel
Sleamaker

 Gabriel
Sleath

 Samuel
Margas

 James
Smith (No 1)

 Simon
Pantin (No 1)

Simon
Pantin (No 2)

Sarah
Parr

 John
Spackman
(No 1)

 Thomas
Spackman
(No 1)

Thomas Spackman (No 1)

  William Spackman (No 1)

 Francis Spilsbury

 Samuel Smith

 Samuel Taylor

 John Sutton

Thomas Sutton

   Samuel Wheat

 Samuel Wheatley & John Evans

 Samuel Wheatley

   Samuel Wood

 Richard Syng

Ann Tanqueray

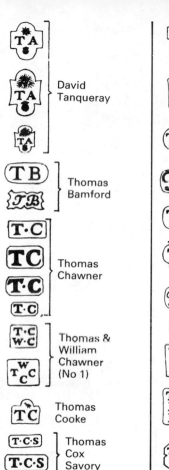

David Tanqueray

Thomas Bamford

Thomas Chawner

Thomas & William Chawner (No 1)

Thomas Cooke

Thomas Cox Savory

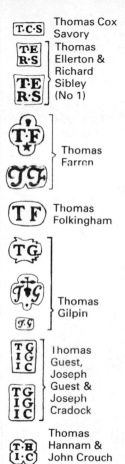

Thomas Cox Savory

Thomas Ellerton & Richard Sibley (No 1)

Thomas Farren

Thomas Folkingham

Thomas Gilpin

Thomas Guest, Joseph Guest & Joseph Cradock

Thomas Hannam & John Crouch (No 1)

451

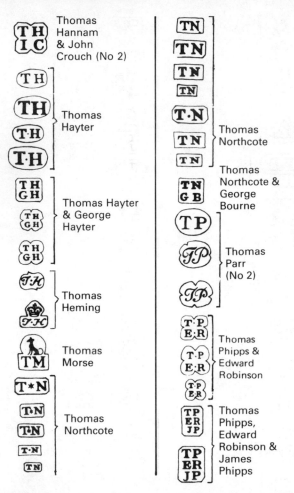

TH IC	Thomas Hannam & John Crouch (No 2)
T H **TH** **T·H** **T·H**	Thomas Hayter
TH GH **TH GH** **TH GH**	Thomas Hayter & George Hayter
T.H **T.H**	Thomas Heming
TM	Thomas Morse
T★N **T·N** **T·N** **T·N** **TN**	Thomas Northcote

TN **TN** **TN** **TN** **T·N** **TN** **TN**	Thomas Northcote
TN GB	Thomas Northcote & George Bourne
TP **TP** **TP**	Thomas Parr (No 2)
T·P E·R **T·P E·R** **T·P E·R**	Thomas Phipps & Edward Robinson
TP ER JP **TP ER JP**	Thomas Phipps, Edward Robinson & James Phipps

452

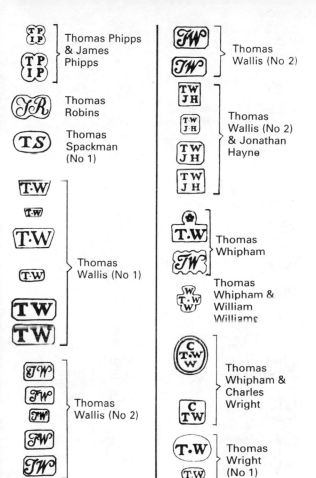

Thomas Phipps & James Phipps

Thomas Robins

Thomas Spackman (No 1)

Thomas Wallis (No 1)

Thomas Wallis (No 2)

Thomas Wallis (No 2)

Thomas Wallis (No 2) & Jonathan Hayne

Thomas Whipham

Thomas Whipham & William Williams

Thomas Whipham & Charles Wright

Thomas Wright (No 1)

453

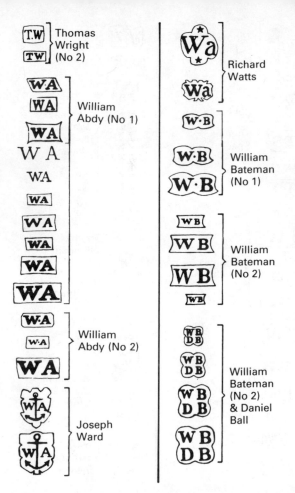

T.W
TW
} Thomas Wright (No 2)

WA
WA
WA
W A
WA
WA
WA
WA
WA
WA
} William Abdy (No 1)

W·A
W·A
WA
} William Abdy (No 2)

Joseph Ward

Wa
Wa
} Richard Watts

W·B
W·B
W·B
} William Bateman (No 1)

WB
WB
WB
WB
} William Bateman (No 2)

WB DB
WB DB
WB DB
WB DB
} William Bateman (No 2) & Daniel Ball

454

William Bell

William Burwash

William Burwash & Richard Sibley (No 1)

William Bellassyse

Walter Brind

William Cafe

Thomas Chawner & William Chawner (No 1)

455

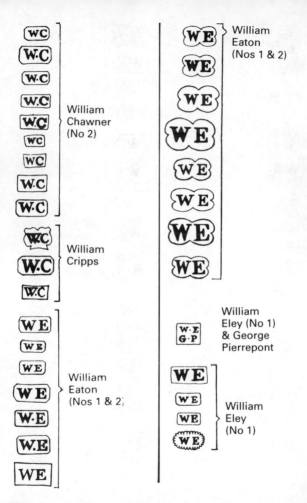

William Chawner (No 2)

William Cripps

William Eaton (Nos 1 & 2)

William Eaton (Nos 1 & 2)

William Eley (No 1) & George Pierrepont

William Eley (No 1)

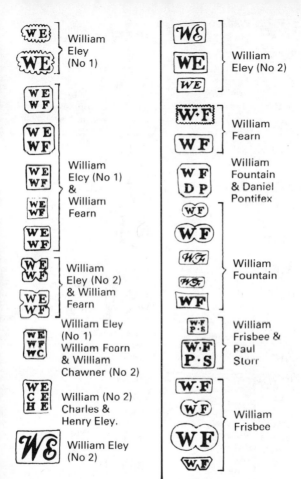

William Eley (No 1)

William Eley (No 1) & William Fearn

William Eley (No 2) & William Fearn

William Eley (No 1) William Fearn & William Chawner (No 2)

William (No 2) Charles & Henry Eley.

William Eley (No 2)

William Eley (No 2)

William Fearn

William Fountain & Daniel Pontifex

William Fountain

William Frisbee & Paul Storr

William Frisbee

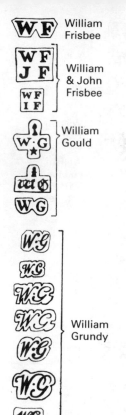

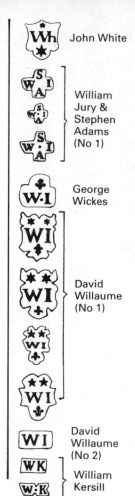

WF	William Frisbee
WF / JF / **WF / IF**	William & John Frisbee
W·G	William Gould
WG	
W·G	
W·G / **W·G** / **W·G** / **W·G** / **W·G** / **W·G** / **W·G**	William Grundy
E·G / W·F	William Grundy & Edward Fernell
Wh	John White
S·A / W·I / **S·A / W·I** / **S·A / W·I**	William Jury & Stephen Adams (No 1)
W·I	George Wickes
WI / **WI** / **WI** / **WI**	David Willaume (No 1)
WI	David Willaume (No 2)
WK / **W·K**	William Kersill

William Lukin

 William Matthew (No 2)

Edward Wood

 William Peaston

William Peaston & Robert Peaston

 William Plummer

 William Priest & James Priest

 William Ker Reid

 William Ker Reid
William Sampel

 William Scarlett

 William Shaw (No 1)

 William Shaw (No 2)

William Shaw (No 2) & William Priest

459

William Shaw
(No 2) &
William Priest

 William
Spackman
(No 1)

 William
Sumner (No 1)
& Richard
Crossley

 William
Sumner (No 1)

 William
Sumner
(No 1)

 William
Sumner (No 2)

 William
Tuite

 Walter
Tweedie

 William
Williams

 460

The Date Due Card in the pocket in-
dicates the date on or before which
this book should be returned to the
Library.
Please do not remove cards from this
pocket.